The Loyal Conspiracy

The Loyal Conspiracy
The Lords Appellant under Richard II

Anthony Goodman

Department of History University of Edinburgh

University of Miami Press
Coral Gables Florida

First published in 1971
by The University of Miami Press
Coral Gables, Florida 33124
Printed in Great Britain
© Anthony Goodman 1971
Library of Congress Catalog Card Number 77–170141
ISBN 0–87024–215–6

Contents

v

Preface

I owe thanks for help in researching for this book to members of staff at the National Library of Scotland in Edinburgh and the Public Record Office and at the other libraries which I have used. Professor Ranald Nicholson, of the University of Guelph, Ontario, kindly criticized a preliminary draft of the chapters, and Professor Denys Hay and Dr Kenneth Fowler, of the University of Edinburgh, made helpful suggestions about chapters four and seven respectively. The Carnegie Trust for the Universities of Scotland has by its generous financial support facilitated publication: I am grateful to the Secretary of the Trust, Dr A. E. Ritchie, for his encouraging advice. Mrs R. Thexton typed the manuscript, for the cost of which the Faculty of Arts of the University of Edinburgh provided a loan. Lastly, I owe a large debt of gratitude to my wife, who has patiently endured the constant and often overbearing presence of the Loyal Conspiracy.

Introduction

The main purpose of this book is to provide biographies of five English noblemen who flourished in the reign of Richard II and who are known from the collective political action which they took in the years 1387–8 as the Lords Appellant. In birth the most distinguished of them was Thomas of Woodstock (1355–97), Richard's uncle and the youngest legitimate son of the previous king, Edward III. Thomas was created earl of Buckingham in 1377 and duke of Gloucester in 1385. Two of the Lords Appellant were closely related to him. One was his nephew Henry of Bolingbroke, Earl of Derby (1366–1413), created duke of Hereford in 1397. In 1399 he succeeded his father John of Gaunt as duke of Lancaster and usurped the Crown as Henry IV. The other was Richard Arundel, Earl of Arundel (1346–97), whose sister Joan was Thomas's mother-in-law.

The two remaining Lords Appellant were Thomas Beauchamp, Earl of Warwick (c. 1339–1401), and Thomas Mowbray, created earl of Nottingham in 1383, Earl Marshal in 1386 and duke of Norfolk in 1397. The principal link between the five of them was that in November 1387 Gloucester, Arundel and Warwick launched an Appeal of Treason against some of the king's friends. The following month Derby and the Earl Marshal associated themselves in the Appeal and in the military and political action taken to support it.

One aim of the book is to outline the causes and results of the Appeal of Treason. The circumstances still hold a certain interest, partly because it was a period when Englishmen felt particularly uncertain about the political and economic future and when many of them found it necessary to reconsider and redefine their attitude to royal authority, to decide anew on the degree of obedience which they should accord to it. The dilemmas experienced and described by Nottingham and by his knight William Bagot—confrontations during Richard's 'tyranny' with manifestly unjust orders and acts—were of a sort unhappily familiar to twentieth-century Europeans.

Introduction

The first three chapters of the book are intended to provide a narrative of the political careers of the Lords Appellant up to 1399. In the following six chapters their personal backgrounds are sketched in. The individual characters of the Appellants can be only dimly perceived. This is the result of the inherent difficulty in writing biographically about English nobles of the later middle ages. Materials concerning them often survive in abundance, but usually such sources illuminate particular aspects of their careers, such as military retaining or estate administration. The whole man remains elusive. We do not even have a clue as to what four of the five Lords Appellant looked like—only a handful of conventional representations. Henry of Bolingbroke's fine effigy on his tomb in Canterbury Cathedral is the only surviving attempt at portraiture. Occasionally chroniclers' reports of the Appellants' words and gestures convey a sense—perhaps a false one—of intimacy. Froissart's Thomas of Woodstock and Henry of Bolingbroke are splendid creations. But are they fictional? In what follows his Bolingbroke has been accepted more unreservedly than his Woodstock. However, Froissart had talked to Thomas: despite his inaccuracies and his prejudice against the duke, his saturnine picture may contain strokes of truth. Courtiers said to the king:

> whan your uncle cometh to you, the whiche is nat often, we dare nat lyfte up our eyen to loke upon any persone, he loketh so hye ouer us. He thynketh we do hym moche wrong that we be so nere about you as we be.*

---

* *The Cronycles of Englande, Fraunce, Spaygne* (etc.), trans. Lord Berners, ii (R. Pynson, 1525), fo. cclxxxvii.

Abbreviations

B.I.H.R.	*Bulletin of the Institute of Historical Research*
B.M.	British Museum
C.A.D.	*Catalogue of Ancient Deeds*
C.C.R.	*Calendar of Close Rolls*
C.F.R.	*Calendar of Fine Rolls*
C.I.M.	*Calendar of Inquisitions Miscellaneous*
C.I.P.M.	*Calendar of Inquisitions Post Mortem*
C.P.	G. E. Cokayne, *The Complete Peerage*, ed. V. Gibbs and others (London, 1910–59)
C.P.R.	*Calendar of Patent Rolls*
E.E.T.S.	Early English Text Society
E.H.R.	*English Historical Review*
P.M.L.A.A.	*Publications of the Modern Language Association of America*
P.R.O.	Public Record Office
R.P.	*Rotuli Parliamentorum*, ed. J. Strachey and others (London, 1767–77)
R.S.	Rolls Series
S.A.C.	*Sussex Archaeological Collections*
Test. Vet.	*Testamenta Vetusta*, ed. N. H. Nicolas, 2 vols. (London, 1826)
T.R.H.S.	*Transactions of the Royal Historical Society*
V.C.H.	*Victoria County History*

The *mark*, the unit of financial account equivalent to 13*s.* 4*d.*, is abbreviated as *m*.

one

The Early Careers of the Lords Appellant (c. 1339–86)

The eldest of the Lords Appellant, Thomas Beauchamp, Earl of Warwick, was already aged about thirty-eight at the accession of Richard II in 1377. He had been born before 16 March 1339, a younger son of Earl Thomas and Catherine Mortimer. Her father, the first earl of March, one of the architects of Edward II's deposition, was executed in 1330. Her husband proved a lifelong friend of Edward III and his family. In 1369 Earl Thomas bequeathed 'an ouche, called the eagle, which the Prince [the Black Prince] gave me' and ' a set of beads of gold with buckles which the Queen [Philippa] gave me'. The chroniclers' obituaries of the earl emphasized his loyalty: 'no one had been found more faithful to the king and realm in his time.'[1] The young Thomas Beauchamp and his brothers were probably eager to emulate their father's distinguished military career. He had been a commander of forces in Scotland in 1335–6, and had served on the Black Prince's expeditions in southern and central France (1355–6) and on Edward III's 1359–60 campaign in northern France. In July 1355 Thomas and his elder brother Guy were knighted by the king when he was preparing to invade France. They may have been educated in the royal household—this tallies with their failure to accompany their father on campaign in 1355. The young Beauchamps acquitted themselves adequately during Edward's brief Picardy campaign—soon afterwards Sir Thomas and Sir Guy were granted respectively royal annuities of 100 $m.$ and £100 for good service. They probably participated in the king's winter invasion of Scotland and capture of Edinburgh. Like their father, the brothers went in 1359 on Edward's imposing and decisive French expedition, during which Sir Guy died, leaving Sir Thomas as heir to the Warwick inheritance. Edward III took the young man more firmly under his patronage, granting him an additional pension equivalent to the one his deceased brother had held. The king, a good judge of men, put a high price on Thomas's services.[2]

In November 1367, during the brief period of peace with France,

Sir Thomas and his younger brother William received royal licence to go to Prussia, with a retinue of nine esquires and twenty yeomen. They were hoping to emulate their father, who had spent most of 1365 crusading with the Teutonic Knights, and, according to a tradition preserved at Warwick, had returned with a Lithuanian prince, 'the Kynges son of lettowe', whose baptism in London he sponsored.[3] With the renewal of the French war in 1369, Sir Thomas once more campaigned across the Channel. In that year he served with two esquires and three archers under the king's son John of Gaunt, Duke of Lancaster, who led to Calais the advance-guard of an army which the king intended to command. The death of Queen Philippa frustrated his purpose, and it was Sir Thomas's father who took the rest of the army across the Channel. Warwick had a blazing public quarrel with Lancaster over his inaction, terminating this unfortunate expedition with a raid into Normandy. On his return to Calais, the earl died of plague, 'nowt lewyng behynde him, after his dayes, non so noble a knizt, ne so orpid* of armes'.[4] It was to be his younger son William, not his heir, who was to make a similar reputation. But in the concluding years of Edward's reign the new earl diligently maintained his family's martial traditions. In 1373, recently installed as a Knight of the Garter, he acted as marshal on the expedition which Lancaster took through France from Calais to Bordeaux. With him served William Ufford, Earl of Suffolk (d. 1382), an amiable noble who had accompanied Warwick on a mission to Cherbourg in 1370. Also present on Lancaster's disappointing expedition was Hugh Stafford, Earl of Stafford (d. 1386), married to a sister of Warwick—Stafford was to be dismissed by Walsingham as a boaster. In 1375 Warwick, Suffolk and Stafford were again together in arms, at the siege of Quimperlé in Brittany. They were commanded by Edward III's third surviving son, the unimpressive Edmund of Langley, Earl of Cambridge, and by the anglophile duke of Brittany, Jean de Montfort. Also present was Warwick's cousin, Edmund Mortimer, Earl of March. The anticipated successful issue of the siege was frustrated by Lancaster's conclusion of a general truce in the Bruges negotiations (June 1375). Warwick was only to fight once more overseas. He was to be the only Lord Appellant who had experienced high command in the French wars of Edward III. Chroniclers of Richard's reign did not mention him as a fierce critic of the king's *détentes* with the French Crown, like Thomas of Woodstock and the earl of Arundel. His greater involve-

* *Orpid*, brave.

ment in a period of reverses may have made Warwick warier of the fortunes of war.[5]

Considering the family connections of March, Warwick, Stafford and possibly Suffolk and their shared campaigning experiences, it may not have been coincidental that they were the four earls whom the aggrieved House of Commons petitioned to consult early in the 1376 session of parliament. Lancaster, as his sick father's representative, bitterly opposed the Commons' interference in government, in which the Lords acquiesced. After the session the duke overturned with comparative ease many of the 'Good Parliament's' measures, rebuffing March, who had backed the Commons. But he and the three related earls belonged to families which owed their fortunes to Edward III; there was no strong opposition from them or other magnates to a firm reassertion of the royal will during what was to be the last year of the reign. However, the Commons' wish to consult Warwick before their 1376 impeachments may indicate that he had a reputation of being independent-minded, prepared to offend princes, though he enjoyed court favour. His father, it was widely known, had berated Lancaster in 1369.[6]

The Lord Appellant next in age to Warwick was Richard Arundel, Earl of Arundel and Surrey, born in 1346, the year in which his father, also named Richard, took part in Edward III's wonderful victory at Crécy and the year before he inherited the Warenne earldom of Surrey. His mother was Eleanor, daughter of Henry, Earl of Lancaster; through her the Appellant was a near kinsman of his future opponents, Richard II and John of Gaunt. His father had been restored to the earldom of Arundel in 1330 and played a leading part in Edward III's military and naval expeditions. During the last fifteen years of his life (he died in 1376) Arundel was less active. Hard living in the field may have undermined his health. But he remained influential at court. In 1375 papal nuncios sent copies of a letter addressed to the king, about the Bruges conference, also to the Black Prince, Lancaster and Arundel.[7] In Richard II's reign the earl's heir was to display eagerness for military activity, but before then Richard Arundel lacked the landed resources or experience necessary to lead a major retinue, unlike Warwick, Stafford, Suffolk and March. In later years he may have regretted his inability to experience high command in the early 1370s, when his family eminently possessed the royal favour necessary for such appointments. As a young man

Richard Arundel was a member of the royal household, where there were opportunities for him to become acquainted with two of his future allies—the king's knight Thomas Beauchamp and Thomas of Woodstock. In December 1368 Richard and his younger brother John were the only esquires listed with the household knights, headed by Beauchamp, for whom robes were to be provided for the Christmas festivities. In 1369 the brothers, now knighted, served in Picardy; this was when Richard was 'first armed'.[8] In 1371 he and his brother-in-law Sir Thomas Holand were at sea in the retinue of Humphrey de Bohun, Earl of Hereford (d. 1373), to whose sister Elizabeth, Arundel was married. Hereford captured a salt fleet bound for Flanders, a profitable but tactless victory which nearly precipitated the count of Flanders into alliance with France against the English. The engagement probably gave Arundel the taste he later displayed for somewhat indiscriminate naval warfare, opening his eyes to the pickings which could be made by raiding Flemish commerce.[9]

Sir Richard continued in Edward's favour. From 1371 pardons were granted at his request and in 1372, at his father's, a licence was granted for the settlement of manors on Sir Richard's daughter Elizabeth and her husband Robert Ufford (d. 1375), Suffolk's son and heir. In 1374 the king granted Sir Richard the valuable Marcher wardship of John Charlton, Lord of Powis. In February 1376, after the earl of Arundel's death, his heir received a pardon for entering on the inheritance without suing out writs in Chancery. The pardon alluded to the late earl's services and to the 'sincere affection' which Edward III had for the heir.[10] During the 'Good Parliament' of 1376 the new earl of Arundel was one of the nobles (who included Warwick's brother Sir William Beauchamp) standing surety for Lord Latimer, Vice-Chamberlain of the Household, whom the Commons wished to impeach. Arundel was also one of the councillors appointed in parliament, possibly chosen as congenial to Edward III and Lancaster. In March 1377 the Crown acknowledged that Arundel and his brother Sir John had advanced 5,000 *m*. They may have been intent on cementing the friendly relations which their father had enjoyed with Lancaster. Thus at the time of Richard's accession Arundel appeared as devotedly loyal to the Crown, in striking contrast to his later reputation.[11]

In 1377 Edward III's youngest surviving son, Thomas of Woodstock, had only just started to assert influence on the affairs of the realm. Thomas, like Arundel, had unfulfilled ambitions. He had been born at Woodstock in January 1355 and appointed nominal guardian of the realm in July 1355 and October 1359. In November 1358 the queen was assigned an annuity for the sustenance of Thomas and his sisters. He was a member of the royal household in the 1360s.[12] Hereford's death in 1373 gave Edward an opportunity to provide for Thomas without loss to the Crown, by marrying him to one of the earl's two coheirs, his elder daughter Eleanor de Bohun (Sir Richard Arundel's niece). Thomas was probably dissatisfied with this marriage, since there was the prospect that the younger daughter Mary would inherit half the Bohun properties and the widow, Countess Joan of Hereford, being young, might long enjoy her dower. In the years 1374–6 Thomas was granted various Bohun properties in Crown wardship, his wife being under age. In June 1376 he was appointed to a Bohun office, the Constableship of the Realm, and in October received the principal Bohun residence, Pleshey Castle in Essex. Thomas's rapid advancement in the last year of his father's life may have been assisted by the value to Lancaster of his political support. It was important to the duke that his brothers should demonstrate faith in his intentions, since, after the death of the Black Prince in June 1376, there were rumours that he had designs on the succession. The hostility in London to the exercise of the Marshal's jurisdiction aligned Thomas with Lancaster, then the Londoners' *bête-noir*. In February 1377 the rumour that the Constable, Thomas, and his colleague the Marshal, Lord Percy (created earl of Northumberland in 1377) were promoting a petition for the replacement of the mayor by a captain and for the exercise of the Marshal's claim to arrest within the city produced a sharp reaction there. Lancaster had to flee for his life.[13]

Thomas's relations with his father seem enigmatic. At the king's death, though aged twenty-two, he was still not an earl; this was to be speedily remedied. Since he was granted the Constableship, it is probable that he had displayed military adeptness, yet he did not receive an important command until the new reign. He may have taken little or no part in his brothers' campaigns. Froissart says that he first fought in France in 1380. Thomas had been knighted by his father only at the 1377 Garter Feast; several of those dubbed with him were much younger, including Prince Richard. The following month Edward from his sickbed commanded Thomas and his elder brother Cambridge to surrender grants of property forfeited in the 'Good Parliament'. They were threatened with loss of the paternal blessing on failure to comply. What must have made these orders more galling (if the account given in Richard's first parliament may be believed) is that they were prompted by the king's low-born mistress Alice Perrers. Thomas may have approved the Commons' attack on her in 1376 for, unlike his brothers, he had been resident in the household when she was establishing her influence.[14] A book which Thomas later possessed (MS. Bodleian 316) had copied in it an account by Walsingham of the 'Good Parliament', with passages derogatory to Lancaster omitted. The chronicler strongly approved of the Commons' impeachments and hinted at their divine inspiration. When Edward died in 1377, Thomas probably looked forward to the new reign for opportunities to make a knightly reputation and become a great landowner. He may have lacked the personal reasons for strong loyalty to the new king possessed by his elder brothers. They had been the campaigning colleagues of the Black Prince. Unlike them, the hitherto insignificant Thomas emerged as an important magnate just when royal authority was experiencing intense criticism.[15]

Richard came to the throne at a bad moment. Within a few weeks a Franco-Castilian force was ravaging the Channel coast. Walsingham, later Arundel's fervent admirer, says that he left Lewes Castle undefended, fleeing in panic from Sussex when the French attacked his manors and offering to send 400 lances to protect his tenants only if the latter paid their wages. The earl certainly did not lose the esteem of his fellow magnates. On 20 July, at the great council which met after the coronation, he was one of the special councillors appointed to assist the chief ministers. In the first parliament of the reign, meeting in October 1377, Arundel and Warwick were among the peers whom the Commons wished to consult. The Commons proceeded to petition for parliamentary control of the initiative enjoyed by councillors and ministers during the minority. They hoped to gain the support of the king's uncles and other magnates because subsidies were needed to deal with the new military emergency. To the royal uncles was entrusted the task of checking that the councillors appointed in parliament did not overstep or abuse their powers.[16] Arundel was not reappointed as a councillor, probably because he wished to go on campaign. On 5 December, the last day of the session, Arundel received his father's old office, the Admiralty of the West, Warwick becoming Admiral of the North. Thomas of Woodstock, created earl of Buckingham in July, was already fulfilling his aspirations to command. The expeditions of 1377–8 were indecisive. Disappointment was reflected in the Commons' criticisms at Gloucester in 1378. They petitioned for the dismissal of the 'continual' councillors. Others appointed included Arundel, a surprising choice if he was widely blamed for the failure of the siege of St Malo.[17] At Gloucester tension between the London citizens and the royal uncles once more came to a head, this time apparently at Buckingham's instigation. In parliament he accused the former mayor, Nicholas Bramber, of 'inexcusable slothfulness' in having failed to prevent rioters led by a 'wexchaundeler' from assaulting his servants on Cornhill and breaking down the doors of their refuge, his London house, alarming him as he lay in bed. Bramber excused himself, but the threats of the earl, his brothers and magnate friends made the London burgesses present fear that a new statute might be promoted infringing the city's liberties. Bramber judiciously appeased Thomas with a gift of 100 *m*. The royal uncles would have done well to settle such disputes less rancorously—the young king was to exploit anti-Lancastrian feeling in the city in the 1380s and Bramber emerged as a dangerous opponent of Thomas of Woodstock.[18]

As regards loans and subsidies for the war, in 1379 London merchants and members of the Commons' House were in a more co-operative frame of mind than the previous, cheerless autumn. In the April parliament there was the generous grant of a graded poll tax. Warwick and his kinsmen March and Stafford were the earls appointed in parliament on a commission to examine royal receipt and expenditure. In the parliament which met in January 1380, the Commons petitioned for new appointments to examine expenditure since the coronation. Those appointed included members of the 1379 group, March being omitted and Arundel added. Thus during the minority Lords and Commons became used to taking measures for the 'reform' and supervision of government, Warwick and Arundel playing a part.[19] There were also calls on their military leadership in 1380. Both the Channel coasts and the Borders were raided. Winchelsea was sacked by a Franco-Castilian force and Sussex levies under the abbot of Battle were defeated. Where was Arundel? Walsingham alleged that he undermined the local will to resist by neglecting the county. Warwick made a positive contribution to security in the autumn by taking a military retinue to the Borders under Lancaster's command. The duke had been appointed chief commissioner to negotiate with the Scots; the display of force was to help secure an extension of the truce.[20]

In May 1381 the Peasants' Revolt broke out in Essex and Kent. On 12 June, when the Essex peasants congregated at Mile End and the Kentishmen at Blackheath, the magnates were gathered in the Tower with Richard II. Among those present were Buckingham, Arundel and Warwick. Cambridge was setting off for Portugal and Lancaster was again negotiating on the Borders. But his son, Henry of Bolingbroke, Earl of Derby, aged fifteen, was in the Tower. The next day after the king's failure to come to terms with the rebels at Greenwich, none of the lords, according to the Anonimalle Chronicler, wanted to give advice or knew what to advise. The king, a year younger than Derby, himself made the decision to meet the commons on 14 June at Mile End. On that day Derby was among those left in the Tower, perhaps in the hope of escaping. He miraculously survived the executions after the Tower had fallen, though a physician was killed merely for being in his father's service. Warwick rode to Mile End in the king's distinguished and apprehensive retinue. Buckingham showed his customary courage by doing so, for he had been closely associated with his unpopular brother the duke, especially in the eyes of the Londoners. The king appointed Arundel as Chancellor in place of the executed Archbishop Sudbury. He held office for three days (14–16 June) for the invidious task of issuing the charters of liberties extorted from Richard. Though the celebrated Smithfield confrontation marked the end of the revolt in London, disorders continued in the counties.[21] On 20 June Buckingham was appointed to restore order and put down risings throughout England, together with the Chief Justice Tresilian. On 7 July the earl was appointed on various local commissions to punish rebels. He commanded the forces which suppressed those remaining in Essex. Warwick and Sir Thomas Percy were ordered by the king to take 1,000 men-at-arms against the Hertfordshire rebels, but the earl was diverted from the task by news of Midlands disturbances. Arundel may have helped put down the rising in Sussex. During the 1381 revolt Buckingham, Arundel and Warwick were among the magnates who courageously supported the king. Buckingham in particular, in the absence of his elder brothers, and with the support of some of his recent campaigning companions, gave his royal nephew sterling support.[22]

From what we know of Richard's impatient and assertive attitude in 1382, it is probable that he was dismayed and enraged after the revolt by the attacks of the House of Commons on the conduct of his household and officials and by the appointment of examining commissioners headed by Lancaster and including Arundel and Warwick. Arundel and Sir Michael de la Pole were entrusted by the 1381 parliament with the duty of residing in the household, to counsel and govern the king. But it seems that the magnates exercised this new tutelage in a half-hearted manner, perhaps because the need for war subsidies seemed less urgent and in succeeding parliaments the Commons grew more parsimonious. In 1382 Richard was himself making some lavish grants of patronage, and under this year Walsingham first alleged that he was prodigal and neglectful of magnates' counsel, overturning 'with his privy council' the ordinances of the 1381 parliament.[23] But kinsmen of Arundel and Warwick were among those enjoying royal favours. Arundel was well rewarded for his help during the revolt: in September 1381 a Chancery fine was remitted, 'by reason of the costs by him incurred in the king's service'; in October he was granted custody of most properties of an alien priory, Fécamp Abbey, and in December a wardship. In 1383 Richard visited the earl's brilliant clerical brother, Bishop Thomas Arundel, at Ely. Soon afterwards, at the bishop's petition, he and the prior of Ely were granted property within their liberty forfeited by the 1381 rebels. The grant alluded to 'the greatness of the singular affection' in which Richard held his 'very dear relative' the bishop.[24] In 1382, according to a tradition preserved at Warwick in the fifteenth century, the king was at the earl of Warwick's Worcestershire manor of Salwarp, to act as godfather to his son Richard, the future earl. In April 1383 licence was granted for the foundation of a religious fraternity by Warwick burgesses, which the earl intended to endow. Masses were to be celebrated for the good estate of the king and his bride, Anne of Bohemia, and of Sir Michael de la Pole, the recently appointed Chancellor. In February a covenant had been made for the marriage of Pole's son and heir, Sir Michael, and Warwick's niece, Catherine Stafford. Her brother Ralph, son and heir of the earl of Stafford, was a particular favourite of the king. In October 1382 he had been licensed to hunt in royal forests, together with other royal companions —the future Appellant Thomas Mowbray, Thomas Clifford, son and heir of the leading Cumberland landowner Roger Lord Clifford, the household knight James Berners and the household esquire John Beauchamp of Holt, a kinsman of Warwick. The death of Ralph Stafford in 1385 and of his father the following year may have weakened Warwick's ties at court.[25]

However, in 1382-3 Richard's relations with Buckingham (who

greeted the arrival of Anne of Bohemia at Canterbury in 1382) and with Derby probably soured, due to the growing tension between himself and Lancaster, which was to become a major political issue in 1384. The failure of English arms in Flanders in 1383 (one of the causes of which may have been this tension) was followed by the first concerted magnate protest against Richard's manner of government. In the November parliament the lay magnates complained that Richard had followed 'insane counsel' and that as a result his household was badly ordered. In reply Richard asserted that he did not wish to be ruled solely by the counsel of the protesting lords, but also moderately and compliantly by that of honest men appointed for the purpose. The peers were angered by his remarks, but the Westminster Chronicler judged that he had behaved prudently, for, the monk wrote, if the lords ruled, they might through negligence bring evils upon the realm, for which the community would blame them. He says that Richard's firm replies aimed at the lesser individuals—presumably the Commons. The episode shows how co-operation between Lords and Commons, always uneasy in the minority, had broken down since 1381. This facilitated Richard's assertions of will, to which he now saw Lancaster as the principal stumbling-block. Soon after the session Richard granted the wardship of Roger Mortimer, heir to the earldom of March (whose profits had previously been reserved to household expenses) to the young man himself and to the earls of Arundel, Warwick, Northumberland and Lord Neville of Raby. Custody of Roger was granted to Arundel, perhaps one of the recent noble critics in parliament, disgruntled over his humiliating failure to get the lieutenancy under Bishop Despenser in Flanders.[26] On 14 December 1383 Arundel was licensed to travel overseas, possibly in the company of Buckingham, who a month later received permission to go overseas on pilgrimage. If they were planning to travel together, this is the earliest known instance of their close association. Buckingham's (and Arundel's) pious intentions may have been laid aside because Lancaster gave his brother the opportunity to accompany him with a military retinue into Scotland (March 1384). To Richard's annoyance the duke in 1384 was still asserting the measure of control over war and diplomacy which he had gained the previous September as a result of the débâcle in Flanders. In January he had concluded a truce with the French. Derby was his father's fellow envoy, receiving his first important appointment.[27]

Discontent came to a head during the Salisbury parliament in May

1384. Arundel bluntly blamed the decline of the realm on bad government, provoking a disgraceful rejoinder from the king. The earl,
despite the favours he had received, may have been trying to revive
the magnate agitation of the previous parliament, but he failed to
win the support of Lancaster, who broke the shocked silence after
Richard's insulting remarks by excusing what the earl had said.
Richard was ungrateful—on hearing an extraordinary accusation that
the duke was plotting his death, he ordered his summary execution.
The lords present indignantly dissuaded the king. Buckingham then
outdid his nephew in impudence, bursting into his presence and
swearing a terrible oath that he would fight or kill anyone who
accused his brother of treason, not excepting the king. Even Walsingham remarked that the earl was guilty of a capital offence, but
Richard remained silent in face of this extreme provocation. In fact,
towards the end of the session, Buckingham received a number
of royal favours. Lancaster's influence remained unimpaired. The
Commons were displaying discontent with magnates' private governments rather than with the king's—and it was the duke who spoke on
behalf of his fellow peers against the statutory remedy they sought,
saying that he and his brothers would set an example by punishing
their own errant retainers. Lancaster was again appointed to head
negotiations with France, this time with Buckingham.[28] But the king
may have hoped that Arundel could be won over from his critics. In
July the nobility gathered at Arundel Castle to celebrate the marriage
of the earl's daughter Elizabeth to the king's companion, Thomas
Mowbray, who had been created earl of Nottingham in February
1383, after the death of his elder brother John. The king and queen
attended the Arundel celebrations. But it seems that the effects of
Richard's graciousness to Arundel and to any other magnates were
outweighed by the alarming manner in which he and his young friends
continued to conduct their struggle with Lancaster. The duke and
Buckingham returned from France with only a short truce, convinced
that the French were bent on serious efforts to revive the war. In the
parliament which met in November 1384 subsidies were granted for
the king to lead an overseas expedition. The attempt by Lancaster
and his brothers to force on their fellow councillors a secure commitment to this undertaking provoked another domestic crisis early in
1385. The duke's threats not to co-operate and his withdrawal from
the council with his brothers were regarded as treasonable gestures by
their opponents. The Westminster Chronicler says that Richard's

friends plotted to kill the duke at a tournament. According to Walsingham, the plot was instigated by young men 'nurtured' with Richard. In 1398 Nottingham confessed that he had once laid an ambush for the duke—he was probably referring to this occasion. When Lancaster was reconciled with the king on 6 March 1385 (without, despite his strictures, effecting any changes in the personnel or manner of government), he forgave the highly respected, elderly earl of Salisbury, Oxford and Nottingham. The plot, like Richard's execution threat at Salisbury, swung magnate sympathies to Lancaster— a measure of Richard's ineptitude. At a great council in March, Archbishop Courtenay said that it was an example which the lords feared the king might follow in future when displeased with them and that as such action was against the law, it would cause dissension in the realm. He was, in effect, accusing Richard of tyranny. Richard made an angry reply and the council broke up. Buckingham, Courtenay's kinsman, tried to effect a reconciliation between king and archbishop. The latter, seemingly not without reason, feared now for his own safety. What may have finally hardened Buckingham's attitude towards his royal nephew was that Richard personally broke the safe-conduct he had procured for Courtenay, actually trying to cut him down with his sword.[29]

In 1385 and the early months of 1386 there were many conciliatory gestures, agreements to launch the Scottish and Castilian expeditions, conferment of titles in August 1385, including that of duke of Gloucester on Thomas of Woodstock, various formal reconciliations and a winter round of dinners and entertainments. At Epiphany 1386 Gloucester entertained Richard's guest Leo de Lusignan at Pleshey. He may have been able to show this crusading propagandist spoils of the sack of Alexandria in 1365, in which his father-in-law Hereford had participated. But it is unlikely that displays of goodwill erased the doubts which magnates had conceived about the judgment of Richard and some of his friends. Moreover, in the 1385 parliament the Commons, once more granting subsidies for the pressing war needs, revived expedients for the supervision of royal expenditure characteristic of the period 1377–81. Richard's determination in 1386 to evade such controls, whilst demanding great sacrifices from the community in face of the expected French invasion, produced a bitter and determined mood in the Commons, meeting in the parliament which convened in October, surrounded by an impressive army summoned to defend London. Richard held out against requests for the dismissal of ministers. He regarded parliament as primarily an instrument for the discharge of business which he laid before it. The king's charges should receive precedence. The reaction to his unexceptionable demand for a Commons' delegation shows how the intrigues of recent years had undermined his reputation; it was rumoured that he intended to have them put to death. Lords and Commons sent Gloucester and Bishop Arundel as delegates to the king at Eltham. Knighton has left the sole account of their angry retorts. It is likely to have been Gloucester rather than the diplomatic bishop who made a threat of deposition. Perhaps the duke thought that his blunt words to the king at Salisbury in 1384 had been effective. Richard's anger, according to Knighton, was turned to melancholy; he agreed to attend parliament and to accept the petitions. On 23 October Suffolk delivered the Great Seal to him at Westminster and the next day he gave it to Bishop Arundel in the presence of Cambridge (created duke of York in 1385) and Gloucester. Suffolk was impeached by the Commons: his punishment was lenient. For Gloucester and the Arundel brothers were not heading a long-matured opposition party, but a movement in parliament of fickle public opinion. Richard probably had more supporters and room for political manoeuvre than has sometimes been implied. He may have held out against the Commons' petition for the appointment of councillors in parliament. Eleven years later Gloucester and the earl of Arundel were accused of procuring the appointment of the commission and of having sent a peer to Richard, who threatened him with death if he refused to assent—the king 'was in great peril of his life'. On 19 November the councillors were appointed, but Richard was able to get concessions over the terms of their commission. He stipulated that their powers, which amounted to a delegation of royal authority, should last for a year only. Apart from a few leading magnates, the council consisted of clerics and laymen with distinguished records of service to Richard and his family, being similar in composition to the councils which often supervised the affairs of magnates during their minority. Since Sir John Gildsburgh, a retainer of Thomas of Woodstock, had petitioned as Speaker of the Commons as long ago as the first 1380 parliament, that Richard should no longer have specially appointed councillors, the 1386 appointments must have been galling to the king's pride. The fact that the council was composed of men especially loyal to his family may have alarmed him—even such as they were prepared to subordinate the royal will to the community's. York and Gloucester for the first time received formal conciliar appointments—an expedient which had not been necessary when Lancaster was in England. It is notable that, apart from Arundel, the other future Appellants, Warwick, Derby and Nottingham (appointed Marshal in June 1385), were not appointed. The king's actions in 1387 turned them into close political allies of Gloucester and the earl of Arundel.[30]

Perhaps the most remarkable political development of 1386 was the emergence of a son of Edward III—in alliance with the sons of one of Edward's best friends—as the first magnate willing to base an attack on the Crown's authority partly on the support of the Commons, harnessing the sense of unity and confidence which had emerged among the shire knights and burgesses in 1376. But the duke's novel political experiment (which invites comparison with those of Humphrey of Gloucester and Richard of York) was ultimately to prove a failure, with himself as one of its casualties. Nobles tended to be equivocal during Richard's reign in their attitudes towards the Commons' pretensions, partly because of their novelty and partly because the Commons in the 1380s criticized aspects of the 'bastard feudalism' developed by magnates as well as royal extravagance. Gloucester might have argued convincingly in 1386 and 1388 that his alliance with the Commons was in defence of the interests of nobles, but he could not provide a permanent justification. Moreover, political disquiet and initiative had increased among the Commons particularly as a result of unsuccessful war and of the royal minority. In less trying times the Commons were more docile, as proved, on the whole, to be the case in the 1390s.

But in the years 1386–8 the prospects of the realm appeared black. Encouragement by a son of Edward III stiffened the resolution of shire knights to persist in their criticisms of the king. In 1386 and in the 'Merciless Parliament' of 1388 Gloucester may have been informally almost as much the leader of the Commons as Sir Peter de la Mare, their Speaker in 1376, had been. But after the excitement of 1376–7, De la Mare could fade into political obscurity as a Hereford-shire gentleman. Gloucester could not, unless he went overseas, as he was to try to do, to Prussia or Ireland. After 1388 the duke remained prominent in the political landscape. His tragedy was to be that he could not repeat his momentarily wild political success or live down the memory of it. He might behave as a loyal magnate, but he was remembered as the man who had defied and threatened a king, in the traditions of Simon de Montfort and Thomas of Lancaster. Richard could never feel assured that he was safe with his uncle.

The extraordinary political drama which unfolded during the 1386 parliament had an exceptionally large audience—the great army which had assembled for a desperate defence of London against the French. The versions of the political crisis taken home by the returning warriors may have been uncomplimentary to Richard, his opponents having presented him as a potential assassin of lords and shire knights. Such adverse propaganda may have prejudiced from the start the success of the policies Richard was to pursue in 1387: he had to contend with a suspicious climate of opinion.

two

The Lords Appellant and the Appeal of Treason (1387-9)

When the propertied classes gathered for the Christmas and Epiphany celebrations of 1386-7, many must have wondered and debated anxiously as to what would be the fate of the realm in the New Year, since the French had recently shown themselves more menacing than within living memory, and the bitterest political crisis for ten years had occurred in parliament. The optimists would have had confidence in the newly appointed councillors—they would have been comforted by the failure of the French to press home their military advantage and by the grant of a subsidy to prevent them from gaining another opportunity. Much may have been expected from the vigour of Gloucester and the earl of Arundel. On the other hand, the pessimists could have pointed out that the realm still had no powerful ally within France, or on its borders, and that the political tension in England made it especially vulnerable. It was not yet clear whether the king would continue to accept the authority accorded in parliament to the council.

In February 1387 Richard and his household left Westminster. It is unlikely to have been widely anticipated that they would be absent for nine months, a phenomenon characteristic of war and emergency, when a king was dealing with Scottish problems or raiding in France. Richard was determined to undermine the authority of the council. His will was strengthened by the support of Archbishop Alexander Neville of York (though he was a member of the council), Robert de Vere (created duke of Ireland during the 1386 parliament) and Suffolk. For the council displayed vigorous activity. With much greater regularity than in the past five years, grants were enrolled on the Patent Rolls with the warrant 'by the advice of the council' or 'with the assent of the council', whereas the warrant 'by Signet letter', characteristic of preceding years, disappears. It cannot be concluded that the king had been completely deprived of the power to initiate grants and appointments, but it is likely that the councillors were scrutinizing his decisions with care. Richard fairly certainly bestowed some favours and offices, assented to by the council, for members of his household continued to be recipients, though not in such large numbers or on such a generous scale as had been the case from 1382 onwards.

A high proportion of the grants made in 1387 went to recipients who were not of the household—mostly benefices and offices whose bestowal did not diminish the money available for household expenses and the defence of the realm. The council fulfilled expectations by showing a concern for retrenchment. Its determined fiscal policy probably irritated the king further. His absence from Westminster, where the secretariats and courts presided over by some of the great officers of the realm customarily convened, probably accentuated his alienation. Frequent physical contact between the king and his ministers, the norm of fourteenth-century government, would almost certainly have given him in 1387 more influence over their decisions. Those appointed in the 1386 parliament were not bound together as a faction or cousinage. The careers of the councillors show most of them to have been pragmatists, eager in the circumstances of 1386 to ensure more circumspect government, but not opposed on any principle to personal rule by the king. It was Richard who was the 'constitutionalist', theorizing, rigid and courageous in adhering to his deductions. He was convinced that the council was illegal and did not take the easier path of dividing and ruling it.[1]

For the ministers and councillors it was probably a disconcerting experience to hold office without ease of access to the king. The situation is likely to have increased the influence of Gloucester and the Arundels over their fellow councillors, just as the king's absence at Eltham in October 1386 had induced parliament to accept their leadership. But the council did not cut Richard off from information about the affairs of the realm. The earl of Arundel almost certainly sent dispatches about his naval operations or about the prizes he had captured. The council sent a messenger to Windsor with a letter from Leo de Lusignan. Now that the threat from France had declined and Arundel had secured the mastery at sea, the councillors may have been willing for Richard to resume his dialogue with Leo, which they had curtly interrupted the previous November. But Richard was not to be appeased. When Gloucester attended the Garter Feast in April, the attitude of some of the household was so menacing that he felt it prudent to withdraw the next day.[2] A crisis in Richard's relations with London at about the same time shows the extent of the initiative which he still held and his inflexibility in using it. On 16 April the mayor, the prudent Nicholas Exton, announced in common council that Lord Zouche (probably William la Zouche, Lord of Harringworth) was urging the king to grant a pardon to the London politician John Northampton and his confederates. They had been condemned to forfeiture and imprisonment in 1384, and Lancaster's efforts to obtain remission of their sentences had been fruitless, partly because Sir Nicholas Bramber had used his influence at court to block their release. In 1387 common council decided that the mayor, alderman and citizens should ride to the king at East-hampstead in Windsor Forest and intercede that no pardon be granted to Northampton. Such a grant would have posed a threat to the control of city government enjoyed by leading capitalists.

The Westminster Chronicler says that the king pardoned North-ampton on 27 April, at the duke of Ireland's instance. In fact no pardon was issued. The king and duke may have been seeking to frighten the mayor and his friends into giving support—sources hostile to Richard report that palace intrigues during the 1386 parliament had failed as a result of Exton's unco-operativeness. On 4 May 1387 a report of the Easthampstead conference was delivered at the Guildhall. Richard had temporized by saying that he would maintain his right to grant the favour of pardon, but would exercise it only after careful consideration. Thus the threat was to be kept hanging over the citizens' heads. In fact Richard would have been taking risks if he had pardoned Northampton. Such a move would have alarmed members of the household enjoying grants of North-ampton's former properties, and would have destroyed the credit in London of Richard's staunchest friend there, Bramber. The fact that in 1387 Ireland or others at court manoeuvred against Bramber's interests shows what little unity of purpose there was among those to whom the king looked particularly for support against the council.[3]

The magnates were soon to show that they were less awed by Richard than the merchants were. Few lords attended the great council which the king summoned to Reading in May. According to the Westminster Monk, Suffolk sought to have his sentence reversed, but nothing was done because of the absence of the magnates. One probably present was the king's elder half-brother Thomas Holand, Earl of Kent. He is unlikely to have encouraged the king in extreme measures: in March he had assisted in mustering the retinues com-manded by his brother-in-law, Arundel. On 9 May he received custody of the Tower for life, the grant being dated at Reading. The initiative for this grant may have been the king's but the patent was issued by the chancery, under Thomas Arundel's control.[4] A number of lesser nobles felt it worthwhile to stay on good terms with Richard. Lord Zouche of Harringworth was probably at court in May 1387, when rumours spread about a pardon for Northampton—he was to be expelled from the household by the Appellants in 1388, as were Lords Beaumont, Burnell and Lovell. In September 1387 the king and queen stayed the night at Groby near Leicester, the residence of Lord Ferrers, Warwick's brother-in-law. There may have been policy in Richard's encouragement of these lords to attend him, for some of his activities were aimed at splitting that new alliance of magnates, lesser lords and gentry which had rendered him powerless during the 1386 parliament. As he progressed, he retained. This was suspected as a preliminary to action against those who had coerced him. The nervousness it aroused was reflected, too, in the arrest near Cambridge of a servant of the king who had been distributing liveries to the gentry of East Anglia and Essex, on receiving which they swore to do military service when summoned by the king, no matter which lords had retained them. It was a shrewd attempt to strengthen ties between king and gentry, at the same time undermining the influence which retaining links gave to magnates in many counties, the effects of which the Commons had complained about in the Salisbury parliament (1384). Perhaps the sergeant tried to win over livery-holders of Gloucester, who was well connected in those regions. In 1387 Richard certainly retained Sir John Russell of Strensham, an important Worcestershire landowner, terminating the contract between Russell and Warwick. Worcestershire was a county in which Warwick's servants disturbed the peace in the 1390s. Russell was then an opponent of the Beauchamp influence and in the last years of Richard's reign was one of his trusted councillors. In the 1390s Richard had some notable successes in detaching retainers of the Appellants. The dismissal of the senior Appellants from the council in May 1389 made some of their servants anxious lest they should be deprived of recently acquired royal grants. Sir Edward Dallingridge of Bodiam (Sussex), an eminent councillor of Arundel and political supporter against Richard, hastened to ingratiate himself with the king, as did another supporter, Sir William Bagot of Baginton (Warcs.), who had long been in Warwick's service.[5]

Richard's 1387 retaining policy may have alarmed the councillors.

It was his judicial policy which led some of them to rise in arms and others to condone such actions. The justices summoned by Richard in August 1387 gave as their opinion that the 1386 commission was derogatory to the king's prerogative, and that its instigators deserved capital punishment. They considered that those who impeached officers without the king's consent deserved punishment as traitors. It is not clear whether the opinions of the justices about the heinous nature of the alleged offences, and even the treasonable nature of some, were sincerely given or induced by coercion—except in the case of the king's partisan, Sir Robert Tresilian, Chief Justice of the King's Bench. Professor Chrimes has related the answers to the existing treason legislation and argued forcibly that, from a legal and constitutional viewpoint, the justices could have arrived at them logically and with clear consciences. Yet they could only do so by condemning, explicitly and implicitly, parliamentary trends of recent but decided growth, of which the 'community of the realm' by and large approved. Though the opinions of the judges may have been a sound and brilliant exercise in judicial logic, in the contemporary political context they were cast in an imprudent and uncompromising form. Their programme shows Richard, confronted with a novel crisis in royal authority, relying heavily on legal remedy. His attitude was in this respect analogous to those of lay magnates who considered their rights threatened by neighbours and tenants. Their councils, on which lawyers figured prominently, remorselessly upheld titles to land, service and judicial rights. Warwick was to give a notable display of obstinacy in the 1390s by pursuing a family of alleged villein status.

The interpretations of the justices may have been impeccably conservative, but they displayed novelty in their categorization of offences and award of appropriate punishments. It is hard to believe that without coercion they would have been shown such temerity. Professor McKisack is one notable sceptic dissenting from those who believe that coercion is unlikely to have taken place. It was difficult for justices to disobey royal commands to give counsel, as they were the king's officers. Like Justice Rickhill, when mysteriously summoned out of bed in 1397, they may not have realized what lay in store. The justices were to plead coercion when impeached in the 'Merciless Parliament', despite the fact that the Appeal of Treason accused favourites of having coerced the justices. A point in favour of their plea appears in their impeachment—the allegation that during the 1386 parliament they had appeared to be in favour of the legality of the council's appointment. The continuator of the *Eulogium* hints that the appellants were particularly incensed against the justices, because they had supported the aims of the king's critics in 1386. Bealknap alleged that he had been threatened at Windsor by Alexander Neville with the king's anger as the 'ymaginour et contrevour' of the 1386 commission.

Nevertheless, it would be surprising if the justices had not been disquieted by some of the proceedings alleged to have taken place in the 1386 parliament. Persuaders such as Tresilian and Neville may not have had to coerce obstinate men. It would have been difficult to disagree that the agitator for the production of the 'statute' by which Edward II had been formally adjudged was worthy of punishment as a traitor. The judges' bad consciences about such a matter may have made it easier to trap them into agreement with propositions likely to appal the 'community of the realm'—for instance, that those who took the initiative from the king in parliament deserved punishment as traitors. The nature of the consultations was kept secret. Even Kent was not enlightened, probably because it was thought that he might place his Arundel relationship before his royal one. The day after the Nottingham council, the secret was imparted to him by a Justice of the Common Bench, Sir Roger Fulthorp, who was of Kent's livery. Fulthorp's indiscretion may have been motivated by dubiety about the rulings. His son and heir, Sir William, gave support to Gloucester and Arundel and was to be granted custody of lands forfeited by his father.[6] It was only a question of time before the judgments became known to the duke. He could recall how courtiers had plotted his brother's death in 1385 and may have considered that the rulings Richard procured were even more insidious. In London Gloucester swore upon relics that he had never intended to infringe prerogative, before an assembly of magnates including Bishop Braybrooke. The bishop (who had reconciled Archbishop Courtenay to the king in 1385) went to court as intermediary. After Braybrooke had spoken, Richard was inclined to believe his former secretary and to trust his uncle, but was dissuaded by Suffolk. The bishop withdrew after an altercation with the latter (who had succeeded him as Chancellor in 1383), leaving Richard furious. The incident (if the sole account of it, by a chronicler hostile to Richard, can be trusted) did no credit to the king's steadiness of judgment.[7]

If Suffolk did sweep aside royal reservations, he surely advised badly. The moment was ideal for a gesture of conciliation. The duke and his fellow councillors had been taken by surprise, but not when Richard had wanted. Walsingham alleges that after the Nottingham council the king and the duke of Ireland gathered soldiers to attack the lords, and in 1388 the impeached chamber knights were accused of having collected forces the previous summer. But it seems unlikely that the king was in arms. If he was, why did he not use force at this juncture? The allegations may have been intended to help justify the rising of the lords and have been based on rumours of royal retaining and fears of the military finance at Vere's disposal for his Irish interests. On 8 September 1387 Richard terminated York's commission as justice of Chester, appointing the duke of Ireland as sole justice and on 10 October appointed him justice of North Wales too. These appointments gave Ireland control of array within his jurisdictions. Cheshire alone produced a large number of levies. In 1386 York had been called on to raise 1,000 Cheshire archers for the defence of London, more than twice the number that any other county was expected to array for the purpose. But in the summer and autumn of 1387 Richard hoped for the attainment of his objectives, the reassertion and recognition of his prerogative on his terms, by peaceful and inexpensive means. He wished to gain the support of London, whose military potential, as organized during the invasion scare of 1386, may have impressed him. This aim was probably encouraged by the ease with which he had recently intimidated the city government at Easthampstead.[8]

Perhaps Bramber encouraged Richard to believe that the Londoners could be relied on. His stock at court is likely to have risen after 21 September, when two friends of his, William Venour and Hugh Fastolf, were elected sheriffs. A few days later, Richard demanded that the city governors should take oaths to support him against anyone who proposed or talked treason. On 6 October Bramber attended the king at Eynsham Abbey near Oxford, bringing the city's agreement. But five days later the cautious Exton was re-elected mayor. The fact that the king's demand for an oath was issued on the authority of the Privy Seal, whose Keeper was the councillor John Waltham, suggests that formal contact and co-operation between Richard and the ministers had not broken down. It is not known whether members of the official council were present at the great councils which Richard held during the year. Some may have been anxious to compromise with the menacing king.

The Chancellor, Thomas Arundel, probably visited court at Wood-stock on 13 October. This visit is evidenced by the terms of a Chancery enrolment, the confirmation of an annuity granted by Ireland to Beauchamp of Holt. The Chancellor may have been attempting to mediate between Richard and Gloucester, as Braybrooke had vainly tried to do. On 28 October Archbishop Neville and Suffolk visited Exton, to enquire whether the Londoners were united in their opinions and prepared to stand by the king. Richard seems to have taken the reply, a somewhat guarded protestation of loyalty, as affirmative. On 10 November he entered London for the first time since the previous February. The city dignitaries met and paraded with their king, wearing his livery of white and red; the crowd cheered. In nine days' time the term of authority granted to the council was due to expire. After his first night at Westminster, Richard summoned Gloucester and the earl of Arundel: a reckoning was at hand.[9]

They refused to come, on the grounds that the king was sur-rounded by their enemies. Both parties then determined to resort to violence, but the nobles proved better prepared. The Westminster Chronicler alleges that Suffolk advised Richard to put Warwick to death, on the grounds that he had counselled Gloucester and Arundel to disobey the summons and resist the king. It seems that Warwick had an armed retinue at Harringay Park (Middlesex). It was not the first time in the reign that a magnate had brought an armed retinue to London, for several had done so at the time of the 1381 parliament, when tension had run high between Lancaster and Northumberland. The chronicler says that Richard refused to countenance the execution of such an eminent man as Warwick. The king showed himself less extreme than Suffolk, as he had at first done in the interview with Braybrooke. Richard's attitude may have been influenced by memories of friendly contacts with Warwick's Stafford relatives and with the earl himself. But Suffolk, if he gave the advice, ignored the ties made by his son's Stafford marriage. Richard wanted his retainers to come armed. Northumberland was ordered to arrest Arundel at Reigate Castle. The earl went through the motions of obeying, but abandoned the task when he found that Arundel was holding his castle in strength. The latter then marched by night, crossing the Thames, to join Warwick who was with Gloucester at Harringay Park—the duke had brought his retinue from Essex. The gentry of nearby counties apparently flocked to join the lords.

Numbers of 'the commons' may have joined too, disgruntled by attempts to enforce servile works and low wage levels, and cherishing grudges against the king for his 'betrayal' of their cause in 1381 and the punishments then meted out to the rebels under his auspices. The effectiveness of the lords' military concentration astonished Richard. He had thought that he was more in command of the situation than when the Commons had 'revolted' in the 1386 parliament. No lords of the present or previous generation had led a revolt against the king despite (perhaps partly because of) memories of Edward II's reign. Gloucester and his allies, by arraying their forces without the king's order and in a menacing manner, were coming perilously close to precedents set recently only by the despised commons in 1381, by Welsh 'traitors' such as Owain Lawgoch and by the disobedient and 'wild' Irish. These were all objects of noble contempt. Richard's assumption that he could return to Westminster when the council's tenure of office was about to expire, resume his full authority and secure it firmly by novel judicial definitions and perhaps punishments, is a tribute to the strength of the loyalty customarily displayed by late fourteenth-century magnates. Richard had not acted in 1387 as if confronted by opponents prepared to use force. He and his partisans seem to have thought that a series of menaces would suffice to destroy the resolution of critics.[10]

Indeed, most magnates did refrain from taking up arms against the king, but they did not defend Richard or openly condemn his opponents. At least one lord felt himself to be in a dilemma—the elderly Ralph Basset, Lord of Drayton (d. 1390), who had served Edward III and the Black Prince with distinction. His instinct was to defend the king, but he could not bear to fight for the duke of Ireland as well. Basset had conflicting personal loyalties, for he was a friend of Gloucester and had been married to a sister of Warwick. In February 1387 he was a surety when Warwick, Stafford, Lord Neville and Sir William Beauchamp received a grant of Stafford's wardship.[11] If the king's leading partisans had not included men as discredited as Ireland and Suffolk, his opponents would not have received such sympathy. The threat of foreign invasion had receded and Richard's judicial case scored some sound points. Suffolk's activities in 1387 were an object of suspicion even to his brother, Sir Edmund de la Pole of Boarstall Castle in Buckinghamshire, Captain of Calais Castle. When, after Richard had accepted the Appeal of Treason, the earl fled to Calais, melodramatically disguised as a poultry-seller, Sir Edmund promptly handed him over to the Captain of Calais, Sir William Beauchamp, who shipped him back to England. Beauchamp kept the Calais garrison neutral and intercepted communications between the English and French courts.[12] De la Pole's treatment of his suspiciously dressed brother does not seem to have been motivated by family coolness, for his business relations with the earl had been close and the latter anticipated a more fraternal reception. After Suffolk's forfeiture, Sir Edmund co-operated with his nephew, Sir Michael, in salvaging some of the inheritance. The heir was also unsympathetic to his fathers' politics, serving as a banneret in Arundel's retinue on the expedition which set off in 1388. Ten years later pardons for support given to Gloucester and Arundel in 1386-7 were sued out by Sir Michael de la Pole, Robert Bolton, clerk, a leading servant of his father, and Robert James of Wallingford, who before 1386 had married Sir Edmund's daughter, but the pardons were cancelled.[13]

The duke of Ireland had made a reputation of sorts for himself in 1387, by deserting his wife and eloping with one of the queen's Bohemian ladies. Since the duchess was a grand-daughter of Edward III, his misconduct was an insult to the king and wide circle of royal kinsmen. Richard's reputation was tarnished in noble circles by his failure to punish the wrong more than by any of his other recent actions. The duke's mother, the countess of Oxford, took her daughter-in-law's part. When Gloucester made his public oath, he declared his implacable hostility to Vere, not to the arguably more dangerous Suffolk, Burley or Bramber. Gloucester realized that his noble audience would sympathize with the feud. Richard, a student of history, might have concluded from Gaveston's example how dangerous it was to allow continuous offence to the *amour-propre* of nobles. However, Richard regarded Edward II as a saint. The scandal of Ireland's elopement was a crucial factor in the failure of York and the absent Lancaster to condemn the rising. Their reactions probably influenced those of other nobles, especially Derby's. The Westminster Chronicler says that all three of the king's uncles were greatly displeased by Ireland's conduct. York, as one of the councillors appointed in 1386, probably also resented the justices' rulings. He had a personal grievance in his dismissal from the Chester justiciary: according to a charge in the 1388 Appeal, Ireland procured his own appointment as Justice without the usual royal commission or sufficient warranty.[14]

On 13 November 1387 there was consternation in the royal household. Gloucester, Arundel and Warwick were in arms a few miles away. Sir Thomas Mortimer, the late earl of March's half-brother, was with them. Some royal partisans, notably Alexander Neville, hoped that the Londoners could be relied on. But other eminent men mediated, including Archbishop Courtenay, Lords Lovell and Cobham. Northumberland protested Gloucester's good faith, as he was to do in 1389. The duke and his allies sent an ultimatum to the wavering city government, alleging that five 'traitors' (Neville, Ireland, Suffolk, Tresilian and Bramber) had induced the king to disturb the realm, making divisions between Richard and 'the lords of his council, so that they were all in doubt and peril of their lives'. The allies gained some support among the Londoners. Ten years later six citizens received pardons for their partisanship—John Chircheman, John Colyn senior (grocers), Walter Donmowe (draper), John West (stockfishmonger, also of the town of Arundel), John Wodcok and John More (mercers). The aid of More, who had been a leading ally of Northampton, may have added to Gloucester's popular support in London. The king soon decided to negotiate, using the good offices of some of the councillors whose authority he had been eager to destroy. In conference with the allies at Waltham Holy Cross, York, Courtenay and others heard their allegations that they had assembled not to attack the king, but the traitors surrounding him. This was a theme which was to be developed (probably with inventive skill) in the charges annexed to the Appeal of Treason in its 1388 form. In the final draft the Appellants—no enemies on principle to regality—adapted Richard's arguments, by posing as the defenders of his prerogative against those who had allegedly abused it by misleading him in his tender years.

It was probably symptomatic of the divided counsels in the household in November 1387 that Gloucester had intelligence of how the unpopular soldier, Sir Thomas Trivet (perhaps anxious to recover his naval command from Arundel), was trying to persuade Richard to have the royal standard raised against him. Richard and the duke were both uncertain as to the best means to attain their objectives: they shared a novel situation. Consequently the mediators were temporarily able to impose their policy. On 17 November the three Appellants rode to Westminster, adamantly leaving their army arrayed and accompanied by 300 men-at-arms. Richard received them in Westminster Hall, seated on the raised marble chair at the end, the symbolic seat of royal authority, from which justice was dispensed. By this reception Richard emphasized the affront to his majesty of their appearance in armour. The Appellants excused their failure to attend when originally bidden and their arrival in arms, on the ground that they were in peril of their lives. Ten years later Gloucester gave the same excuse: ' . . . I came armed into my Lordes presence, and into his Palais . . . I dede it for drede of my lyf.'

Richard Lord Scrope of Bolton (a member of the 1386 commission, whose dismissal from the Chancellorship Richard had insisted on in 1382) spoke on behalf of the Appellants, challenging the five alleged traitors to combat. But the king referred the Appeal to parliament, an expedient about which he was apprehensive, but which would give his accused friends a breathing-space. The Appellants had to accept the royal promise, for if they had tried to coerce a king attending to their grievances, they would have alienated moderate magnates such as Courtenay and Northumberland, who had no desire to replace the rule of the duke of Ireland by that of the duke of Gloucester. After the public conference, Richard and the Appellants retired to a chamber and took wine together with seeming amicability. The king was adept at concealing his emotions, when he had rehearsed his demeanour: he was to put on a fine show at Conway in 1399. By deserting the camp for the council chamber, the Appellants had lost coercive power, but they had appeared moderate and the king had made a commitment. Afterwards Richard could not contain his fury at the rising and his subjects' failure to oppose it. He was inclined to authorize the armed action which some had urged all along, but he did not break completely with the mediating councillors who were trying to hold him to the bargain. The ambiguities of his policy probably reflected his continued uncertainty, increased by conflicting advice. The accused were too divided among themselves to offer a firm front. Suffolk was determined to get abroad, Neville and Tresilian went their separate ways into hiding. Only two of the five, Ireland and Bramber, offered resistance to the Appellants, and their activities do not appear to have been well co-ordinated. The duke headed for his Chester command, armed with royal letters on whose authority his deputy, the able Sir Thomas Molyneux, quickly assembled an army from Cheshire, North Wales and Lancashire. Meanwhile Bramber assisted the king in more efforts to win London support. Towards the end of November the king ordered a proclamation in the city, that no one defame the five appealed of treason or members of the household. On 28 November Exton was bidden to attend at Windsor. There he and the aldermen were asked by the king to estimate the armed men they could furnish him with if required. In reply they hedged, refusing to commit themselves. Richard's approaches to the craft gilds were similarly rebuffed.[15]

How was Richard able to approach the Londoners, when the Appellants were still in arms? His negotiations could hardly have remained secret. The citizens had probably been manning their defences since the assembly at Harringay Park, as they were to be when the Appellants' army returned in December. Though there was sympathy with Gloucester in the city and the king had been unable to prevent his army's purchase of supplies there, it is unlikely that the majority of citizens wanted to admit an army, of whatever political complexion. Unwillingness to force the issue with the city may have been one of the determining factors in the Appellants' decision to compromise by appearing in Westminster Hall. Nevertheless, distrustful of the king, they kept their army in being. They may have found it politically and logistically inexpedient to stay encamped near London and have withdrawn northwards in search of supplies and reinforcements. Richard summoned a great council to Westminster. This time it was he who failed to appear when it convened, just as he had absented himself during part of the 1386 parliament. His absence and the hostile remarks he was reported to be making about the Appellants showed his renewed confidence. In vain bishops and lay lords tried to maintain their conciliatory policy. It may have been during this council that a 'Prelate of the Realm' (Thomas Arundel?) prayed Burley to advise the king against intending to raise forces, so avoiding the threatened destruction of the king and realm. Burley was said to have replied 'in a haughty manner' that if the prelate raised the matter again, he would turn the king's anger against him.

In these alarming weeks, a momentous development took place, which helped the Appellants to win the brief civil war, but altered the political character of their movement and undermined what little cohesiveness it possessed. This was the adherence to the Appeal of Henry of Bolingbroke, Earl of Derby, and of Thomas Mowbray, Earl Marshal. The two were themselves odd allies, for Derby was an affectionate son of Lancaster and the Earl Marshal had been one of the courtiers 'nurtured' with the king who had plotted Lancaster's death in 1385. It is uncertain whether the newcomers were devoted to the persons and aims of the senior Appellants, though Derby was Gloucester's nephew and the Earl Marshal was Arundel's son-in-law, and though Favent thought that they joined the Appellants because of ties of kinship. The marriage of Derby to Mary de Bohun, so unwelcome to Thomas of Woodstock, had resulted in lengthy and possibly strained negotiations over the division of Hereford's inheritance. The Earl Marshal's boon companionship with the king predated his marriage to Arundel's daughter and he had a claim, which he pressed when opportunity arose, on Warwick's Lordship of Gower. Why did the two young earls take to arms at this point? They may have feared that, if Ireland won, his influence at court would be impregnable. Derby, controlling the county palatine of Lancaster, may have been affronted by Molyneux's recruitment there. On the other hand, Derby and Nottingham may have been suspicious and apprehensive about the Appellants' intentions and determined to gain influence within their counsels.[16]

On 12 December Henry of Bolingbroke and Thomas Mowbray consulted the senior Appellants (and Sir Thomas Mortimer) at Huntingdon. This was a good strategic centre, between the court and the north, well placed for a march on London or the Midlands. It is probable that Appellant supporters from the Midlands and East Anglia joined the rising at Huntingdon. Knowledge of the council at Huntingdon is unfortunately derived mainly from the charges made on the king's behalf in 1397. The Westminster Chronicler recounts a speech made by Warwick concerning a deposition proposal, likely to have been made there, in which he argued that deposition would bring shame on their families and that it was strategically necessary to march against the duke of Ireland. The chronicler says that Warwick's proposal was unanimously accepted. It is credible that he argued against deposition, since his family had enjoyed Edward III's favour and he had not, as far as we know, had bad relations with Richard II. The Westminster Monk probably had special knowledge of Warwick's views as a result of the earl's link with the abbey in 1387. Ten years later he confessed that he had opposed Richard partly as a result of the advice given by the monk-recluse of Westminster. His consultation is an indication of the perplexity felt by at least one of the original Appellants, who was not an ambitious and unscrupulous rebel, but a middle-aged man with a lifetime of loyalty to the Crown behind him, seeking a safe and honourable deliverance from a novel dilemma. One factor which probably aided the adoption of Warwick's political and military strategy was the problem of choosing a successor to Richard. Mortimer, Warwick and perhaps Arundel would have been likely to advocate March's claim, which Derby and probably Gloucester could accept only with reluctance. If the Appellants had marched to depose the king, there might have been a reaction in his favour, swelling the duke of Ireland's force with new recruits and increasing the chance of a prolonged civil war. However, at the time the decision taken must have seemed equally hazardous—the allies were intending to cut loose from their eastern bases, turning their backs on London and the king, over which they had no control. They may have genuinely feared that Richard would seek French aid, a more plausible manœuvre now that the English had maintained an army in Spain, scored successes at sea, threatened Flanders and reinforced Brest. Knighton and other English chroniclers refer suspiciously to supposed contacts between the English and French courts in 1387, contacts reaching a climax after Gloucester and his allies had risen in arms. Burley's offices as Constable of Dover Castle and Warden of the Cinque Ports facilitated communications. The confederates were already hinting at tentative royal negotiations in November, as their letter to the Londoners shows.

The decision to intercept Ireland's army turned out to be the right one: the Appellants had correctly estimated his and the king's capacity. Richard merely waited for his lieutenant to succeed, though, according to the 1388 Appeal, he had arranged that the duke

> should take the field with all of his Power that he could assemble, and that the King should meet him with all his Power, and that the King together with him should hazard his Royal Person.

If Richard had advanced through the Chiltern Hills with even a small force, his threat and presence in the field might have affected the outcome, raising the uncertain morale of the duke of Ireland's force and depressing that of their opponents. Moreover, the Appellants' retinues had become vulnerable as they spread out through the western Midlands in order to block the duke's lines of approach to London. Why did Richard fail to act? Throughout his reign he professed himself eager to chastise his enemies; his Crown seemed in danger, as it had been in 1381. Then he had temporized brilliantly, but it had been Knolles and Walworth who deployed the force trapping the rebels at Smithfield. Richard does not seem to have developed any talent for the exercise of command—in Scotland in 1385, in England in 1386, in Ireland in 1394–5 and in Ireland and Wales in 1399, he relied mainly on the advice and activity of those he trusted. In 1399 his reliance on the counsel of his favourite cousin, Edward of Norwich, Duke of Aumale, and on the military capacity of John Montague, Earl of Salisbury, was disastrous. To be fair, in 1399 Richard did take energetic personal action in an effort to stave off disaster, whereas in 1387 he depended on the initiative of Robert de Vere, who had given him what turned out to be sensible military advice in Scotland in 1385, and on the Cheshiremen, whose martial reputation was high. In December 1387 Richard II is likely to have been paralysed by conflicting advice. Some members of the household were reluctant to ride against the Appellants. Bramber was probably anxious for him to hold London securely. If Richard was contemplating a treaty with Charles VI, he needed to keep open his communications with the Cinque Ports.[17]

Meanwhile the Appellants marched south-west into the Cotswolds, probably recruiting successfully on their march. Thus William Harwedon may have joined them not far from his home at Great Harrowden (Northants.) and their proclamation at Northampton may have drawn in the townsmen William Barry, Simon Bosyate, John Loudeham, John Trig, besides Thomas Percy from Roade, not far from the town, and a well-to-do local landowner, John Longville of Little Billing (also lord of Wolverton, Bucks.). The Appellants were diligent with propaganda among peers as well as gentry and townsmen: on 19 December, according to Dr M. E. Aston, a letter addressed to Bishop Wakefield of Worcester was delivered, which explained the cause of their rising. In fact the bishop read it the day before Ireland's army was routed in Oxfordshire. The death of Molyneux and the flight of the duke completed the demoralization of the Cheshiremen. The Appellants probably executed some prisoners, but allowed the majority to go home, deprived of their arms. The capture of the duke's correspondence provided evidence that the king had authorized his actions.[18] One unremarked incident of the campaign may typify small contributions to the Appellant victory made by relatively unimportant supporters. This was the destruction of the bridge over the Thames at Lechlade in Gloucestershire, which Thomas of Woodstock ordered, to block one escape-route which Vere's army might have taken. In March 1388 pontage to pay for its repair was granted to Richard Smyth, Prior of the Augustinian Hospital of St John at the head of the bridge. Smyth was later pardoned for giving support to Gloucester and Arundel—perhaps he helped to break down the hospital's own bridge. Another Lechlade supporter of the Appellants was a butcher, John Colett.[19] Four days before Ireland's defeat, the king was not moving to adventure his person in the duke's company (a failure which Richard may have regretted for the rest of his life) but in the opposite direction. He went from Windsor to keep Christmas in the Tower, which he garrisoned strongly. Bramber's attempt to hold London for the king was unsuccessful. The victorious Appellants once more marched north of the city, entering with guarantees of good behaviour. Bishops, York and Northumberland, mediating again, arranged for the surrender of the Tower. The Westminster Chronicler says that the Appellants, after their entry, threatened Richard with deposition, if he did not refrain from opposing them, and alluded to his heir as being of full age. Richard was stupefied. The late Miss Clarke and V. H. Galbraith suggested that the Appellants may actually have withdrawn their allegiances for three days. Their main authority was a continuation of Higden's *Polychronicon*. The writer says that after Richard had been deposed, consultations as to who should succeed him failed to produce agreement and therefore he was restored. The 'commons' wanted Gloucester as king, but this was opposed by Derby, who protested that his descent gave him the better claim. Miss Clarke and Galbraith thought that Gloucester may have been referring to this incident in his 1397 confession:

> I among other communed for feer of my lyf to zyve up myn
> hommage to my Lord, I knowlech wel, that for certain that I
> among other communed and asked of certeins Clercs, whethir
> that we myght zyve up our homage for drede of our lyves, or
> non: and whethir that we assentyd therto for to do it, trewlich
> and by my trowth I ne have now none full mynde therof, bot I
> trowe rather ze than nay.

His uncertainty as to whether a deposition had been agreed on is understandable, if there was noise and wrangling in the Tower. The Appellants' hesitations stamp them as confused and half-hearted rebels, not determined usurpers like Henry of Bolingbroke in 1399. It is likely that in 1387 he and the Earl Marshal were unwilling that

Richard should be deposed. In 1397 it was alleged that they had upset the deposition proposal at Huntingdon. The Earl Marshal was a friend of the king and there is no positive evidence that Derby was not in the 1380s, though Richard's treatment of his father probably strained relations. Walsingham says that after Richard had consulted the Appellants, he retained Derby alone in his company 'as a pledge of his love'.[20]

The failure to carry through the deposition of Richard in 1387 showed realism. It was easier for Henry of Bolingbroke in 1399, for potential claimants were dead. In London in December 1387 there were reasonably neutral lords such as York and Northumberland, who were not yet prepared to welcome a deposition. Moreover, now that the Appellants had won, this hazardous measure appeared less necessary. Richard's embittering experiences in the last months of 1387 made his political touch cautious. He became more convinced that it was his mission to raise royal authority from the dust into which he felt his subjects were inclined to cast it. From the nadir of December 1387, he worked on the whole with tact, persuasiveness and forbearance to restore his personal prestige and to assert royal authority as embodied in the justices' rulings. The task took him not twelve months, but ten years. The patience required probably strained his nerves and distorted even further his naturally extravagant political judgment. He had this advantage: that the words and actions of Gloucester and his allies, from 13 November 1387 onwards, provided him with a more certain justification for his aims than he had previously had. This moral advantage made the magnates anxious to appease him in the 1390s. But the king remained acutely conscious of what had happened, of the legacy of precedents and statutes and of the fact that all his principal opponents were alive and influential ten years later. There was a sound instinct behind the wish to depose Richard, for as long as he continued to reign, the manner in which he had been coerced put those responsible in personal jeopardy. The armed baronial protest, with its honourable feudal origins, had become more equivocal since the deposition of Edward II, as later exponents, such as Archbishop Scrope in 1405 and the duke of York in the 1450s, were to show. Twice the Appellants were on the point of deposing the king, their principal motive probably being a justified fear for their future security. The failure to carry out this intent was, in part, a comment on political stability—on the prevalence of loyal and moderate attitudes towards the Crown among the nobles, despite awareness of the precedent of Edward II's deposition; on the need for broad backing from the 'community of the realm' for successful initiatives. The Appellants belonged to a nobility which had become especially close-knit in Edward III's reign and which had shown suspicion in Richard's minority of any attempt to dominate the Crown. Magnates with such a background were unlikely to believe that they could rule for long, individually or collectively, as mayors of the palace.

An important factor in the success of the Appellants was their large stake in the propertied wealth of the realm, with its concomitant local political influence. This wealth was necessary for their rising, partly because soldiers expected to be 'waged' in advance. A large proportion of the £20,000 granted to the Appellants in the first 1388 parliament was probably swallowed up by their debts for military wages. Derby had brought to their aid the resources of the largest English lay inheritance. Lancastrian property, scattered over many counties, was concentrated in the Midlands and north. Otherwise the Appellants had few estates in the north. Warwick had four lordships in the bishopric of Durham and the Earl Marshal had some Yorkshire manors. He also held the Lordships of Bramber (Sussex) and Axholme (Lincs.). The fact that he was Marshal probably added prestige to the cause: the continuator of the *Eulogium* described how one of Ireland's knights lost heart on seeing the arms of the Constable and Marshal displayed. In Wales and the bordering counties the Appellants could command considerable influence, to some extent balancing Richard's over the principality and the earldom of Chester. Arundel was the leading landowner in the northern marches, ruling the Lordships of Yale and Bromfield, Chirk, Oswestry and Clun; he had many Shropshire manors too. His neighbour Owain Glyn Dŵr may have fought for him against Ireland, certainly contracting to serve in the earl's overseas retinues in 1387-8. Among the earl's bannerets for service in March 1387 were Sir Fulk FitzWarin of Whittington (Salop) and the Herefordshire landowner Sir Richard Talbot, a Bohun by descent, whose wife was related to Arundel. Other members of Arundel's retinue with interests in the region were his Shropshire relative Sir Roger Strange and the Marcher Sir Reginald Grey, son and heir of the Lord of Ruthin.[21]

Furthermore, the Appellants could exercise some influence in the lordships of the greatest landowner in the middle Marches, Roger Mortimer. Since 1383 his inheritance had been in the wardship of Warwick, Arundel, Northumberland and Lord Neville. They appointed his uncle Sir Thomas Mortimer to head the council supervising the administration of Roger's estates. In March 1387 Sir Thomas led a retinue of eighty-two on Arundel's naval expedition and he supported the Appellants so forcefully in arms and counsel that Richard singled him out for punishment ten years later. There were other estates and lordships held by Gloucester, Warwick and Derby in the middle and southern Marches. The Appellants were influential in the Midlands—Warwick was the dominant landowner in Warwickshire and Worcestershire. From February 1387 onwards the Stafford inheritance was in the hands of Warwick and his nephew Stafford, Lord Neville and Sir William Beauchamp. In western and eastern England were Bohun, Arundel, Beauchamp, Mowbray and Lancaster manors: Bohun holdings were concentrated in Essex, Arundel ones in Sussex. It may have been useful to Gloucester, Arundel and Warwick that they had their principal groups of estates within easy reach of London. In south-east England there were few lay landowners rivalling Gloucester and Arundel. Robert de Vere may have been handicapped because a large part of his inheritance was held as jointure by his mother, whereas Gloucester's territorial influence had been extended by the 1385 grant to him of the Moleyns wardship, mainly in Buckinghamshire.[22]

In 1398-9 the lieges of London and of sixteen counties were forced to sue out pardons for the support they had allegedly given to the Appellants. The counties were Kent, Surrey, Sussex, Hampshire, Wiltshire, Oxfordshire, Berkshire, Buckinghamshire, Bedfordshire, Huntingdonshire, Cambridgeshire, Norfolk, Suffolk, Essex, Hertfordshire, and Middlesex. This list does not tally with areas where the Appellants were territorially predominant, apart from Essex, Sussex and perhaps Buckinghamshire, but it does include the whole of south-eastern England, of regions which formed economic hinterlands to London, where information about the politics of the realm and city was more easily obtainable. The counties fined by Richard correspond to a remarkable extent with those in which the Peasants' Revolt had attracted most support.

The tentative conclusion may be put forward that, though the territorial influence at the Appellants' command in the provinces was of crucial importance to their rebellion, their success partly depended on winning the approval or at least acquiescence of the politically sophisticated part of the realm. The territorial influence which

Gloucester and Arundel in particular wielded there probably helped them in the task. The patronage that kings could exercise from their chain of residences in the counties around London should have aided Richard. But in 1387 he had concentrated on securing support in the provinces and in distant royal appanages.

The composition of the military retinues which Gloucester and his allies arrayed remains hypothetical. The Lincolnshire landowner and Lancastrian retainer Sir John Bussy may have taken up arms with Derby, for in May 1398, according to a Patent Roll entry, he was pardoned

> for adhering to Gloucester and Arundel, when they assumed the royal authority in the tenth year by commission under the great seal in derogation of the king and his crown, drew after them Warwick and others in insurrection at Harringay and elsewhere, came to the king in his palace at Westminster, and plundered, imprisoned and killed many lieges in divers parts of the realm, which commission was declared by Parliament to be high treason, and for any other offences connected therewith.

At the same time an identical pardon was granted to the Northamptonshire landowner Sir Henry Grene.[23] Useful comparisons, throwing light on the support which the Appellants obtained, can be made between the list of counties pardoned in 1397–8 and the individual pardons granted, lists of which were enrolled on two Pardon Rolls—attention has been drawn to these lists by Mrs C. Barron. In many cases the individual's place of residence (which may have changed in ten years) is given or can be worked out. In some cases status or profession is stipulated and sometimes even changes in these or place of residence. In the lists there are six monks, including the abbots of the Benedictine house of Bardney and the Cistercian house of Revesby, both in Lincolnshire, the Cistercian abbot of Waverley (Surrey), whose patron was Bishop Wickham, and Hugh Veretot, who was associated with Arundel in the farming of Fécamp Abbey properties. There was also a monk of Peterborough. There were 12 secular incumbents, 13 clerks and 3 chaplains. 42 of the laymen pardoned styled themselves knights in 1397–8 and 29 styled themselves esquires. From towns came 4 who styled themselves merchants (one each from York, Bristol and Nottingham and one formerly of Chesterfield in Derbyshire) and there was a Coventry mercer. Also listed were a notary of Ipswich, a leech, a barber, a harper, a draper from Pershore

(Worcs.), where Warwick held the manor of Wadborough, a tailor, a weaver of Lincoln, a saddler, two butchers, two fishers (one of Bristol), a sawyer of Leicester, a fletcher, two carpenters and a smith. Some minor officials sued out pardons—the subconstable of Lincoln Castle, three parkers, one warrener, a former manorial bailiff and five former servants, including a barber's from the Lancastrian manor of Pontefract (Yorks.). Though many of those listed of indeterminate status or profession can be shown from other evidence to have held property befitting an esquire, others were almost certainly of humbler rank. Probably large numbers of the lesser folk who were pardoned had been in arms in 1387, for it is unlikely that they could have given the king's opponents useful support in any other way. The John Wryght who identified himself in his pardon as the man 'Whych hath Weddyd the doutir of William Bonde of West le' probably had little to offer of use to the Appellants except his strong right arm.

There follows a list of the numbers individually pardoned resident in counties whose communities petitioned for grace. A large number of those pardoned, albeit a minority, have not been allotted to particular counties, and there has been some arbitrariness in the allotment, when individuals are stated to have been of more than one county or have been identified as possessing property in more than one.

London	6	Bedfordshire	9
Kent	3	Huntingdonshire	4
Surrey	14	Cambridgeshire	4
Sussex	57	Norfolk	30
Hampshire	5	Suffolk	10
Wiltshire	0	Essex	16
Oxfordshire	2	Hertfordshire	6
Berkshire	3	Middlesex	1
Buckinghamshire	7		

The scarcity of pardons from some counties which Richard considered culpable is surprising, particularly in the case of Kent, where, it might have been expected, hostility to Richard would be widespread after 1381. The Appellants had little territorial influence in the county. But such influence is probably reflected in the large number of pardons for Sussex and Essex—Sussex produced more than any other county. Servants and livery-holders of Gloucester and Arundel were probably anxious to sue out pardons, in view of the implied threats to them and Warwick's men in royal proclamations and commissions of 1397. Sussex men pardoned included eight from Arundel's town of Arundel, two from his town of Lewes and two from Billingshurst and Tortington, where he held manors. But the majority of Sussex partisans whose place of residence was named did not come from the earl's manors—a fact which suggests that he was able to recruit the support of neighbours. Prominent Sussex retainers and friends of Arundel who received pardons were Sir William Percy, John Cocking esquire and John Stevens. One man came from Nottingham's manor of Findon, another from Sir Edward Dallingridge's manor of Bodiam. Other Sussex gentlemen who gave support to the king's opponents were Sir William Fiennes, Sir Henry Husee and Sir William Waleys. Arundel's military concentration at Reigate probably included, besides many of the Sussex men, five from Reigate, a carpenter from neighbouring Merstham, a man from the earl's manor of Dorking and another Surrey man, William Miltone, who was Arundel's servant and 'henksman'. Other servants of Arundel who took out pardons were Sir Hugh Browe, to whom he granted Cheshire manors in March 1388, his clerk Robert Publow, his retainers William Rees and John Bonham, Richard Alderton, who was granted an Essex manor by the earl in October 1387, Stephen Hyndercle, former yeoman of his chamber in 1397, and two Hampshire men holding property in the county of his grant in 1397, Walter Rotherfield and John Yattere of Chawton.

Counties in which, as in Sussex, leading gentlemen sued out pardons were Cambridgeshire, Huntingdonshire, Norfolk and Suffolk. Influential in the first two counties were Hugh Lord la Zouche, who had associations with Gloucester, the latter's retainer Sir William Castleacre, Sir William Moyne, who had sat for Huntingdonshire in the 1386 parliament, and Sir Payn Tiptoft, who had acquired a manor for life from Arundel by May 1388. Partisan East Anglian gentlemen included Gloucester's acquaintance Lord Morley, Sir Simon Felbrigg, Sir Ralph Bigot, Sir John White, Sir Roger Drury and Sir John Mauteby. It is likely that Arundel was able to call up contingents from his Norfolk properties of Castleacre, Mileham and Beeston, for six men from Castleacre sued out pardons, three from Mileham and two from Beeston, including the parson Roger Routon. One Appellant supporter came from Warwick's manor of Necton (Norfolk). From counties other than those whose communities sued out pardons the following number of individual suppliants have been identified:

Cornwall	2	Northamptonshire	39
Derbyshire	9	Nottinghamshire	5
Devon	3	Rutland	2
Dorset	1	Shropshire	4
Gloucestershire	10	Staffordshire	7
Herefordshire	7	Warwickshire	33
Lancashire	1	Worcestershire	22
Leicestershire	23	Yorkshire	4
Lincolnshire	20		

In fact the number pardoned from these counties is slightly greater than the number pardoned from counties which were fined. This statistic serves to emphasize that the Appellants received considerable support in regions besides south-east England and East Anglia. It is surprising that only a handful from Shropshire (and three from the Marches) were pardoned. The large number from Northamptonshire, Warwickshire and Worcestershire probably in part reflects the influence of the earl of Warwick, underlining the importance of his adherence to the cause. Among the Appellants' partisans were his influential knights William Bagot and Nicholas Lilling, his well-rewarded esquire John Daniel senior and his servant William Spernore. Warwickshire gentlemen pardoned included William Clinton of Maxstoke (whose brother Edward, also an Appellant supporter, was in Nottingham's service in 1391), John Charnels of Bedworth and William Peyto, probably of the same family as Sir John Peyto, Nottingham's knight in 1388. Two men from Napton (Warcs), whose advowson had been held by Arundel, were pardoned—both may have been drapers. A number of supporters came from Warwick's Worcestershire manors: three from Salwarp (one a carpenter), a chaplain from Yardley and two men from Elmley and Comberton. Four came from his Northamptonshire manors of Potterspury and Cosgrave, one from his Buckinghamshire manor of Hanslope. Three Bedford men were pardoned—Nottingham had property there. Northamptonshire landowners pardoned were Sir Giles Malory (later high in Warwick's service), Sir Henry Grene, Sir John Trussell and Thomas Wydeville esquire. But most of the partisans from identifiable places in the Midlands did not hail from properties of the Appellants.

Some of the large number of supporters from Leicestershire and

Lincolnshire may have joined as a result of the influence which Derby could exert through his control of the Lancastrian lordships there. Seven men from Lancaster's borough of Leicester were pardoned, a larger number than from any other town. Their participation helps account for Knighton's detailed information about the Oxfordshire campaign, on which J. N. L. Myres commented. In Lincolnshire, as in Leicestershire, there were some influential gentlemen supporting Gloucester, such as the Lancastrian retainer, Sir John Bussy, and Thomas Missenden, who by 1388 had probably entered the Earl Marshal's service. Staffordshire, Derbyshire and Nottinghamshire all provided some significant supporters, but, surprisingly (especially in view of Lancastrian influence) only a handful from Yorkshire and Lancashire took out pardons. The Border counties and Wales are scarcely represented. These blanks may reflect Richard's ability to capture support in the principality, and the neutrality of the northern lords. The rising was so sudden that the Appellants probably did not have time to mobilize what support they could command in the far north and the far west. The pardon for Sir William Heron, Lord Say, appears exceptional—he was probably a Northumberland landowner. He may have been in the south in Arundel's service when the crisis arose, for he went on his overseas expeditions of 1387–8. It may be that northern society was not so deeply stirred by the political conflicts which preoccupied lowland England. In the Borders the main issues were relations with the Scots and between the affinities aligned behind the leading families. It was the Appellants, not Richard, who exacerbated feelings there by the failure of their northern policies.

But as regards lowland England, the names on the Pardon Rolls demonstrate how widespread adherence to Gloucester and his allies was from 1386 onwards. Most of the servants and tenants, artisans and burgesses who adhered to them possibly did so because of the need to show loyalty to landlords and patrons. But can it be assumed that such lesser folk were indifferent to the issues at stake—to the ruinous consequences to the realm which, it had been noised abroad, would ensue from the malpractices of traitors? Paucity of evidence makes a definite answer impossible. An important point is that magnates were asking men outside their lordship as well as within it to make a *chevauchée* within the realm. This was a novelty for that generation of Englishmen, therefore the Appellants considered that to win zealous supporters it was necessary to justify as well as to order or request, as did fifteenth-century demonstrators in their public bills and manifestos. The Appellants' propaganda was perhaps one stimulus to the involvement of lesser men in noble politics, a phenomenon familiar under the Lancastrian monarchy, when the 'commons' continued to be used as tools for noble ambition and on occasion articulated their own grievances.[24]

In the parliament which contemporaries called 'Wonderful' or 'Merciless', the Lords Appellant secured the condemnation by the Lords for treason of those whom they had 'appealed' at Waltham Cross and Westminster and again in the Tower, after the king had capitulated. They also secured the impeachment by the Commons and conviction by the Lords of others who had been the king's partisans in 1387. Therefore the parliament marked the culmination of their success. It conferred legality on their rising and on the defeat of their opponents. It gave approval to the exercise of influence over government which they had acquired. Yet the fact that contemporaries applied such contrary epithets to this parliament shows how divided they became about its judgments and acts. Divisions of opinion among its members soon appeared. The Lords grew restive as Gloucester, Arundel and Warwick pressed for convictions and capital punishments, in alliance with the Commons. The Commons became even more impatient with the Lords than their predecessors had done in earlier parliaments of the reign. Derby and the Earl Marshal inclined to the side of the moderates, breaking up the precarious unity of the Lords Appellant. Now that the king's partisans had been routed, magnates were less willing to tolerate the ascendancy of Gloucester and the earl of Arundel. In order to remain predominant, they had to appease over policy and the distribution of royal patronage. Their hold on government depended on continued uncertainty about Richard's intentions, but after the shock of the past months, he was being more circumspect.

In December 1387 the victorious Appellants had ensured their safety by taking control of government, which they were to retain for seventeen months. On 31 December they went to Westminster and took control. They decided to reduce drastically the size of the household and to arrest supporters of the king's extreme policies. The New Year was heralded by the detention of some of Richard's favourite household knights and clerks, including Burley, Beauchamp of Holt and Berners. Also arrested were some distinguished soldiers—Sir Thomas Trivet, Sir Nicholas Dagworth and Sir William Elmham. The only one of the five appealed of treason whom the Appellants were able to detain was Bramber, who presumably had remained in London loyally backing the king, as he had done in 1381. Some of the chamber knights were neither imprisoned nor banished from court. Their services were necessary, for the Appellants could not dissolve the royal household. One distinguished household knight who seems to have been trusted by the Appellants was Philip la Vache of Chalfont St Giles (Bucks), who had served in Edward III's chamber and in the household of Princess Joan, Richard's mother (d. 1385). Vache had a talent for surviving political upheavals. According to his friend Geoffrey Chaucer, he was an upright man who became depressed by court intrigue. He was friendly with Sir Richard Adderbury and Lady Margaret Moleyns, who were forced to leave court in 1388. Probably for the only time in his life, Vache was returned as knight of the shire for Buckinghamshire and as a member of the Commons' House took part in the impeachment of his former colleagues. The Appellants were so well disposed towards him that in May 1388 he was appointed to the key office of Captain of Calais Castle, in succession to Sir Edmund de la Pole.

The Appellants were concerned to effect economies. For example, in February 1388 Richard Braundeston was appointed to replace William Hanney as Controller of the King's Works, because he offered to serve with a wage reduction of one-third. His patent was warranted 'by the advice of the council'. It is difficult to be sure who the councillors then were, apart from the Appellants. Bishop Arundel had never been dismissed from the Chancellorship, nor had the other two ministers whose appointment the king had so resented in 1386. Early in 1388, according to the Westminster Chronicler, the existing councillors appointed a group 'for the continuous government of the king' consisting of Bishop Wickham, the Treasurer Walter Skirlaw, Lords Cobham and Scrope and Sir John Devereux. The last was appointed Steward of the Household, and, to Richard's gratification, his retainer Sir Peter Courtenay was appointed Chief Chamberlain. All these were appointments likely to be approved by the magnates, for the Appellants did not dare to pack council and household with their own retainers.[25]

Parliament met on 3 February 1388. It aroused more interest among contemporaries than any previous one since 1376, judging by the number of private accounts which have survived. The charges made in it were sensational, the legality and reversibility of its

judgments continued to be a political preoccupation for the rest
of Richard's reign and, indeed, after it. The Appellants had some
retainers, friends and sympathizers sitting as shire knights. Essex was
represented by the former Speaker, Sir John Gildsburgh, and by
Thomas Coggeshall, who was to be pardoned for the support he gave
to Gloucester and Arundel. They were probably both then retainers
of the duke. Sir Gerard Braybrooke the younger sat for Bedfordshire:
the nephew of Gloucester's close friend and political sympathizer, the
bishop of London, he was to be a retainer of the duke and to rise high
in the confidence of his family. Sir Gerard and some of his Bedfordshire friends were later pardoned for giving help to the Appellants—
the influential Sir Roger Beauchamp of Bletsoe, Ralph Walton of
Sharnbrook, a minor landowner, and William Tyrington of Aspley,
a lesser official of the royal household successfully insinuating himself
into county society. Sir Gerard (or his father of the same name) was
appointed in March 1388 to take oaths in Bedfordshire to maintain
the Appellants' cause. Sir Richard Waldegrave, a former Bohun
retainer, was elected for Suffolk—his 1397 pardon may indicate that
he gave Gloucester support in parliament, which would have been
weighty, for, like Gildsburgh, he was a rich and well-connected
gentleman who had been Speaker of the Commons.

Arundel's councillor and retainer Sir Edward Dallingridge was
sitting for Sussex, with Sir William Waleys, who received a pardon for
supporting Gloucester and Arundel in 1386–7. Other shire knights
connected with the earl were the Cheshireman Sir Hugh Browe
(Rutland), similarly pardoned, and Sir John Dauntsey (Wilts.).
Retainers of Warwick were Sir William Bagot, shire knight for
Warwickshire, and Sir Nicholas Lilling (Worcs.). Sir Giles Malory
and John Wydeville (Northants.) may also have been his retainers.
All of these possible Beauchamp servants except Wydeville received
later pardons for their support of the Appellant rising, as did the other
shire knight for Worcestershire, Sir Hugh Cheyne, and one of the
burgesses for Worcester, Roger Irchfield *alias* Swynsor. Dallingridge,
Dauntsey and Bagot were appointed to take oaths pledging support
for the Appellants in the shires which they represented. Other likely
supporters of the Appellants in parliament were Sir John White
(Norfolk) and Hugh Quecche (Surrey), the latter of whom was
appointed to take oaths in his county. Both of them were to sue out
pardons for the support they had given to Gloucester and Arundel in
1386–7. Other shire knights who administered oaths on behalf of the

Appellants in the shires which they represented were Sir John Irby (Cumb.), Sir Thomas Walsh (Leics.), Sir Thomas Fogg (Kent), Adam Francis (Middx.) and Sir Walter Atlee (Herts.).[26] Sir John Botiller, one of Lancaster's most important duchy officials, sat for the county palatine. Thus, out of a total of 74 shire knights, 19 have been firmly identified as likely supporters of the Appellants. Richard's publicly expressed hope that members would be elected who were impartial in recent controversies was substantially unfulfilled.[27]

On the first day of the session the Appeal of Treason was read. The king ordered the justices present to advise on how it should be dealt with. During the session Richard's right to play a formal part in the proceedings enabled him to score points—he was not elusive, as early in the 1386 session. But his credit was too low for him to defeat the aims of the Appellants. However, they too were vulnerable to criticism; before the Appeal was read, Gloucester publicly knelt before the king and excused himself from the charge of plotting to seize the Crown, a charge which he said had been relayed to the king. Richard declared that he held the duke pardoned. The Lords then showed determination to assert their jurisdiction in treason cases. They declared by common accord that, in cases such as the Appeal, trial should take place in parliament and not according to common or civil law. The justices had prepared the way for this assertion by their reply to Richard's preliminary question, saying that the Appeal did not meet the requirements of one or the other. The Lords temporal proceeded speedily to judgment. Alexander Neville, Ireland, Suffolk and Tresilian were found guilty by default and sentenced to forfeiture and (except in Neville's case) execution. The Lords' acceptance of the accusations in the Appeal established the legality of the Appellants' more questionable activities. On behalf of the confederates, Gloucester protested in parliament that the military assembly and expedition they and their friends had made was for the good of king and realm and to upset the malice of traitors. With the assent of king and parliament this was approved.

Bramber was now produced for trial. On 16 February Richard, in the presence of the Lords, commanded the Steward of the Household, Devereux, to bring him before parliament. Richard then withdrew. Bramber was denied counsel or the right to answer the charges in detail. His offer to prove his innocence by combat was rejected, the Commons wishing to have his treason declared manifest. Some peers may have been disquieted by these proceedings, a situation which probably encouraged Richard to intervene by declaring that he did not believe Bramber guilty. The Appellants threw down their gloves to maintain their charges, an example followed by a large number of lords and shire knights. The king had been too bold in challenging the Appeal, but he had influential sympathizers in the Lords. A committee of twelve secular peers was appointed to examine the charges against Bramber, headed by York, Salisbury, Kent and Northumberland. Their findings were that Bramber had done nothing worthy of death. The Westminster Monk says that grave discord would have arisen between the Appellants and the Lords, but for the opportune discovery of Tresilian hiding in the precincts of Westminster Abbey. Gloucester and Cobham organized his forcible extradition, he was brought before parliament and the sentence passed against him was confirmed, despite his protests. Tresilian seems to have been more unpopular than Bramber, for his appearance reanimated flagging enthusiasm for the Appeal. The Lords questioned leading London officials concerning the charges against Bramber. Their patent willingness to abandon the defence of their fellow citizen helped the Appellants to secure, at last, a rigorous conviction (20 February).

The session had now lasted over two weeks. No more trials took place until early in March, when other offenders were impeached by the Commons. The Appellants were probably relieved to share the burden of accusation. Among the first to be tried were the dismissed justices. The Lords sentenced them to death and forfeiture, but Archbishop Courtenay, speaking on behalf of the bishops, begged for commutation. The queen also intervened. The Chancellor, Thomas Arundel, announced that the king had granted the former judges their lives, and they were exiled to Ireland.

On 12 March four former knights of Richard's chamber were brought before parliament to hear the Commons' impeachment. They offered to acquit themselves like knights. Burley's bearing made a good impression on many. The next few days were taken up with less controversial business, partly with the grant of a subsidy to finance the expedition which Arundel was undertaking. Then followed a recess for Easter, which gave Richard a chance to canvass for his imperilled companions. Some nobles were in a receptive mood, for Gloucester and his partisans rather than Richard now appeared determined to introduce inflexibly harsh punishments into political life. The trial of the highly respected, if undoubtedly ambitious, Burley, to a large extent destroyed what unity parliament and the Appellants themselves had displayed. In mid-April the second session commenced. The Commons immediately requested that the former chamber knights should be adjudged. Scrope, Cobham and Devereux petitioned that they should be allowed to answer the charges in detail. But the Commons wished their guilt to be declared and the Appellants canvassed for a fortnight in favour of this, against strong opposition in the Lords. On 27 April York said that Burley had been faithful in all the business of the king and realm, a declaration which helps account for the favour which Richard showed to him and his son and heir Edward of Norwich, Earl of Rutland, in the 1390s. Gloucester replied that Burley was a traitor and offered to prove it with his right hand. The brothers called each other liars before their peers and would have come to blows on the spot, had not Richard (displaying more propriety in family affairs that he had done over Ireland's elopement) intervened to pacify them. Heartened by these divisions, he pleaded with the Commons for Burley's life, but they would not relent. He sent York and Cobham to beg in vain that the knight should be allowed to answer the charges. On 5 May Burley was condemned unheard. The queen spent three hours on her knees before Arundel asking for his life. It was alleged in 1397 that he had been condemned in the absence of most peers. Then Gloucester, Arundel and Warwick were accused of having met the king in a secret place in Westminster Palace, to reveal Burley's offences to him. It was said that Richard had refused to accept their allegations. This may have been the meeting to which Adam of Usk heard Richard refer, in a speech during parliament to Arundel:

> Did you not say to me, at the time of your parliament, in the bath behind the White Hall, that Sir Simon Burley, my knight, was, for many reasons, worthy of death? And I answered you that I knew no cause of death in him. And then you and your fellows traitorously slew him.

It is likely that these fellows did not include Derby and the Earl Marshal, for the Kirkstall Chronicler says that it was the three original Appellants who ignored Richard's requests and insisted on Burley's execution.

The rest of the chamber knights were condemned without a hearing on 12 May. Did Gloucester, Arundel and Warwick take the right decision in pressing for the executions, knowing that their insistence was losing them important friends? Burley was the first at whose conviction they aimed who had a high reputation in campaigning circles, dating from Edward III's reign. Execution as a political weapon had been unknown in England for over fifty years and much of the animus which had grown up against Richard from 1384 onwards resulted from suspicions that he intended to reintroduce it. This background of fear steeled the determination of Gloucester to act mercilessly. As a result, Richard began to appear the champion of a moderation which he had been the first to discard.[28] The harshness of Gloucester and his colleagues also sprang from the knowledge that, as they had failed to depose Richard, his obnoxious privy councillors, or equally disliked new ones, might soon creep back to court and inspire him to punish them for their rising. Tout stressed that 'the purge of the household was never very complete'. The Commons would have liked more drastic measures against it, petitioning that all those whom the council did not wish to be there should be removed. Only a limited royal assent was given: individuals might be removed if any lord showed that they were incompetent or unworthy. Therefore the aim of the executions was to ensure that the victims never again asserted their influence and that other intimates of the king did not advise him in a similar manner. Another expedient was to appoint 'official' councillors during parliament, as had been done in 1386. In May 1388, with the assent of parliament, Bishops Wickham and Braybrooke, the earl of Warwick and Lords Cobham and Scrope were appointed as councillors, to supervise the king. Their consent was to be necessary to royal decisions.

Gloucester and his allies had been able to secure the sentences against the chamber knights only because the Commons were implacable. The Commons' impeachments did more harm to Richard's friends than the Appeal of Treason. But the impeachments put Lords and Commons once more at odds, a situation reminiscent of the parliaments of the early 1380s, when, as a consequence, Richard had been able to assert a measure of personal authority. In the 1386 parliament the unity of the two Houses had been a necessary ground for opposition to the exercise of royal authority. As the 1388 session continued, it became increasingly difficult to hold Lords and Commons on the same course. The senior Appellants' endorsement of the Commons' intransigence made it necessary for them to appease their fellow peers in matters of policy and patronage.[29]

Parliament was not dismissed till 4 June. Two days earlier, the king's younger half-brother, the ambitious Sir John Holand, was

created earl of Huntingdon. He was led formally into the Lords by
the two senior earls, Salisbury and Warwick. Apart from his royal
relationship, Holand was important as Lancaster's son-in-law. He had
recently served as constable of the duke's army in Spain and was one
of the few Englishmen to make a reputation on that lethargic expedition. His return may have been the result of Lancaster's and his own
anxiety about political developments in England. The man who had
earned execration by killing Sir Ralph Stafford in 1385 now had
rewards showered on him: on 7 April 1388 he was granted an inn in
Lombard Street which De la Pole had forfeited and in July he
received two manors which had belonged to the former justices.[30]
The appeasement of the absent Lancaster was probably regarded as
important by the senior Appellants. The duke had always refrained,
despite great provocation, from taking extreme and publicly coercive
measures when at odds with Richard. His armed protest in 1385, in
response to the court plot against his life, had been of a different
kind from Gloucester's in 1387. Like York, John of Gaunt probably
thought well of Burley. One of the accusations in the Appeal of
Treason was intended to identify the rising of the Appellants with
the duke's interests: the accused were said to have planned his arrest
when he set foot in England again. A week before parliament ended,
he was appointed lieutenant in Aquitaine. His negotiations with the
Castilians were approved, though they were in breach of his agreements with the Crown. Arundel's accusation in the 1394 parliament
shows that he felt strongly about this breach. By appeasing the duke,
the Appellants were bringing his interests in some respects into line
with Richard's. For the duke, in order to fulfil the ambitions which
he now transferred from Castile to Aquitaine, became anxious for a
permanent settlement with France, a policy which Richard was convinced must be carried out if the Crown was to be freed from financial
dependence on parliament.[31]

The principal Border magnate, Northumberland, was well
rewarded for his acquiescence in the Acts of the 1388 parliament. A
few weeks after it ended, his son and heir Sir Henry Percy (who was
to sue out a pardon for the support he had given to the king's
opponents) replaced the rival Lord Neville as Warden of the East
March. Shortly afterwards Lord Beaumont was appointed the Warden
of the West March, superseding Neville's son and heir Sir Ralph
and Richard's friend Clifford. The Percy family gained greater control
over Border defences than before, at novel high rates of pay.

Froissart says that this resulted in animosity between them and the Nevilles, as a consequence of which the Scots under the earl of Douglas were able in August 1388 to penetrate to the gates of Newcastle. Henry Percy attacked their camp at Otterburne and in the celebrated fight was defeated and captured. Yet the Percies had shown early in the reign that they were incapable of defending the Border without the co-operation of the other leading families. The Appellants' principal military appointments in 1388 did not lead to success. Percy failed as Warden and Arundel's summer offensive overseas brought no territorial gain or alliance. However, Sir William Beauchamp carried out profitable raids from Calais, a second Scots incursion, around Berwick, was held and a favourable commercial treaty was concluded with the Teutonic Knights in Prussia.[32] Above all, since the arrest by the duke of Brittany of Olivier de Clisson and the English attacks on Philip the Bold's Flemish commerce, French interest in invading England had not revived. Philip was anxious for an accommodation and he had written to Gloucester, saying that, at Leo de Lusignan's request, Charles VI was prepared to negotiate a truce of several years, during which peace might be negotiated. Gloucester did not reply till 12 June 1388, excusing his tardiness on the ground of absorption in domestic affairs. He said that he had presented Burgundy's letter to the king and council and was replying as a result of their advice. He had protested that he 'would do nothing of his own motion therein'. This probably indicates only a concern for constitutional niceties, for he and his fellow Appellants would have encountered criticism if they had undertaken foreign negotiations on their own initiative. It cannot be concluded from Gloucester's slowness to answer and from his disclaimer that he was unalterably opposed to a policy leading to peace with France. In the 1390s he was to object to terms which he considered unfavourable.

From the English viewpoint the summer of 1388 was an opportune time to consider new negotiations. Gloucester may have realized this and seized the initiative by pressing king and council to respond to Burgundy's letter. It was in the duke's interest to bring the war at least to a temporary halt, for both John of Gaunt and Richard had been discredited as a result of the recent difficulties in conducting it and he would ingratiate himself with his brother by promoting a truce. On 26 November 1388 envoys were appointed, including Bishop Skirlaw of Durham, Sir William Beauchamp, Devereux and the royal retainers John Clanvowe and Nicholas Dagworth. Negotiations by these and succeeding envoys culminated in June 1389 in a truce of three years, which was to be continuously extended, allowing time for intermittent peace negotiations. By initiating negotiations in 1388 the councillors whom Richard had been forced to accept paved the way for a solution of problems which had hampered the Crown from the last years of Edward III's reign onward and had inhibited Richard's assertion of his personal authority.

Moreover, the coercion of Richard and the harsh punishment of his partisans had set Lords and Commons at odds again. This was apparent in the parliament which met at Cambridge in September 1388. The roll of its proceedings is unfortunately missing. A principal reason for summons may have been to procure a subsidy for action against the Scots. On 13 August king and council had ordered the chancellor of the duchy of Lancaster to have it proclaimed that the duchy forces were to join the king by the end of the month, to march against the Scots. The writ outlined the course of the Scots invasion, penetrating almost to York 'to our shame and dishonour', and declared that Richard had taken a resolution to fight in person, by the advice and with the assent of the council. The king is likely to have been furious at the Scots incursion, a violation of the truce which his 1385 expedition had helped to procure. His display of resolution underlined the failure of the councillors to safeguard the realm. The Westminster Chronicler says that a royal council met at Northampton on 22 August, in which Richard proposed that he should lead an expedition. But he was overruled by the magnates and it was decided to postpone the expedition to the New Year. They may have considered an autumn campaign in the Scottish Lowlands to be a bleak and unpromising proposition and the prior grant of a subsidy in parliament a necessity. One point agreed at Northampton was that members of the leading Border families, and not just the Percies, should have the authority in the defence of the Marches. A writ dated 20 August, endorsed by king and council, assigned Northumberland and Neville to undertake the defence and raise soldiers.[33]

In the Cambridge parliament the Commons were more interested in petitioning about their grievances than in financing military schemes —a familiar stance. They complained once more about the consequences of lavish distribution of liveries by lords. They reiterated that recipients were emboldened to commit wrongs against neighbours who did not enjoy the same protection. The Commons wanted a statute which would curtail the grant of liveries, a remedy which their predecessors in the first 1384 parliament had requested. In 1384 Lancaster had merely promised on behalf of his brothers and fellow nobles that they would punish erring livery-holders. At Cambridge Gloucester was unable either to prevent the Commons from sticking to their demands or to induce the Lords to agree to them. It was Richard who intervened as mediator, so gaining the goodwill of the Commons. This was indeed a reversal of the previous parliament's alignments. The king ostentatiously set the Lords an unwelcome example, by declaring that his servants could give up the wearing of his livery. The Lords refused to comply, to the fury of the Commons, so he licensed them to continue the use of liveries until the next parliament met. There is an analogy between the Lords' defence of their rights and Richard's past defence of his, which shows that he and they had a parallel interest. Richard was determined that no statutes should give a lasting sanction to the infringement of his prerogative, in his relations with the Crown's servants. Magnates were now defending their prerogative of using their patronage without statutory limitation. Over the past two years the granting of liveries and the prevalence of unlawful maintenance may have increased in volume, due to the need for private retinues to defend the realm and to the political tension. A few grants of annuities and manors made by the Appellants in the years 1387–8 are recorded. The fact that Richard was busy in the summer of 1387 retaining and granting liveries suggests that he was copying and trying to outbid his opponents. A number of those who joined the Appellants' army in 1387 may have received badges of their livery and used them for private advantage. The increase of such activities was likely to undermine the renewed alliance of Lords and Commons against the Crown, part of the Appellants' political basis.

In 1388 Richard kept Christmas at one of his favourite country houses, Eltham in Kent. The Westminster Chronicler remarked on the magnificence of the festivities, in contrast to the previous Christmas, when the king held the Tower, fearful of siege and deposition. A great council met on 20 January 1389 at Westminster, which was probably attended by influential people besides magnates. Richard may have once again seized the opportunity to woo the lesser property owners; the secretive discussions held were perhaps on the subject of liveries. His proposed Scottish expedition was discussed and it was decided that Nottingham should have custody of the East March, and Northumberland, Beaumont and Clifford that of the West March until the end of July 1389, when the king and his retinue would cross the Border. The proposed Wardens would supersede Sir John Stanley, formerly Vere's lieutenant in Ireland, who had been appointed to his Border command during the Cambridge parliament. In the Percies' eyes Nottingham's appointment to the East March was probably an unwelcome intrusion into their sphere of influence. Mowbray had hitherto held commands in subordination to his father-in-law, Arundel, and this was to be his first important independent command. He may have considered that political alliance with Arundel and Gloucester, eager like himself for Crown patronage and military opportunities, gave limited scope for his ambitions. Richard was probably cultivating Nottingham and Derby—the latter received a breastplate as a royal gift. The reluctance of these two earls to uphold the influence over government exercised by the senior Appellants may have been one factor which facilitated Richard's *coup* of May 1389. Another probable factor was the discontent of Border magnates about defence provisions against the Scots. The Westminster Chronicler believed that the appointments made to Border commands were unwise, since they set the northerners at odds and starved them of funds. In March Nottingham had been granted continued custody of the East March for a year, to commence on 1 June, and the following month Northumberland's hold on the other March was strengthened by his appointment for a like period, together with John Lord Ros and Ralph Lord Neville (son and heir of John). None of the Wardens were granted the coveted higher rates of pay. In June 1389 a Scots force ravaged as far south as Tynemouth. Nottingham and Neville could not muster a large enough force to hold them. Northumberland does not seem to have co-operated.[34]

At a council meeting held in Westminster on 3 May, Richard had declared his intention of ruling in person, on the grounds that he was now of age. He proceeded to dismiss some of the officials whose appointments he had been forced by the Appellants to accept. At 12 o'clock, in the Marcolf Chamber in Westminster Palace, Thomas Arundel (who had succeeded Alexander Neville as archbishop of York) resigned the Great Seal and the next day, in the same place, Richard handed it to one of the councillors forced on him in 1388, the venerable Bishop Wickham. Present were Archbishop Courtenay, Bishops Gilbert of Hereford, Brantingham of Exeter and Waltham of Salisbury, and York, Derby and Northumberland. The equally venerable Brantingham was appointed Treasurer. Courtenay, Wickham, Brantingham and Waltham had all been members of the 1386 commission appointed to exercise royal powers, but now they were intent on stressing the king's personal authority.

To reassure public opinion, a proclamation was issued a few days later. It asserted the king's intention to rule. The decision that he should do so, it was said, had been made by the advice and with the assent of the magnates. Richard intended to govern by the advice of the council and in a manner likely to ensure better peace and justice. He and his heirs would not reverse the sentences of 1388. Riots and maintenances, in disturbance of the peace and hindrance of the law, were forbidden on pain of forfeiture. Complaints about such misdoings were to be addressed to the king and council. Thus the redress of grievances of the lesser property owners, to which Richard had shown himself sympathetic at Cambridge, was linked with a threat against violent attempts to reverse the assertion of personal authority. Walsingham hints that Richard's declaration in council came as an unpleasant surprise to the magnates. But it is more likely that his intention had the prior support of influential ecclesiastical and lay peers, such as those who were present at Wickham's appointment. The latter and Brantingham, who owed their fortunes to Crown service, may have helped plan the *coup*, finding Richard for the first time a willing pupil. Wickham was capable of fearless political initiatives, as he had shown in the 1376 parliament. Possibly Gloucester, Arundel and Warwick were caught unprepared by Richard's declaration. Walsingham says that the duke's detractors told the king that he was preparing another rising. The fact that critics of the duke were once more influential shows how far the political situation had changed. Such criticisms were reminiscent of the summer of 1387, but now the king had the moderates firmly behind him. He had their support only at heavy cost to his concept of prerogative—his confirmation of the 1388 judgments. Richard dared not make a false move, otherwise Gloucester would once more command support. The duke knew he was out-manœuvred. His protestations of innocence failed to allay Richard's suspicions. For the rest of Thomas's life, his relations with his nephew were to be poisoned by such insinuations, however hard he tried to act like a loyal subject.[35]

After the May *coup* rewards were handed out. On 13 May the Earl Marshal was granted custody of the Border towns of Berwick and Roxburgh and days later Huntingdon was appointed Admiral of the West and Lord Beaumont Admiral of the North. At the end of the month they were superseded in both commands by Sir John Roches, a royal retainer and former admiral who had been Arundel's lieutenant as Captain of Brest. These appointments prematurely terminated the grant of the admiralties in March 1388 to Arundel, by the terms of which he was to hold them for five years. On 22 June Huntingdon and Beaumont were reappointed in place of Roches.[36] Three weeks earlier Arundel had obtained licence to go abroad, intending to make a pilgrimage to Jerusalem. But the licence was soon revoked. The genuineness of his religious motives need not be queried. He had probably intended to go on pilgrimage in 1384 and his will of 1392 reveals his piety, to which the remains of Holy Trinity College at Arundel are to some extent a monument. It was symptomatic of the transformation of the political situation that a man who had recently been at the peak of influence contemplated leaving the realm on a prolonged and dangerous expedition—the earl of Stafford had not survived his Jerusalem journey in 1386. Arundel may have changed his mind because he and his friends were worried about the issue of events in England. On 18 June at Leulighem, envoys (who included Richard's friend, the elderly Salisbury) concluded a truce of three years. In the same month Northumberland travelled south and, according to the Westminster Monk, was made the king's chief councillor. On 9 July the king dismissed from his household many whom he considered had been too friendly with the Appellants. The senior Appellants and their friends were in close contact, for the next day two Essex manors forfeited by Berners and bought by Gloucester were granted to the duke's feoffees, who included the recently dismissed Chancellor, Thomas Arundel, Bishop Braybrooke and the earls of Arundel and Warwick. The political outlook remained uncertain, for the dismissals of May had been a bold measure, a leap in the dark. Richard and probably many others believed that there was only one person who could arbitrate the divisions between the king and his kinsmen. The frequently resented ability and authority of John of Gaunt had become the hope of king and realm.[37]

three

The Court and the Appellants
(1389–99)

The political eclipse of the senior Appellants is reflected in their absence from the lists of those present at council meetings after May 1389. At Windsor on 20 August none of the former Appellants attended the council, though a strong household contingent did. At Clarendon just over three weeks later, when proposals for negotiations with the French were discussed, there was a good attendance by lay magnates, including Derby and the Earl Marshal. The latter was granted a sum in addition to the one he had received for the custody of the East March, and his appointment to the Captaincy of Calais was considered. The earl of Northumberland interceded on behalf of Gloucester and Arundel, saying that they very much wished that good love, unity and concord might be established between themselves (and also Warwick) and the king and lords of the council. 'And that neither parties hold the other in suspicion or enmity.' It was agreed that a reply would be given to Arundel when he came to Westminster on business after 30 September. But no complete reconciliation then took place. The king may not have felt the need to oblige Northumberland or his former opponents so urgently, now that the return of Lancaster was being hastened. At a Westminster council on 15 October Richard showed his willingness to assent to the Earl Marshal's request for an extension of his custody of the East March for five years and angrily rejected conciliar opposition to a grant of it with high scales of pay. Northumberland was appeased with the Captaincy of Calais and the grant of the West Wardenship to his son and heir Sir Henry Percy for five years. Richard considered it most important to retain the renewed friendship of the Earl Marshal, who was, after all, Arundel's son-in-law and who may have been disquieted by the prospective reassertion of Lancastrian influence—as may have the king, though it was necessary to his security.[1]

John of Gaunt landed at Plymouth in December, anxious, according to Walsingham, to heal the dangerous rift between his nephew and the senior Appellants. Richard and Gloucester competed to show their affection for the duke. The king took off the livery collar which Lancaster wore round his neck and put it on himself. Gloucester presented his brother with two very fine tapestries of Arras. At the great council which met at Reading on 9 December Lancaster formally reconciled the three Appellants with the king and, at the royal instance, put aside his old enmity towards the earl of Northumberland. In the parliament which met in January 1390 Lancaster and Gloucester were formally appointed councillors. The subservience to parliament of the Chancellor, Bishop Wickham, together with these appointments, checked any inclination, if it existed, to give support to the senior Appellants, or to undo the settlement of May 1389. Gloucester's return to favour at court was reflected in the February grant of a licence for three gentlemen to travel abroad, made at his request. The same month, Lancaster, Gloucester and Northumberland petitioned the Crown on behalf of Abbot de la Mare of St Albans. At a March council meeting ordinances for official conduct were laid down, supplementing those of the previous August: no grant was to be made which might decrease revenue, without the advice of the council and assent of the king's uncles and the Chancellor. These aims were reminiscent of those of Richard's critics. It is clear that the councillors on whose support Richard had leaned since May 1389 were determined that business should be done efficiently and without undue favour. They may have been annoyed by the way in which Richard had imposed his will on them in October 1389 over the Wardenship, ignoring the interests of economy. In March 1390 the councillors probably had the support in their business-like aims of Lancaster, who did not wish a favourite such as Mowbray to undermine his influence at court, as had happened in the 1380s.[2]

In July 1390 John of Gaunt held a magnificent hunting-party at his town of Leicester. The king and queen attended, as did York, Gloucester, Arundel and the Earl Marshal. Lancaster, who had not been backward in exploiting the royal need for his support, asked the king to pardon his dependant, the imprisoned Londoner Northampton. Richard fenced cleverly in reply, implying that he now lacked the authority to grant such a pardon. He complained of his lack of power and inability to help his exiled friends. According to the Westminster Chronicler, this conversation marked a significant *rapprochement* between the two. Probably partly to please Lancaster, in 1390 and 1391 Gloucester (but not Arundel or Warwick) was granted a number of royal favours, setting a pattern for the period up to his arrest in 1397. At the Canterbury council in September 1391 Gloucester obtained royal permission to go to Prussia for a crusade. Crusading enthusiasm had revived among the magnates as a result of the 1389 truces. After the Anglo-French jousts at St Inglevert (March–April 1390), in which Derby and the Earl Marshal participated, a number of English knights undertook to go on Louis de Bourbon's proposed Tunis crusade. Derby tried to join it, but was diverted to Prussia, whence he returned in the spring of 1391, having gained a great reputation. Gloucester was probably spurred to emulate his nephew's achievements. The duke's Essex neighbour and former campaigning companion, John Lord Bourchier, may also have interested him in Prussia—he owned a house in Danzig, in which Derby stayed. Lancaster had probably reconciled Gloucester with his son. The former's herald Croyslett was present with Derby on his crusade.[3]

It was a good time for Thomas of Woodstock to go abroad and make a crusading reputation, since his brother had to some extent restored his political standing and was guaranteeing it, but was, as of old, overshadowing him. Moreover, Thomas may have wished to boost further the prestige of the 'way of Prussia' as an alternative to Mediterranean crusading, which, as his meeting with Leo de Lusignan in 1386 would have made him aware, required French co-operation and could be used as an incentive to make a hasty and perhaps unfavourable peace with France. Lancaster, in order to put his ambitions in Aquitaine on a secure basis, was anxious to revive the stagnant peace negotiations. Therefore he was probably glad to see his brother go overseas. On 5 September 1391 royal orders were issued for the arrest of ships and sailors, to assemble at Orwell (Suffolk) for Gloucester's voyage. Next day two of his officials made a recognizance of 1,000 *m.* to Lancaster, possibly as part of a loan transaction to help finance the expedition. The royal brothers probably attended the council held at Eltham early in September, after the arrival of the French envoys who had failed to appear at Canterbury. On 13 September Gloucester was granted the marriage of a wealthy ward, without rent, the grant being dated at Eltham. On 16 September he was given royal authority to negotiate with the Master General of the Teutonic Order in Prussia. He embarked in mid-October. With him went Warwick's nephew, Thomas Earl of Stafford, who had come of age in 1390 and in the summer of 1391 had married Gloucester's daughter at Pleshey.[4]

In the parliament which met in November 1391 the Commons showed unprecedented confidence in Richard's government, stimulated probably by the absence of high subsidy demands and the continuing display of royal sympathy for grievances against the private governments of magnates, which had been a feature of Richard's policy since the Cambridge parliament of 1388. General confidence in the council was probably enhanced when on 27 September, in *le Parlour* below the King's Chamber at Windsor, Richard received the Great Seal from the aged Wickham, and handed it to the Appellants' arch-supporter, Thomas Arundel.[5] Attitudes to royal authority were of urgent interest to Richard in case of a renewal of the war, with its concomitant financial and political difficulties for the Crown. A great council met at Westminster in February 1392 to settle the issue. On the first day, when Lancaster, Derby and Nottingham were among those present, the composition of a formal embassy to France was settled. The next day Gloucester, a chastened man, attended. It may have been his impetuosity that had led him to embark for Prussia in an uncertain season. The weather hazards ruined his expedition, storms scattering his fleet. The Westminster Chronicler's account of Gloucester's terrifying experiences may have been derived from him in person. Eventually his ship reached the eastern coast of Scotland and, hugging the shore southwards, put in at Bamburgh Castle (Northumberland) just before Christmas. After a stay at Tynemouth, the disappointed duke returned to Pleshey.

On the second day of the great council (13 February 1392), measures were drafted in preparation for a campaign against the French. By 15 February, the day after the earl of Arundel had joined the councillors, Richard proposed that the judgments on Alexander Neville and Robert de Vere should be reversed. This proposal was flatly rejected by the magnates, but they showed some anxiety to appease Richard, promising loyalty to him on behalf of themselves and their retainers. They swore to join in arms with the king against anyone who broke these engagements. In return Richard pledged that he would not harm anyone for past actions and declared that it was not his intention to restore those who had forfeited in parliament.[6]

The following day instructions for the envoys to France were concerted. It was noted in the minute that Gloucester had agreed that Calais might be held of the French Crown. Froissart says that, unlike his brothers, he was pessimistic about peace-making, telling his friends secretly that he would only agree to peace if the territories acquired in France by the Treaty of Brétigny (1360) were restored. Many lay lords, according to the chronicler, agreed with him, especially Arundel, but they dissembled their opinions on seeing Richard's enthusiasm for peace. If this timid and ineffective muttering was the extent of Gloucester's and Arundel's opposition, it shows how politically ineffective they now were—as long, Richard had discovered, as he did not upset the 1388-9 settlements. Gloucester's opposition may have been muted because he was interested in acquiring the lieutenancy of Ireland, to which the Westminster Chronicler says he was appointed during the council. He had hankered after the duchy of Ireland early in 1389. It was agreed in 1392 that he should lead a major expedition, receiving a total of 34,000 m. from the English Exchequer over a period of three years.[7] Now that the duke's Prussian plans had collapsed and it seemed as though French relations might be dominated by the king's and Lancaster's peaceful ambitions, he may have grasped at the Irish nettle as providing him with a worthy field of endeavour and influence. But, according to Froissart, his opposition to the peace policy was more forthright at a council held to consider the proposals brought back from Amiens by Lancaster and York. This may have been the great council held at Stamford (Lincs.) in May 1392. Among those present may have been the earls of Warwick and Stafford, besides gentlemen summoned from the counties. A visiting prince, William of Jülich, Duke of Guelders, publicly urged Richard to form an alliance against the French Crown. His stirring words probably impressed the ancient knights present more than the magnates, who were likely to be better informed about Guelders' limited resources and restless ambitions. Possibly he was being used by Gloucester and Arundel to prejudice consideration of the peace terms—for the 1387 alliance with him against the French Crown had been made under their auspices. Lancaster's exposition of the proposed abandonment of the claim to sovereignty and of the formation of a Lancastrian principality in Aquitaine under the French Crown seems to have been unfavourably received. Froissart credits Gloucester with the declaration that the proposals could not be accepted until a parliament was summoned. This was accepted, as 'they dared not oppose him, for he was too popular with the commons of England'.[8] Whether this opposition cost him the Irish Lieutenancy, or whether he relinquished it because he had decided that it would prove too expensive, is not clear. Certainly after visiting Ireland in 1394–5 Gloucester was to talk scathingly about the opportunities there. However, in 1392 preparations for his expedition had got well under way. On 7 May the council had ordered the collection at Bristol of ships, mariners and supplies, to be ready by 1 July. The duke had recruited a retinue. But at the end of the month the earl of Ormonde was made justiciar for a year (an appointment at which he expressed dismay) and on 23 July Richard wrote from Windsor to the bishop of Meath that Gloucester had been discharged 'with the assent of the great men of our said realm and of other of our Great Council'.[9]

Gloucester continued to enjoy royal favour. He was the only former Appellant present at a great council at Windsor in the last week of July, when with York he took a leading part in passing judgment on the citizens of London at Eton. This restriction of their liberties, on account of the offence the king had taken at the failure to make a loan requested by him, would have delighted Thomas in his youth. By 1393 the king often wore Gloucester's livery and walked with him arm-in-arm, as he did with his other uncles. The duke had particular need of royal favour, to relieve the debts incurred over the Irish Lieutenancy and to retain control of the Stafford inheritance after the earl of Stafford's untimely death in July 1392. Moreover, Lancaster may have by now bought his brother's support for the proposed Lancastrian principality in Aquitaine; the Westminster Chronicler says that in 1394 it was thought that Gloucester continued to support the plan because the duke had promised him lands. Perhaps these were fiefs in Aquitaine, where Thomas had had his first grant of properties.[10]

The Winchester parliament, commencing in January 1393, approved the continuation of the peace negotiations. Gloucester was appointed with Lancaster on the new delegation, which also included Nottingham, who was to become increasingly involved in Anglo-French diplomacy. Froissart says that Gloucester was appointed to appease those who favoured continuing the war. He represented the duke, who told him at Pleshey about his role at the conference, as a stiff and suspicious bargainer, on his guard against French trickery. Nevertheless, he correctly reported that Gloucester concurred in the provisions made at Leulighem for the truce and peace.[11] The Cheshiremen who rebelled in 1393 complained that Lancaster, Derby and Gloucester intended to surrender Richard's title to the French

Crown. Gloucester, who had been appointed justice of Chester in succession to his enemy Robert de Vere (1388), was placed in the invidious position of having to suppress rebels with some of whose complaints he sympathized. Arundel, on the other hand, some of whose lordships neighboured Cheshire, was equivocal in his attitude to the rebels. In September he was stationed at Holt Castle with an armed retinue and remained inactive, awaiting the outcome of the rebellion. Lancaster and Gloucester felt the lack of his help keenly— in the 1394 parliament the former acrimoniously accused him of supporting the rebels.[12]

The Cheshire Revolt may have focused discontent about the peace policy, which came to a head in the 1394 parliament. Arundel may have hoped to exploit this mood by his public attack on Lancaster, in which he emphasized how the duke had directed foreign negotiations to his own advantage. He branded John of Gaunt as a favourite who ruled the king and who 'often in Councils and Parliaments spoke such rough and harsh words that the said Earl and others often did not dare give their opinions plainly'. Arundel was probably furious that Gloucester, his closest ally, had succumbed so completely to Lancaster's influence. Perhaps he was angling for the support of young nobles such as his son-in-law Nottingham, who were almost as impatient of Lancaster's influence as had been courtiers in the early 1380s. Arundel may even have been flying at the highest game of all, trying to win royal favour. Richard was preparing to pay a very high price for peace, the alienation of Aquitaine, from which Lancaster, Derby and possibly Gloucester would have benefited, not the king's particular friends. But Arundel's attack misfired—it may have been too reminiscent for the king's liking of the accusations against favourites alleged to rule the king which Arundel and his allies had made in 1387. Richard personally defended his uncle in parliament with skill and moderation, saying that he treated him no differently from his other uncles. Arundel was isolated and had to make a public apology to the duke. Feelings continued to run high between them, for in 1397 Lancaster was eager to participate in Arundel's condemnation. The earl had only worsened his political position; he sued out a pardon for all treasons committed. Gloucester remained firmly allied with his brother—they petitioned in parliament for the punishment of some of the 1393 rebels, as having conspired to kill them and other magnates, an aim which they alleged a ringleader to have largely confessed in Derby's presence.[13]

Arundel's insulting lateness at Anne of Bohemia's funeral on 3 August 1394 involved him in more trouble. Richard put him in the Tower. A week later the earl came into the royal presence at Archbishop Courtenay's Lambeth residence, in a small room by the *wydrawyngchaumbre* of the principal chamber. There he swore to behave loyally and to make no riots or unlawful assemblies. A surety of £40,000 was pledged for his observance of the oath, by lords who then entered the room. They were his brother Archbishop Thomas Arundel, the Chancellor, his brother-in-law the earl of March, Warwick, Nottingham, Aubrey de Vere, Earl of Oxford (uncle and heir of Robert de Vere), Warwick's brother Sir William Beauchamp, the Marcher Reginald Grey, Lord of Ruthin, Northumberland's brother Sir Thomas Percy, the Shropshire landowner Lord Burnell and Lord Lovell. Gloucester was conspicuous by his absence. He was with Lancaster and York at Pontefract (Yorks.) on 26 August, when John of Gaunt wrote to the king protesting his own loyalty, in connection with a slanderous accusation made at court. That the duke should have had to endure attack may reflect his decline in favour. Richard failed to punish the Cheshire rebels as harshly as his uncles wished, and favoured (as in the early 1380s) a younger set of noblemen, especially York's son Rutland, Huntingdon and Nottingham, who were not concerned with rules restricting royal initiative.[14]

It was these younger nobles who played the leading roles on Richard's Irish expedition of 1394–5 and profited most from it by confirmations of old titles and new grants. Only two of the former Lords Appellant went, bearers of high military office—Gloucester, the Constable, and Nottingham, the Marshal. The duke was outshone by his colleague; he was once more eclipsed by court favourites, now that Lancaster had again gone overseas, in an attempt to enforce his ducal authority against the Gascon opposition which threatened to wreck his peace policy. It is no wonder that Gloucester's memories of Ireland were to be sour. He landed at Waterford early in November 1394, a fortnight after the king's arrival. The duke was granted lands in Wicklow, but he did not preside at any of the formal ceremonies in which Irish chiefs submitted and performed homage, for early in the New Year he returned to ask parliament for subsidies, a duty which he performed successfully. On the other hand, the Earl Marshal had been granted the Lordship of Carlow before the expedition set out for Ireland and his forays against hostile strongholds and villages were well publicized in letters from the king and others. In January 1395 the Earl Marshal had the delicate and crucial task of meeting the Irish chief Art MacMurrough and negotiating the terms of his evacuation of Leinster, and the following month he received the homages of the Leinster chiefs.[15]

Thus Richard triumphed in Ireland and returned eager to solve the French problem. Gloucester was absent from the council meeting at Leeds Castle (Kent) on 8 July 1395, at which envoys were appointed to discuss the French marriage proposals. The lay envoys were Rutland, the Earl Marshal and Lord Beaumont. But the duke attended the great council summoned to Eltham on 22 July, to consider the Gascon petition against the grant of Aquitaine to Lancaster, and the king's proposed marriage. There are two accounts of the council—that of Froissart, visiting the English court for the first time since Edward's reign, and an official minute on the Gascon business. Before the meeting the Gascon lord Jean de Grailly, basing his views on English opinions, told the chronicler that Gloucester was considered as overbearing and unpopular with the commons and as responsible for Burley's death and for the deaths and banishments of royal councillors during Lancaster's previous period abroad. Grailly asserted that the duke wished to establish his pre-eminent influence by marrying one of his daughters to Richard II, who excused himself on the grounds of consanguinity, because he was determined to marry a daughter of Charles VI. For the proceedings of the council Froissart relied on the weighty and significant testimony of the old knight Richard Stury, a royal retainer and councillor. Among the leading magnates at the council were York, Gloucester, Derby, the Earl Marshal and Arundel. Asked what reply should be made to the Gascon petition, they seemed afraid to speak. The bishops wished to refer the matter to the royal uncles, who, however, excused themselves. No opinions were expressed until Gloucester spoke in favour of his brother's grant. His remarks were not generally well received, but no one had the courage to oppose what the duke said, 'as he was much feared'. The council then dissolved into muted discussion groups. Derby, who had supported his uncle, dined with him and the duke then took leave of the king, riding to London. The council soon broke up, the Gascon petitioners being unable to obtain a certain answer. Froissart went on to say that Gloucester was continually soliciting favours from Richard, and was violently averse to the Gascon cause, just so that he could keep his brother out of England. The official minute corroborates, among other points, the presence of Stury and vouches for that of several magnates not mentioned by Froissart, including Warwick. It indicates that on the second day of the council clerks and lords gave opinions in favour of the Gascon petition, Gloucester and Derby putting in stipulations on Lancaster's behalf.

The two accounts show plainly that most magnates were hostile to Lancaster's grant. Yet, despite what Stury said about their attitudes, in John of Gaunt's absence it was surely reasonable that they should hesitate to press for an unfavourable judgment, deferring particularly to the views of his nearest relatives. Richard may have been annoyed that the special circumstances enabled Gloucester to seem dominant. But Thomas may have only been intent on safeguarding his brother's interests, a policy unlikely to re-cement political relations with his old ally the earl of Arundel. The court gossip picked up by Froissart shows how members of the household were busy making accusations against Gloucester in 1395 and continued to be so until his arrest in 1397. According to the chronicler, he virulently opposed the French alliance, even after it was a *fait accompli*, holding discontented conversations with London citizens, with Bishop Braybrooke and with the young earl of March, all of whom visited him at Pleshey. It is very likely that there were tale-bearers, envious of Thomas's enjoyment of royal patronage, who imputed sinister motives to his absences from court and his country entertainments, to his silences and indiscretions. No one ever forgot how Thomas had treated Sir Simon Burley. Richard's 1395 negotiations for a marriage alliance with the French royal house may have caused a deterioration in his relations with the duke, because the king at the same time abandoned the peace policy to which Thomas had subscribed in 1393. The hostility and belligerence which the duke displayed towards the French, in the conversations reported by Froissart, were not caused solely by his belief that campaigns in the rich and vulnerable provinces of France would be profitable—he was convinced that the king had been duped by his adversaries. During the negotiations of the early 1390s Gloucester had insisted that the French Crown must be forced to make territorial surrenders. Eventually his conditions (over which he had shown flexibility in 1393) were totally disregarded.[16]

In Paris Rutland and Nottingham settled the terms of the marriage alliance and truce (March 1396). In August the king went to Calais with Lancaster and Gloucester to meet the duke of Burgundy. In September he went again for the marriage ceremony, Derby and Nottingham being present as well as the king's two uncles. The

'Religieux de St-Denys' stressed the leading roles which the uncles played (at least formally) on these visits; in September, with Rutland and Nottingham, they held secret council with Burgundy and Berry. On the king's return to England with his bride, Isabella, Thomas Arundel, the Chancellor (who was to receive the archbishopric of Canterbury), resigned the Great Seal into the king's hands at Dover Castle. Gloucester and the earls of Derby, Nottingham and Arundel were present. Arundel may have come to Dover to pay his respects to the new queen. Those present in the castle were soon to be involved in the third great crisis of the reign.[17]

The reasons why Richard arrested Warwick, Arundel and Gloucester in July 1397 are as puzzling now as they were to contemporaries. The Meaux Chronicler, of whose house the duke was patron, believed that the king had him murdered because of slanders. Considering Lancaster's fear of court rumour in 1394 and the interpretations which Froissart heard placed on Gloucester's activities in 1395-6, this is plausible. The plot which the duke is alleged to have woven, as retailed by the anonymous French apologist for Richard and by other French sources, may have been related to him at court in the period 1397-9. It may have been circulated to justify the arrests, which were at first proclaimed to be for new offences. On the other hand, the plot may have originated in fictions relayed to the susceptible king by courtiers, elaborated around some of Gloucester's friendships and entertainments. The apologist has Thomas Mowbray betraying the plotters, just before the king set out to dine with Huntingdon at the latter's town house. Mowbray was inclined to be an *intrigant* and had a motive for trying to destroy Warwick. He had just won the Lordship of Gower from the earl, who was unlikely to accept the loss passively for long. If Gloucester had recently made insulting remarks to the king publicly after dinner, as the French apologist reported, Richard would have been in the mood to believe and act on denunciations. He was certainly irritated in January 1397, when it was reported to him that the Commons were opposed to the grant of a subsidy to finance retinues under the Earl Marshal and Rutland, whom it was proposed to send to Italy, in support of Charles VI against Giangaleazzo Visconti. In May the two earls were involved in other royal schemes—they attended the Diet at Frankfurt, ostensibly to support the Anglo-French plans to end the Schism, but also to promote Richard's ambition to be elected king of the Romans in place of

Wenzel. Walsingham, puzzled by the July arrests, put forward a theory in this connection to explain them. He says that about 24 June the dean of Cologne and other German envoys arrived at court, declaring that the king had been, or was about to be elected king of the Romans. They suggested that those who disagreed with this in England should be won over by gifts and favours. The chronicler was unsure whether their remarks aroused the royal anger against the senior Appellants, but from that point onwards, he says, Richard began to 'tyrannize'. Thus there are a few hints of opposition to Richard's ambitious and novel foreign plans in 1397. Gloucester and his friends may have suspected that Richard wished to introduce a novel, Roman jurisdiction into England.[18]

On one point the conflicting accounts of the July arrests were agreed: they were carried out in haste and without careful preparation. According to Walsingham, Warwick was arrested after dining amicably with the king; according to the 1399 Parliament Roll, he was detained when at the bishop of Exeter's hostel outside Temple Bar. Richard then ordered Archbishop Arundel to persuade his brother to give himself up, swearing that he would suffer no bodily harm if he surrendered. To deal with Gloucester at Pleshey, the king made the mayor of London gather a force. Rutland, Huntingdon, Kent, the Earl Marshal and members of the household also accompanied the king on the march into Essex, Rutland being sent on ahead to spy out his uncle's defences. But most of Gloucester's retinue were on vacation. Richard was amazed, 'since it had been reported to him by slanderers, whom he had always listened to, that the duke had prepared himself for a siege, having secretly collected 1,000 men-at-arms'. Thomas, a sick man, met the king and his soldiers in procession with the priests of his new college at Pleshey. Richard had him arrested and placed in the Earl Marshal's custody, to be dispatched out of harm's way to Calais, where the Earl Marshal was Captain.

Arundel, who had obeyed the king suspiciously, was also placed in Mowbray's custody and sent to the Isle of Wight, of which Rutland was guardian.[19] On 12 July, styled 'the King's brother', Rutland was granted Gloucester's cherished Constableship and on the same day the Constable of the Tower was ordered to receive Warwick. On 13 July the keeper of Arundel's castle at Reigate was told to deliver it up without delay and Huntingdon was dispatched to seize and hold Arundel Castle. It was proclaimed that the arrests had been made 'for the peace of the people and to save them harmless' and that

Rutland, Kent (the young Thomas Holand), Huntingdon, the Earl Marshal, Somerset (Lancaster's son John Beaufort), Salisbury (John Montague), Thomas Lord Despenser and Sir William Scrope had given their assent to the proceedings. Allegedly the peers had been placed in custody with the agreement of Lancaster, York and Derby. The mayor and sheriffs of London were told to arrest all servants and livery-holders of the three peers who might be found armed or making assemblies and those 'who are going from place to place within the said city and suburbs, sowing evil words and inciting people against the king'. Another proclamation referred to the common fear that the arrests had been made because of 'their assemblies and ridings within the realm' (i.e. in 1387) and that other arrests would follow for the same reason. The king stated his intent that neither members of the three Appellants' households nor others in their company ten years before should be troubled for what they had done. On 20 July the sheriff of Warwickshire was strictly ordered to array the local forces and have them ready to bring to the king's presence when required. On 28 July keepers of the peace in Sussex, Surrey, Kent and Essex were told to detain all those stirring against the arrests. These measures reflected Richard's fear of insurrection—a likely contingency after the arrests and one which would surely have deterred him from carrying them out unless he had thought they were necessary to his security.[20]

After the arrests and orders for the seizure of properties, Richard summoned a great council to meet at Nottingham. On 5 August 'en la grant Sale' of the castle, eight lords, including the Earl Marshal, presented to the king a Bill of Appeal accusing Gloucester, Arundel and Warwick of treasonable acts in 1386 and in the following period. Temporary grants of the confiscated properties were made: the Earl Marshal received his father-in-law's Lordship of Lewes, Sir William Arundel received Reigate; Warwick's castles of Warwick, Castle Barnard and Elmley went respectively to Sir John Clinton, Sir William Scrope and Thomas Lord Despenser. Huntingdon kept Arundel Castle. The new Appeal was made in the parliament which commenced on 17 September. Four days later Arundel was produced and took his stand bravely and defiantly on the pardons he had received. His condemnation and execution on Tower Hill were hustled through on the same day and he was interred at the London church of the Austin Friars, in Broad Street. Walsingham may have derived from the earl's confessor, a friar, his long and edifying account of the earl's courage at the execution. This friar may have been the distinguished Thomas Ashbourne whom the chronicler mentions as one of those who failed to discourage veneration at the earl's tomb by the 'vulgus commune'. Ashbourne was the confessor whom the earl had appointed executor in 1392 and whom he had shown the place behind the high altar of Lewes Priory where he wished to be buried.[21]

On 24 September, after being ordered to produce Gloucester in parliament, the Earl Marshal announced that he was dead. Nevertheless, he was condemned and the next day a confession was read. Its nature, and the testimony of its recipient, Sir William Rickhill, Justice of the Common Pleas during Henry's first parliament, established its authenticity, though the version publicized was doctored to exclude the duke's moving protestations of loyalty and remorse, and his piteous pleas for mercy.[22] For the circumstances of Gloucester's death, chroniclers of Henry's reign relied on what are still practically the sole sources of information, Rickhill's and John Halle's accounts. A writ dated 17 August ordered Rickhill to accompany the Earl Marshal to Calais and there fulfil the instructions which the earl gave him. According to the justice the writ was delivered to him at midnight on 5 September, when he was staying in his country house. Crossing the Channel on 7 September, he went that evening to the earl's Calais hostel and was given by him a commission dated 17 August, commanding him to interview Gloucester and report under his seal what he should say. Rickhill said that he was astonished 'because the Death of the said Duke had been announced to all the people both in Calais and England'. He received the duke's confession in Calais Castle on 8 September, but was not readmitted the following day and returned to England.

The 1399 confession of Halle, Mowbray's 'vadlet', was even more intriguing. Oversleeping one day in September 1397, he was hauled from bed by the earl's esquire John Colfox and summoned before his master. In answer to a question from the earl, who was in a testy mood, Halle said that he supposed Gloucester to be dead. The Marshal replied that he was not, but that the king had ordered him to have the duke killed and that royal esquires and Rutland's esquires had been sent as observers. The earl ordered Halle to go along on his behalf, coaxing him with 'a great blow on the head'. Halle was taken to a building in the Princes Inn, where Gloucester was brought (presumably from the Castle). On seeing two of the newcomers from

England, the duke said 'Now I know that I will be alright' and enquired after the king's health. Assuming that Halle's account was reliable, it is likely that the duke was hoping desperately that the visit betokened a merciful reply to his recent plea. But he was brusquely told the king's will, shriven and smothered under a feather-bed. In the inquisitions into Gloucester's forfeited property, the date of his death was given as 17 or 15 September, fitting in with the justice's and the valet's evidence. It is difficult to find any reason why they should have postdated his demise in 1399, as has been suggested. Richard may have decided in the first weeks of August that he dare not produce his uncle to answer the Appeal in parliament, but have had sufficient scruples to put off the necessary murder until the day on which parliament met. In October Mowbray was ordered to deliver Thomas's body for transport to the widow Eleanor, for burial in Westminster Abbey. Richard had second thoughts about this, probably as a result of the cult that sprang up at Arundel's tomb: the duchess was ordered to surrender the body for burial at Bermondsey Priory (Surrey), obscurely in the suburbs.[23]

On 28 September Warwick had been produced in parliament, after being brought from imprisonment at the Cornish royal castle at Tintagel, in a county where events in the 1390s had shown that the earl had few sympathizers. He made a complete confession of guilt and was sentenced to forfeiture and death, but at the petition of the girl-queen Isabella and other notables this was commuted to life imprisonment in the Isle of Man, where he was placed in the custody of Sir William Scrope and of his brother Stephen.

The king was petitioned by his 'povres oratours' Thomas and Margaret Beauchamp, the former earl and countess, that they might be allowed to have some necessities, including two beds with sets of sheets and pillows, a dinner service, napery and kitchen utensils, vestments and plate for a chaplain to celebrate mass, and, for Margaret, some clothes, including her furred gown, and wardrobe accessories. She also requested means of transport, to go to the coast and return to the king. Perhaps she wanted to see her husband off when he embarked for the Isle of Man. On 16 November 1397 Sir Giles Malory and others were ordered to grant her a list of necessities. Richard had already allowed her to have her personal ornaments at Windsor, before parliament met. In May 1398 Margaret was granted 250 *m.* per annum during her husband's lifetime. Walsingham alleged that she and Thomas endured hardships, as the sums Richard had promised for their maintenance from the former Beauchamp properties were unpaid. Later in 1398 she received papal permission to live with three honest matrons for as long as she liked in the London convent of the Minoresses Without Aldgate. Her sister had been professed there, and if she went there she would find sympathizers and companions in misery, Gloucester's daughter Isabel and, on her visits, Gloucester's widow.[24]

Ample excuse was made in the 1397–8 parliament for the two unscathed Appellants of 1387–8, Mowbray and Bolingbroke. After the forfeitures they were elevated as dukes of Norfolk and Hereford. In the second session of Richard's notorious parliament, meeting at Shrewsbury in January 1398, Hereford alleged that in the previous month Norfolk had suggested to him that rivals including William Scrope, John Montague and Thomas Despenser, respectively earls of Wiltshire, Salisbury and Gloucester were about to procure their downfall through their participation in the 1387 movement. Unless Hereford's accusation was true, it is hard to see what his object was in making it. He was probably incensed by Norfolk's reputed part in Thomas of Woodstock's demise, but only a fool would have tried to ruin Norfolk by implicating himself in a politically dubious conversation which drew attention to his own past treasonable associations. Norfolk's judgment may have been so shattered by the recent events that he rashly confided in a man who regarded him as untrustworthy, the creature of a tyrannous king, and who therefore felt compelled to make his version of the conversation public. For Hereford this cannot have been a happy course, for the suspicious king might wonder what else the two nobles had said. At Coventry on 16 September 1398 Richard sentenced Hereford to exile for ten years, later commuted to six. He was licensed to go with a princely retinue of 200 and £1,000 for expenses. Norfolk was exiled for life and forfeited his inheritance, because of alleged maladministration as Captain of Calais, but was allowed to keep property to the value of £1,000 *p.a.* He forfeited lands granted since the 1397 Appeal on the grounds that he had not fulfilled his allotted role as recent Appellant to the king's satisfaction. Norfolk was to stay in Germany, Bohemia and Hungary and to cross the Mediterranean on pilgrimage: he was not to stay in other parts of Christendom on pain of treason. This demarcation may have been intended to deter him from meeting and trying to plot with Hereford. Norfolk's absence was not perhaps meant to be as final as it appeared, provision being made that his homage should be respited for any land that he might inherit during exile 'until it shall please the king that he return to do the same in person.'[25]

The forfeitures by Arundel, Gloucester, Warwick, Sir Thomas Mortimer and Lord Cobham in the second 1397 parliament encouraged Richard to make a new territorial settlement of estates, probably with more deliberation than the Lords Appellant had done—in 1388 no magnate with wealth comparable to Arundel's and Warwick's had forfeited. Many of the manors confiscated in 1397 were kept in the Crown's possession to be granted out individually to royal retainers for life. More remarkable was the annexation of the Arundel lordships in the Northern Marches to the new Principality of Chester. On 28 September 1397 the following grants of Arundel properties were made in tail male—the Lordship of Arundel and the bulk of the Sussex properties to Huntingdon (elevated in the second 1397 parliament as duke of Exeter), the Lordship of Lewes and other Sussex manors to the Earl Marshal; in October Norfolk properties to the duke of York and Shropshire properties to Thomas Percy, newly created earl of Worcester. In January 1399 the Lordship of Reigate was entailed on Exeter.[26] The first grants of former Beauchamp properties had been made in September 1397. The king's nephew Thomas Holand, Earl of Kent (created duke of Surrey), received Warwick Castle and extensive properties in Warwickshire; Thomas Despenser, Earl of Gloucester, was granted Elmley Castle and Worcestershire properties, and William Scrope, Earl of Wiltshire, was granted the Marcher Lordship of Pain's Castle and the Durham lordships. Other Beauchamp property grantees were Rutland (duke of Aumale), Exeter, Norfolk, Somerset (marquess of Dorset) and Sir Henry Grene.[27]

Thus before the 1399 confiscation of the Lancastrian inheritance, Richard had built up the landed power of the Crown and of the noble families which he trusted, in the largest estate-holding revolution of the century among magnates. As far as the beneficiaries were concerned, his achievement received a measure of forlorn justification in their bid of January 1400 to recover these gains by putting him back on the throne. But forfeitures on such a majestic scale were likely to produce tensions among the magnates inimical to Richard's aim of stabilizing royal authority. The forfeitures of Edward II's reign were still producing uncertainties and antagonisms, as Norfolk's alleged remarks to Hereford in December 1397 bear witness. Richard's forfeitures created a new group of the 'disinherited', a source of embarrassment and danger. There was Arundel's son and heir Richard, placed in Exeter's custody in October 1397, who probably died in captivity. His younger brother Thomas, then placed in his brother-in-law Norfolk's custody, escaped from Exeter's callous treatment at Reigate in 1399 to join his exiled kinsmen Bolingbroke and Thomas Arundel, former archbishop of Canterbury. Then there was Warwick's heir, his young son Richard, who with his wife Elizabeth was in October 1397 in the custody of Surrey, his father's supplanter at Warwick Castle. Gloucester left a son under age, Humphrey, carefully educated—the hope of many, according to Walsingham. He was a force to be reckoned with, as he was heir to the moiety of the Bohun inheritance held by his mother and grandmother. Richard kept him under surveillance, as he did the other Bohun heir, Bolingbroke's son Henry of Monmouth. The king took the young cousins to Ireland in 1399 and on his return left Humphrey in Trim Castle. On his way back Humphrey died of plague on Anglesey, 'to the great grief of the land'.[28]

In the first parliament of Henry's reign the titles and inheritances of the earls of Arundel and Warwick were restored to them. Warwick made himself look ridiculous in parliament by his attempts to deny that he had confessed to treason in 1397. But he attended the council on occasion in the first months of the reign and in January 1400 may even have taken the field in support of the new king against the rebel earls. He died on 8 April 1401 and his son Richard succeeded to the inheritance in February 1403 and to the dower lands which his widowed mother held in March 1407. Richard Earl of Warwick (d. 1439) achieved more chivalrous and military fame than his father had done: a staunch Lancastrian, he was to be entrusted with the supervision of Henry VI's education. Thomas Earl of Arundel (d. 1415) also fought well for Henry IV and Henry V. Gloucester's kinsfolk rallied to the new dynasty. His son-in-law Edmund Earl of Stafford died fighting for Henry at the battle of Shrewsbury in 1403. Richard II, by attacking the senior Appellants of 1387-8, drew their families together once again, so that Henry could rely on their services against the assaults on his rule. There was one notable exception. The duke of Norfolk, having been to Palestine, and heavily in debt, died at Venice on 22 September 1399. He was buried there. His son and heir Sir Thomas Mowbray had been born in 1385. He had expectations of the restoration of his full inheritance and the duchy of Norfolk, for he was married to Henry's niece Constance Holand. But Sir Thomas's associations may have made him anti-Lancastrian—

his father had quarrelled with Henry, he had been brought up in the household of Richard's queen Isabella, and his father-in-law Huntingdon had died rebelling against the usurper. In 1405 Mowbray, still a minor, became involved in Archbishop Scrope's equivocal demonstrations against Henry's rule. Bolingbroke executed him without compunction.[29]

four

The Character of Thomas of Woodstock

Thomas of Woodstock is a complex, often puzzling and always shadowy figure. The knowledge of his character which can be gleaned outside of national politics is uncertain, due to the ambiguous nature of some of the scanty evidence. Thomas emerged in his nephew's reign as an intelligent and assertive politician, a man of positive opinions, whose explosive temper sometimes helped to carry his points, but in the long run damaged his reputation. In 1384, 1387 and probably in 1386 he spoke intemperately in the royal presence. According to the confession attributed to him

> Also, in that I slandered my Lord, I acknowledge that I did evil and wickedly, in that I spoke it to him in slanderous wise in audience of other folk. But by the way that my soul shall to [i.e. travel], I meant no evil therein. Nevertheless I know and acknowledge that I did evil and foolishly . . .

In 1388 the duke probably lost credit by quarrelling in parliament with York and in 1397 he may have publicly insulted Richard after dinner. Even if some of these incidents are fictitious or garbled, it is significant that contemporaries regarded them as plausible.

In the highly charged atmosphere of the last two months of 1387, the duke of Gloucester may have temporarily let his ambition and faith in his own abilities overcome his judgment of what was practicable. It is fairly certain that he then revealed designs on the Crown, a policy as unwelcome to his fellow magnates as was to be the claim of Richard Duke of York (his great-nephew) in 1460. Gloucester's ambition probably hastened the defection of Derby and Nottingham from the Appellant cause. However, during most of the years of crisis (1386–9) the duke displayed keen political awareness; he and his allies were masters of propaganda, managing to keep the sympathy of public opinion until the autumn of 1388. Thomas's willpower was an important factor in holding together for many months a potentially divergent coalition of magnates, lesser lords, gentry and royal officials. Isolation was the price which he eventually paid for success in forcing his royal nephew to govern less extravagantly and more tactfully. He may have toyed with the idea of procuring Richard's deposition partly in anticipation of such an isolation. As long as the king ruled without threatening the 1388 settlement and its authors, magnates were happy to dispense with the pre-eminence which this sterner brother of Lancaster had recently exercised in councils and parliaments. Though Gloucester strove to act correctly in the 1390s, he could not live down the reputation which he had gained as Richard's opponent in the field and in the council chamber. Any criticism which he made of royal policy was greeted both with approval and alarm. Eventually Richard could no longer stand the strain of gauging his uncle's reactions and arrested him.

In the period 1393-5 Gloucester tended to be at odds politically with the earl of Arundel, but he appears to have kept on friendly terms in the 1390s with most of his major political allies of the period 1386-9. Lord Cobham was one of his executors in 1391 and his deputy in the Court of Chivalry in 1392. In that year Sir Thomas Mortimer negotiated on his behalf with the royal council and acted as a fellow feoffee. Archbishop Arundel, Bishop Braybrooke and the earls of Arundel and Warwick were among the duke's feoffees in 1394 and among his attorneys (excepting the first earl) in 1395. Cobham and Richard Lord Scrope were also attorneys then. From October 1395 onwards the former was one of his feoffees in the wardship of Warwick's nephew Edmund Stafford, who was heir to the earldom of Stafford. Gloucester's continued connections with former political allies may have helped to sustain the king's suspicions.[1] On the other hand, worries about Richard's intentions, besides family and business connections, probably fostered relations between the former allies. Thomas's long-standing connections of one kind and another with magnates may also be a tribute to attractive sides of his personality. From afar, at least, he could inspire devotion, evident in Walsingham's obituary—'the best of men', 'the hope and solace of the whole community of the realm'. Walsingham may have had violent and unreliable prejudices, but in this case (as will be seen) he is likely to have been informed by personal observation. Two lords who had known the duke well, Morley and FitzWalter, bitterly denounced his ' betrayal ' and death in Henry IV's first parliament.[2]

An interesting account of Gloucester was given by the chronicler of the Cistercian abbey of Meaux (Yorks.). It reveals some of the characteristics which made the duke feared and respected—and his insensitivity to the constitutional rights of others, the insensitivity of a practical and impatient man. In 1390 the king granted to him the reversion of the Lordship of Holderness (Yorks.), with its appurtenances, which included the patronage of Meaux. The reversion was dependent on the death of Anne of Bohemia; in September 1394, having received seisin of the lordship, Gloucester visited it (not long after his entertainment by John of Gaunt at Pontefract). He stayed for three days at Meaux, at the house's expense. Addressing the monks in chapter, he requested a search of their records and then a recognition of his rights to the patronage: they willingly complied. His determination to secure the claim had been prompted by a conversation with Archbishop Arundel, who had asserted his right to the patronage. The duke (sometimes so vociferous in politics) kept silent about the matter until he was able to secure his interest in person. After he had done so, the abbot of Meaux rashly mentioned to him in private that he wished to resign the abbacy. Gloucester (who seems to have enjoyed sitting in chapter with the monks) promptly proposed the resignation, which they, in fear of him, reluctantly accepted. Once their overbearing guest had departed, they persuaded the former abbot to retract his resignation, since the manner in which it had been proposed might have provided Gloucester with a precedent for further intervention in their affairs. The abbot sent the duke a gift of £20 to appease him, but later proposed his resignation again, this time to the abbey's visitor, the abbot of Fountains. This wavering exasperated Gloucester, who was aware that previous election disputes had produced bad effects at Meaux and considered the monks to be undisciplined and their abbot lax. He wrote firmly to the visitor, advising him to deal harshly with any monks who would not accept the proposed resignation and a new election. He also wrote round to the neighbouring gentry, asking them to assist the abbot of Fountains.

The information which the Meaux Chronicler provides about Gloucester shows a man who knew when to be silent in order to forward his claims, but who brusquely intervened to settle the affairs of an abbey. Here was a prince whose presence commanded obedience, who was officious and domineering, but prepared to spend time in organizing some rather obscure monks. The chronicler recognized the duke's reverence for the house and was proud of his patronage: 'he prized our monastery highly, in which he would have chosen to be

buried, if he had enjoyed his earlier liberty at the end of his life.'
The assertion about his burial was wishful thinking, perhaps based
on a flattering remark by the duke, who in fact chose to be buried in
Westminster Abbey. For the Cistercians of Meaux his body would
have been a valuable acquisition, considering his posthumous fame.
In January 1400 Pleshey Castle was to be surrounded by the inhabitants of some of his former Essex manors, who demanded that the
countess of Hereford should surrender Richard's favourite, Huntingdon. They proceeded to execute the earl on the spot where Gloucester
had been arrested in 1397. The duke, suppressor of the commons'
rebellion in 1381, may have already won popular fame in 1387.
According to one account, the 'commons' wished to place him on the
throne, after Richard had surrendered the Tower.[3]

Thomas of Woodstock's tastes befitted those of a leading magnate,
the son, brother and uncle of kings. He attached importance to the
solemn code and courtly values of chivalry. In his youth he formed a
'company of May', whose companions he remembered fondly in later
life, and who may have celebrated the coming of spring with poems
and carols. He was fond of music: at one time he kept a blind harper
in his household, and in his London house in 1397 there was an organ
and the hall tapestries were decorated with angels playing musical
instruments.[4] Froissart, no mean judge in such matters, was impressed by his encouragement of 'deeds of arms' on the 1380–1
expedition. During the march through France, Thomas interested
himself in a challenge made by a French esquire, seeing that an
opportunity was provided for it to be met, and rewarding the esquire
well for his noble conduct. When the army wintered in Brittany, the
earl held tournaments at which both Breton and French knights
were welcome. These entertainments took place when the English
were in dire straits, but they did not strike Froissart as incongruous.
He says that the French sang Thomas's praises, one of them remark-
ing that he spoke like a king's son, a compliment that the earl would
doubtless have relished. Moreover, he took his duties as Constable of
the Realm seriously, writing before March 1390 a treatise addressed
to Richard II on the order of battle in the Court of Chivalry. In this
work of codification he remarked on the number of duels fought
recently, the lack of ordinances for their regulation and the diversity
of customs.[5] Justice Rickhill's account of his visit to Gloucester in
September 1397 shows that the duke was literate. In December 1360
£4 had been paid to Robert de Holm, chaplain, 'for the expenses of

Edward Palmer, for the youngest son of the Lord King, in the custody of the same Robert, to be instructed in the science of grammar'. None of Gloucester's royal kinsmen indulged in any kind of literary composition as far as is known, not even Richard II. The only exception was the duke's nephew Edward of Norwich, who turned to translation and composition during a spell in prison.[6]

Gloucester was especially interested in the most noble kind of chivalrous enterprise—crusading. There was the example of his father-in-law Hereford to emulate. One of the duchess's treasured possessions, which she singled out as a bequest to her son, was a coat of mail with a brass cross attached, which had belonged to her husband. This may have been part of the duke's crusading armour.[7] In 1386 he entertained the deposed King Leo of Armenia at Pleshey and in 1395 the propagandist known as Robert the Hermit. Both were visiting England to advocate peace with France, so facilitating a joint crusading venture in the Mediterranean. Froissart reports in considerable detail Gloucester's arguments against Robert's schemes. The duke was too level-headed to sacrifice what he considered to be the interests of the realm for the sake of crusading. But the sincerity of his desire to take the cross is shown by the Prussian expedition. Success in this venture might have raised his prestige among the young nobles coming of age in the 1390s, who had been minors when he had won honour by marching through France. The young men seem to have been content that the duke should play a minor role on the Irish expedition of 1394-5.[8]

It is sometimes difficult to be certain when noble tastes are more than perfunctory gestures to convention and fashion. However, Walsingham was not alone in attributing to Gloucester a sincere piety. Some of his religious interests and patterns of behaviour may have flowed from this piety. The duke's appeal for Richard's mercy in 1397 was based on devotional invocations typical of the period:

> that he will, for the passion that God suffered for all mankind, and the compassion that he had for his Mother on the Cross, and the pity that he had for Mary Magdalen, that he will vouchsafe for to have compassion and pity . . .

Both Gloucester and his royal nephew are likely to have been familiar with sermons, prayers and paintings which expressed this kind of religious emotion. The duke had a special devotion for St Thomas of Canterbury ('my special patron and advocate'). A reverence for

Becket and an interest in crusading are characteristic of Richard too. Aspects of Gloucester's behaviour which may have been influenced by his piety were his temperateness of diet in middle age (Froissart says that he sat little at dinner and supper), the absence of evidence for sexual licence and the soberness of his apparel, if the 1397 inventories can be accounted a reliable guide to his wardrobe.[9] He took care to provide for the female recluse living at his village of Kneeshall (Notts.) in a house at the church's end. In 1395 he granted her 40s. from the manorial revenue. Gloucester had a special regard for the Minoresses Without Aldgate. In 1394 he arranged for the appropriation of an advowson to their convent. His London house was near that of the nuns, who allowed him to make a door so that he could enter their church as he pleased.[10]

Thomas's piety and tastes in literature and art may have been influenced by the traditions of the family into which he married, the Bohun family. His widow, who was staying in the Minoresses' house when she died, bequeathed twelve books in the will made shortly before her death, most of them devotional in character. To her daughter Joan she left 'a book with the psalter, primer and other devotions . . . which book I have often used'. It may have been the surviving volume consisting of Psalter and Hours (National Library of Scotland, MS. 18.6.5), which contains prayers for her father, Richard II and Bishop Braybrooke. The collection indicates the devout nature of its owner, the *peccatrix*.[11] According to Duchess Eleanor's will, her favourite possession was a crucifix. Her uncle the earl of Arundel, in his 1392 will, left her 'a tablet of gold' containing a crucifix, whereas he left cups to his sisters, the countesses of Hereford and Kent. Isabel Duchess of York, in her will (proved January 1392) bequeathed to Eleanor 'my tablet of gold, with images, also my psalter with the arms of Northampton' (i.e. the Bohun arms). Eleanor's daughter Isabel had when very young been placed in the London convent of the Minoresses (where the duke wanted Mary de Bohun to be professed). Isabel lived there, reverenced by Richard II, and eventually became abbess of the house. In 1401 her great-uncle Archbishop Arundel, considering that only one other of Gloucester's children was living (Anne Countess of Stafford) and that the inheritance might devolve on 'strangers', petitioned the curia for permission to interview Isabel, to enquire whether she was prepared to forgo the religious life. If he made his enquiry, she certainly refused.[12]

The duchess and her husband are found sharing what may have been a devotional interest in 1391. They were granted an indult to enter enclosed monasteries—possibly to procure prayers for the success of the duke's crusade. At Pleshey in 1397 he had probably one of the finest lay collections of religious and secular books in England. Miss M. V. Clarke analysed the inventory then drawn up for the Crown, which listed other furnishings as well. The chapel of the castle possessed 39 service books, the library 83 books, 21 of them devotional in character, besides several sets of the Gospels and Bible in English. Most of the books were in French or Latin. There were French miracles of Our Lady, Passions of the Saints and a Life of St Thomas of Canterbury. There were theological and canonical works. Religious subjects figured prominently in tapestries at the castle: two depicted 'lestorie de Nativite de notre seigneur et de la Nativite Presentacion et Purificacion notre dame'.

It is arguable that the contents of the castle library did not necessarily reflect Gloucester's tastes. Probably many of the books and hangings were commissioned and acquired by his father-in-law Hereford. However, a significant pointer to one field of the duke's interests is 'a Chronicle of France in French, with two clasps of silver enamelled with the arms of the duke of Burgundy', which the duchess mentioned in her will. This chronicle is likely to have been a gift from Philip the Bold. A surviving volume which Gloucester almost certainly had made for him (MS. Bodleian 316) and which he presented to his new college at Pleshey, shows a predominant historical interest. It contains Higden's *Polychronicon*, Walsingham's account of the 'Good Parliament' and the same author's recently written short chronicle of English history (1328–88), besides a tract by Higden on the composition of sermons. Gloucester's interest in romances is reflected by the book he bought from the executors of Sir Richard Stury, the elderly royal councillor who gave such a hostile account of the duke's policies to Froissart in 1395. This was a *Roman de la Rose* (British Museum, 19 B xiii). The books listed in Gloucester's London house may have reflected his and his wife's reading habits: there were a *Meistre des Istories*, a book concerning nuns and their rule, *Vitae Patrum*, the remnant of a psalter with French glosses, *Godfrey de Boilon* and *Seven Psalmes*, the latter glossed in French, Latin and French Bibles, the *Legenda Aurea*, missals, psalter and primer. This selection has much the same range as in the Pleshey library. Historical and crusading romances were well represented there, for instance, by books about Hector of Troy and the Battle of

Troy, the Romance of Alexander, Merlin, the Romance of Lancelot, Bevis of Hampton, Tancred and Godfrey of Bouillon. Godfrey's crusade, whose history was also to be found in the London house, was the subject of fifteen Cloths of Arras in the castle—the crusading hero Charlemagne was the subject of another set there. Some of the tapestries were in less solemn vein—one showed 'The history of the battle between Gamlayn and Launcelot', others jousts, a mythical knighting, 'the history of an assault made on Ladies in a Castle' and 'the history of a discomfiture of a Wodewose [wild man of the woods] and a Lion and other histories'.[13]

The books which the duchess intended to leave to her only son Humphrey in 1399 may have been selected as ones which would edify and inform the boy in ways of which his father would have approved. They were the chronicle of France, which had belonged to the duke of Burgundy, Giles's *De regimine principum*, a book of 'vices and virtues'[14] and a poem of the *Historie de Chivaler a cigne*, a version of the romance which held a special significance for the Bohun family.[15] There was also a richly illuminated psalter which had belonged to the duchess's father. Gloucester is known to have given one book as a present, a breviary. The recipient was Sir Henry Scrope (*c.* 1373–1415), who succeeded his father Sir Stephen in 1406 as lord of Masham (Yorks.) and was executed in 1415 for his part in Cambridge's conspiracy against Henry V. The Scropes of Masham were related to the Appellants' ally, Richard Lord Scrope of Bolton (Yorks.), who in his will of 1401 made a bequest to Sir Stephen. In his will Sir Henry Scrope ordered the celebration of masses for Gloucester and his wife. The likelihood that Sir Henry shared devotional interests with them is suggested by his bequest of a volume containing works by the Yorkshire mystic, Richard Rolle of Hampole —his *De Incendio Amoris* and commentary on *Judica me Deus*. Another religious link between Gloucester's family and the Scropes of Masham is their connection with the London Minoresses. Sir Stephen Scrope (who was to leave his widow a cross which had once belonged to Gloucester) had a widowed sister-in-law, who became abbess of the house, and his daughter Matilda entered into the religious life there.

The Scropes had long-standing Bohun and crusading links. Sir Stephen's father Henry had campaigned in Scotland in the retinue of Hereford's father Northampton. Sir Stephen was present, like Hereford, at the capture of Alexandria in the crusade of 1365, as was his brother Sir William, who had campaigned with Hereford in Italy. The eldest brother, Sir Geoffrey, had died whilst crusading in Prussia in 1362. The Sir Henry Scrope who was Gloucester's friend went on the Tunis Crusade of 1390. Mutual interest in crusades may have been one factor which brought Gloucester and the Scropes together.[16] A few scattered references hint at other facets of Gloucester's friendliness and piety. In 1382, at his request, a royal pardon was granted for a sum due from the widow of a soldier who had died on the Breton expedition. In 1394, in his college statutes, the duke decreed that masses were to be said for all those who had died in his army in 1380–1.[17]

As was customary with men of Gloucester's station, he maintained friendly relations with a number of religious houses. He was *persona grata* at the great Benedictine houses of St Albans and Westminster. He was received as a member of the confraternity of St Alban in June 1378 and his wife was received in 1386. In 1384 he procured a royal favour for the abbey's Northumberland cell at Tynemouth. Abbot Thomas de la Mare, who may have been one of the duke's godfathers, helped persuade Warwick to adhere to his rising in 1387. The duke gave Abbot Thomas a ring containing part of the True Cross, which the future Cardinal Beaufort was to covet. The monk recluse at Westminster was also Gloucester's political supporter in 1387.[18] In December of that year the duke and duchess agreed with the Westminster monks that their anniversaries should be celebrated by the convent. In 1393–4 two Westminster monks paid a visit to the duke with a present of cloth of gold. In 1390, at his request, a royal favour had been granted to a cell of Westminster, Malvern Priory (Worcs.). Other houses which benefited by his patronage were Barking Abbey (Essex), whose nuns were granted a request at his petition in 1392, and Walden Abbey (Essex), a house patronized by the Bohuns to which in 1393 he was licensed to alienate Haddeston (Norfolk).[19]

The religious foundation on which Thomas lavished most money and attention was not a monastery but a college of secular priests, which he founded next to his principal residence in honour of the Holy Trinity, like Arundel's foundation similarly dedicated and situated by the castle wall at Arundel. In January and February 1394 the duke was licensed to found at Pleshey a college of nine chaplains (including a master), two clerks and two choristers, and to alienate to it the advowson of Pleshey church and two parcels of land there, on one of which he proposed to rebuild the church together with the college lodgings. Statutes drafted by Bishop Braybrooke were in February ordained by the duke and subsequently ratified by the bishop, and the dean and chapter of St Paul's. Paul Kirketon was appointed first master and warden. In July 1394 Thomas Albyn, rector of Pleshey, formally resigned the church into the bishop's hands, in a 'great chamber' in the castle, where were present Thomas Feriby, Archdeacon of Ely and others including Nicholas Myles, rector at the duke's living of Debden (Essex). The statutes reveal his intentions in making his foundation and the circle of kinsfolk and friends for whose souls affection or duty determined him to make provision. They were ordained by him 'to the praise and honour of God Omnipotent and in augmentation of divine worship' and for the good estate of himself and others living—the king, Lancaster and York, Archbishops Courtenay and Arundel, Bishop Braybrooke, the earls of Arundel and Warwick, Countess Joan of Hereford, Elizabeth Lady Despenser, Joan of Brittany Lady Basset, Lord Cobham, Sir John Harleston, Sir George Felbrigg, Thomas Feriby clerk, the duke and his wife. The souls to be especially remembered were those of Gloucester's parents and sisters, of Hereford and of Mary de Bohun, Countess of Derby.[20]

Among the college's original endowments were Barnston manor (Essex), purchased by the duke in 1389 and the reversion of properties granted to him which had been forfeited by Vere but were held for life by his mother, the countess of Oxford. These were the manors of Welbury (Herts.), Bockingfold and Whitstable (Kent), with the advowson of Whitstable. The duke and duchess were eager for the college to flourish: in July 1396 they were licensed to augment its personnel. They granted to Kirketon and his fellow chaplains the Bohun manor of South Fambridge in perpetuity. In the same month the countess of Oxford granted her life interest in Bockingfold to the duke, who quickly alienated it to the college. In or before 1397 the duke and duchess also granted the college the warren and lordship of Thurrock (Essex).[21] Gloucester's pride in his foundation, and the speed with which he established and built it, contrasting with the dilatoriness of some founders, were apparent in his reception of Richard at Pleshey in 1397. He met the king and his army in procession with the priests of the college, walking probably towards their church. Richard did not consider it incongruous to join in the procession, and he could not forbear expressing his admiration to his hated uncle, when he saw the interior of the new collegiate church, which Gloucester is known to have built on a magnificent scale.[22]

Thomas of Woodstock, who shared a number of traits and interests with his nephew, was probably a connoisseur of beautiful and luxurious ornaments. According to E. G. Millar, Duchess Eleanor's Psalter and Hours show that she patronized the outstanding school of illuminators which her father had employed, though the decorations in her volume are less fine and lavish than those in the small group of his surviving manuscripts. Millar considered that the illuminations in her psalter are also related to those in one of the outstanding manuscripts of Richard's reign—the Litlyngton Missal, commissioned by the abbot of Westminster who died in 1386. The inventory of goods at Pleshey lists many luxurious furnishings. It is impossible to be sure whether they reflected Hereford's tastes rather than the duke's. But it is likely that Gloucester and his wife prolonged and enhanced the canons established by her father. Among the books in the chapel was at least one new one in 1397—a 'Book of Gospels glossed in English'. The compilers of the inventory were moved to comment on the excellent quality of some of the manuscripts—one in the chapel was described as 'bien escripts', another as 'bien esluminez'. The duke probably possessed a number of panel paintings. Listed were a 'tablet of two leaves [i.e. a diptych] embroidered with gold of Cyprus with a crucifix [of Our Lady] flourished with pearls' and 'three tablets each of three leaves [i.e. triptychs] painted with divers images'. Their small value suggests that they were of no great size, nor highly prized. The most highly valued furnishings were the tapestries, the best beds with their elaborate coverings and hangings, ecclesiastical vestments and the plate. At Pleshey there were sixteen valuably furnished beds. The best, assessed at £182 3s., had blue satin curtains decorated with garters of gold, in allusion to the duke's membership of the Order of the Garter. There were sets of vestments for the use of visiting bishops who celebrated mass in the chapel. One of the two best copes, valued at £60, was worked with the Garter emblem and motto. At London the duke had another fine bed and an elaborate 'hanap'* which may have been for his personal use.[23]

Further evidence for the duke's possession and love of beautiful objects appears in some of the gifts which he and the duchess made to the abbeys of Westminster and St Albans. In December 1387 they indented to give the abbot and convent of Westminster vestments of

*Hanap, henap, drinking-vessel.

cloth of gold embroidered with their initials, a silver-gilt thurible adorned with images of saints and two silver candlesticks, carved in the shape of angels, bearing shields with the arms of the earls of Essex and Hereford. In 1391 the duke gave the convent a set of altar and mass furnishings and plate, whose jewelled magnificence evoked superlatives from the Westminster Chronicler. Gloucester was later to retrieve these useful assets from the convent. In February 1388 he gave to St Albans Abbey 'a golden circlet, in the middle of which is a white swan with wings outstretched as if to fly'. The appreciative description in the 'Liber Benefactorum' is illustrated by a miniature of the duke, holding the lifelike gift, his emblematic swan, a more graceful figure than the donor.[24]

The surviving references to the devotional, literary and artistic patronage of Thomas of Woodstock and Eleanor his wife help to put in perspective chronicle references which show his somewhat unattractive political activities. The references also provide a few comparisons with the connoisseurship of Richard II and some of his friends, which has recently been praised. If Richard did indeed become an outstanding patron of arts—the evidence for this is not voluminous—it may have been partly because he was trying to outshine his uncles Lancaster and Gloucester. John of Gaunt's marriage to Blanche of Lancaster and Thomas of Woodstock's to Eleanor de Bohun exposed these two sons of Edward III to the influence of the two most interesting English lay patrons of the mid-fourteenth century—Henry Duke of Lancaster and Humphrey Earl of Hereford. Their beautiful houses, the Savoy and Pleshey Castle, were admired by contemporaries. We have no visual evidence about the form and content of these houses, but chance has preserved Richard's fine woodwork in Westminster Hall. Lancaster's and Gloucester's experience of international diplomacy brought them into contact with two of the most remarkable lay patrons in later medieval Christendom—Charles VI's uncles of Berry and Burgundy. Richard met them only in 1396 and had hardly, unlike his uncles, travelled in France. The magnificence which Richard cultivated may have been copied partly from the style of his uncles.

It appears that materials no longer exist for a certain, rounded and convincing character sketch of Thomas of Woodstock. But there are enough references to suggest that he was a man of more varied interests and talents than the superficial features of his career indicate. His activities in cultural spheres were similar to those of French princes, whom he probably wished to emulate, however much he distrusted their policies. Aspiring crusader, patron of nuns, monks and collegiate priests, possessor of devout, learned and entertaining literature, lover of precious plate and tapestries, he held court at Pleshey, a place admired by the much-travelled Froissart. There the duke preferred to reside, especially in the 1390s, when he supervised the speedy establishment of his fine college and held entertainments. Thomas of Woodstock could be an implacable enemy, but he made lasting friendships, with cultivated nuns as well as with veteran professional soldiers. As a boy he captivated his devout aunt, Elizabeth of Hainault, and his godfather, the able Bishop Hatfield of Durham (d. 1381), left him the expectation of a 600 *m*. debt and his bed 'embroidered with signs of Wodewose and trees'. It was appropriate to Thomas's rank that he should possess beautiful and costly furnishings and ornaments, such as the presents which he and members of his family gave to Richard's bride during the wedding festivities at Calais in 1396. On the eve of Isabella's marriage the duke gave her a golden eagle adorned with precious stones and pearls and on the wedding day she received a golden crown from him, a great covered gold cup from the duchess and six other 'henaps' from their children. As will be suggested in the next chapter, a mainspring of Thomas's political activities was the need to receive honours, rewards and opportunities for profit from the Crown, in order to sustain his rank. New standards in princely luxury and munificence were being set across the Channel. Gloucester, austere in some of his habits and preoccupations, could not bear to forgo such dazzling magnificence any more than could Richard.[25]

five
The Properties and Servants of Thomas of Woodstock

To understand the influence which Thomas of Woodstock could bring to bear on the affairs of the realm, it is necessary to survey his propertied wealth, its locations, the inherited local influence which was one of its most important appurtenances and the ties which he formed through the personal and administrative services required by a magnate. The extent to which lords in the later fourteenth century expected support of a political nature from those who received their fees and annuities—especially for those who were their life retainers—is not clear. Neither is the extent to which the expectations of lords in the matter were fulfilled. A survey of Thomas's servants gives indications—mostly of a tentative nature—that he received considerable support from them in the crisis of 1386–8. In 1397 Richard acted as if he had special reason to fear the reactions of the servants of Gloucester, Arundel and Warwick: shortly after the arrests, orders were sent to the mayor and sheriffs of London and to the sheriffs of counties in which the three had a lot of property, to arrest any of their men and servants found armed or making unlawful assemblies, besides 'others of their retinue and livery whatsoever' found so compromised.[1] But it is not clear whether the intense political support which Richard suspected his opponents' servants and retainers might display, and which he expected from his own in 1397 and the following years, was normal. Whether support was given to magnates probably depended on circumstances—on the political situation, the nature of the individual's personal and financial ties with his lord, their significance in comparison with other ties of the same kind which the retainer might possess and the influence of opinions expressed by kinsmen and by neighbours in his 'country'. The valet who was a minor in a noble household, the groom who was of humble origin, were more likely to trespass and riot, even take up arms against the king at their lord's command, than the landed gentleman, usually a more complex political animal. One fairly safe conclusion is that the magnate who was an able politician, sensitive to the opinions and interests of the circles from which his retainers were drawn, was more liable to receive the calculated support of the important men who were his friends and servants. Thomas of Woodstock was in the category of fortunate lords who could rely in 1387 on considerable support from such men. But if he had revolted in 1389, as Richard suspected he might, it is doubtful whether he would have commanded the same amount of support, since political circumstances had become so adverse to his interests. This doubt may have been one reason why Thomas did not stir then: he had the art of nicely calculating the odds. In the adverse circumstances of 1399, Richard failed to command the support of the numerous and well-rewarded annuitants on whom he had relied so heavily, perhaps in imitation of the Appellants' reliance on theirs. The 'perfidy' then displayed towards the king, whose badge of the white hart his servants quietly discarded, shocked French observers such as Jean Creton and Janico Dartasso. Such conduct reflected the complexity of relationships in the English propertied classes. Ties with kinsmen, neighbours and comrades in arms made for divided loyalties among the king's retainers, at a time when the king had been so foolish as to antagonize different sections of society. Political trimming was respectable in England long before the end of the seventeenth century. Such a mentality on the whole favoured the tranquillity of the realm.

In 1368 Thomas of Woodstock was holding the lordships of Melle, Chizée and Civray in Poitou: letters patent of the Black Prince gave full power to his brothers Lancaster and Cambridge and to his cousin Arundel to receive Thomas's homage for them. The conquest of the boy's first lordships by the French helps account for his later demands for the enforcement of the Treaty of Brétigny, leading to their recovery, as a basis for peace. In the articles for peace drafted in 1393, to which Thomas was a party, his former lordships were specifically renounced by the English (clause xii). Lancaster may have promised to compensate his brother for loss of his claim.

The first grant of English properties to Thomas was made by his father on 3 April 1374, 'to hold until the full age of Eleanor whom the said Thomas will take to wife, or until further order'. The object of the grant was 'that he may more fittingly maintain his estate'. He was to receive annual fees from the counties of Essex and Northampton, which had been enjoyed by the earl of Hereford, Eleanor's father, and nine of the earl's former manors—Kirtlington, Deddington and Haseley (Oxon.), Farnham and Shenfield (Essex), Wheatenhurst and

Haresfield (Gloucs.), Upavon (Wilts.) and Long Bennington (Lincs.).
The valuations set on these manors in 1380 (exclusive of Haresfield
and Upavon) totalled £171 17s. The profits from these properties,
together with the royal annuity of £300 which Thomas had to maintain himself and Eleanor, may have given him an income of about
£530. In addition, in August 1376 Thomas was granted 1,000 m. at
the Exchequer, £243 of which was converted the following October
into custody of Bohun properties: the castle, town and manor of
Pleshey, the manors of High Easter, Waltham, Wix and two-thirds
of Hallingbury, the court of the honour of Mandeville at High Easter,
the view of frankpledge at Chishall (Essex), the manors of Kneeshall
(Notts.) and Ascot (Oxon.) and the courts of the honours of Gloucester
and Farleigh. On 24 May 1377, less than a month before his father
died, Thomas was granted Bohun properties for the remaining part of
his 1,000 m. annuity. These were the Marcher Lordships of Brecon,
Hay, Huntingdon, Caldicot and Newton, yielding an anticipated
income of £533 6s. 8d.[2]

These grants, from which Thomas may have received about £1,200
p.a., were confirmed soon after Richard's accession, on the same day
as he was granted a life annuity of £1,000, assigned at the Exchequer,
to maintain his newly acquired status as earl of Buckingham. The
increase in his income in 1377 helps account for his ability to muster
retinues for expeditions in the next few years. On 5 July 1379, with
the assent of the council, the new annuity was assigned during royal
pleasure on the revenues from alien priories in the king's hands for the
duration of the war with France. This arrangement may have given
the earl a personal interest in opposing peace, since he was concerned
that his annuity should be firmly assigned. 1380 was the crucial year
for the development of Buckingham's fortunes, financial and political,
for Lancaster's marriage of Derby to Mary de Bohun in that year
deprived him of the hope that he might gain the whole of the Bohun
inheritance in right of his wife. Froissart tells the story of how a great
lady of the Arundel family spirited Mary de Bohun away from
Pleshey. Buckingham, on his return from Brittany, was furious with
Lancaster: as the wedding had taken place at Arundel Castle, he may
have been annoyed too with his future Appellant ally, the earl of
Arundel. The lady who was determined to marry Mary off in despite
of Thomas was almost certainly her mother, Arundel's sister Countess
Joan of Hereford. She received the custody of Mary on 16 January
1380. In March 1381 Lancaster ordered payments to be made for the

expenses of the day of Derby's marriage. Among those present at the feast had been ten of the king's minstrels and various officials of the countess of Hereford, including officers and valets of her chamber. Perhaps Lancaster promoted his brother's leadership of the 1380 expedition in order to facilitate the marriage. By the time Thomas's daughter Anne was born, relations between him and his brother seem to have been amicable. The duke attended her christening at Pleshey. On 6 May 1383 payments were ordered for presents he had given to the infant, including a pair of matching basins with collars and swans engraved on the rims, and with blazons of Buckingham's arms. The total cost was £96 3s. 5d. An esquire of the earl was rewarded by the duke for bringing news of the birth and on the baptismal day he gave presents to the countess's damsels. He gave other sums to the damsel assigned to be Anne's mistress, to the countess's midwife, the baby's nurse, rocker, valet of the chamber and page.[3]

As a consequence of Derby's marriage, Thomas for the rest of his life was dependent on Crown grants rather than on inherited resources to maintain the income of a leading magnate. He could not afford to be outstripped in favour by rivals at court. On 22 June 1380 orders were issued to escheators to give Buckingham and his wife seisin of her moiety of the Bohun inheritance, comprising Pleshey, High Easter, Waltham, Wix, Shenfield, Farnham (Essex), the court of Hertford and the view of frankpledge at Hoddesdon (Herts.), Haseley, Kirtlington, Deddington and Pyrton (Oxon.), Kneeshall and Arnall (Notts.), Long Bennington (Lincs.), Fulmodestone (Norfolk), two-thirds of Spene (Berks.), the view of frankpledge in Sawston (Cambs.), Wheatenhurst (Gloucs.) and, in the Marches, Huntington and Caldicot Castles, Newton and appurtenances. These releases included many manors which Thomas had held since 1374 and 1376, but not all of them. Whereas the Bohun properties which Thomas had held by his father's grants, during Eleanor's minority, were valued at £838 10s. 4d. p.a., the properties he received in her right (exclusive of the value set on advowsons) were estimated at about £500. The fall in income was anticipated by the grant to him in May 1380 of Mary de Bohun's share, without rent, until she came of age. He may have hoped by persuading her to enter the London Minoresses as a nun to keep this moiety permanently; instead he had to relinquish it to Derby in 1384. There are some indications that Buckingham's financial state was sound in the early 1380s, despite the high costs which the 1380–1 expedition probably entailed for him. In 1383 he contemplated a pilgrimage overseas, an expensive undertaking for a man of his station. In March 1385 he was granted the wardship and marriage of William, son and heir of Sir Richard Moleyns of Stoke Poges (Bucks.), for which he paid in advance £700. This was a worthwhile investment, since the heir had been born only in 1378, giving the earl long-term prospective enjoyment of a considerable inheritance, the main constituent of which was fourteen Buckinghamshire manors. It may have been as a result of careful management that he was able to take the third largest retinue on Richard's Scottish expedition. On 6 August 1385 he was created duke of Gloucester and granted another annuity of £1,000. These favours were confirmed to him in parliament on 12 November following. The ducal annuity amply recompensed the recent loss of Mary de Bohun's wardship, giving Gloucester an estimated income of about £2,500.[4]

One of Gloucester's subsequent aims was to have the ducal income, at first received at the Exchequer, attached to a firm source. Therefore, at his petition, half of it was assigned on the ancient custom of wool and wool-fells in the ports of London and of the east coast. On 17 May 1386 he was granted the castle and honour of Castle Rising (Norfolk), to be held in tail male as part satisfaction of the annuity. On 24 August following, at his petition, the council granted that he could take half of the annuity assigned on the ancient custom from the subsidy as well, as he could not get full payment. During the period of his political ascendancy Thomas tried to increase the financial benefits which he derived from the Crown. On 2 May 1387 farmers of alien priories were ordered to pay arrears of his comital annuity. On 15 July the king granted him the wardship of FitzWalter manors in Essex—Burnham, Woodham Walter, Little Dunmow, Henham and Raindon, for a rent of £180 11s. 4d. On 13 March 1388 he was granted one-third of Egremont manor (Cumberland), a FitzWalter possession. It was probably in the same year that he petitioned for both his royal annuities to be secured on properties forfeited in the first 1388 parliament. The petition was endorsed as granted by the king with the assent of the council, but remained unfulfilled, probably as a result of Gloucester's dismissal in 1389. One favour he had procured in September 1388 was a grant of all the Caen Abbey properties in the king's hands. These were granted in fee tail in June 1389, to the value of 400 m., as part payment of his comital annuity. The month afterwards, he was licensed to treat with the abbess and convent for the purchase of their English possessions. This is an indication that the

Appellant movement had not crippled him financially—probably because of the large indemnity granted to the Appellants. In 1389 Gloucester purchased Berners's forfeited Essex manors of Barnston and Roding Berners, for £600 paid on his behalf by Archbishop Arundel and others.[5]

But after the duke's loss of influence at court, not much in the way of royal favour came to him until Lancaster's return from Aquitaine. In 1390 Richard made a tardy attempt to put a large part of Gloucester's annuities on a landed basis, at least in reversion—a less satisfactory arrangement than the one for which the duke had probably petitioned in 1388. In May 1390 he was granted the Yorkshire Lordship of Holderness, in reversion after the death of the queen, and also reversionary interests in the Lordship of Oakham and shrievalty of Rutland. The Rutland properties had recently been granted to the duke's nephew Edward of Norwich (who seems to have been no friend of Gloucester) during the lifetime of his father York. Holderness, valued at £600, was to be held by Gloucester in deduction of his comital annuity: he had seisin of it in 1394, after the death of Anne of Bohemia.[6]

In 1391 Gloucester had received considerable favours from the Crown, which Richard's anxiety to appease him and Lancaster may have expedited. In February 1391 the duchess of Gloucester was granted the wardship and marriage of the heir of Sir Thomas Mandeville of Black Notley (Essex). Sir Thomas had served her father and had been in the military retinues of her husband. In September 1391 the duke was pardoned debts on any accounts and farms owed to the Crown and was granted the marriage, without rent, of Alan Buxhill. His executors were granted the privilege of holding lands, rents and reversions which he enjoyed by Crown grant for two years after his death. This and other favours bestowed in September 1391 were intended to facilitate his crusade to Prussia. It is indicative of his growing obligations that in 1380 his executors had been granted the right to hold the comital annuity for only one year after Thomas's death, to discharge his debts. Though the crusade resulted in heavy financial loss for the duke, it was not ruinous, for in the following year he was appointed to an expensive office, the lieutenancy of Ireland. The revocation of the lieutenancy in July 1392 left the duke heavily indebted to the Crown for prests received. In February 1393 his executors were granted the right to hold his properties, including annuities, for three years after his death. The next month he was pardoned 9,500 *m.*, received in prests at the Exchequer for the governorship of Ireland and the next day acknowledged in Chancery a debt of 5,000 *m.* received for the office. £1,000 of this was remitted in June 1394.[7]

However, Gloucester's fortunes were bolstered in the last years of his life by his connections with the rich Stafford comital family. The duke married his daughter Anne to Thomas, the young earl of Stafford. The account of Stafford's receiver-general, Nicholas Bradshawe (1390–1) records payments on the occasion of the wedding to the clerks of Gloucester's chapel at Pleshey and to the minstrels and heralds present. It also records disbursements to the Crown and members of the earl's council in connection with the marriage, payment to a goldsmith for the repair of a swan badge (the duke's livery) and Stafford's expenses for his expedition to Prussia in his father-in-law's company. Stafford died on 4 July 1392 : his heir was his younger brother William, who had been intended for the Church. The day after Stafford's death, the king ordered that the profits from properties in wardship as a consequence of William's minority 'be reserved to the king's use and wholly applied to the expenses of the household'. In the next few weeks the custody of various Stafford properties was granted to royal servants, but on 24 July Gloucester was granted the wardship of the late earl's inheritance, except for the dower due to his daughter, Countess Anne. The duke was also granted the right to arrange William's marriage. He received these favours during a great council gathered at Windsor, perhaps in compensation for his surrender of the Irish Lieutenancy and as reward for his part in condemning the government of London on Richard's behalf.[8]

In 1395 Thomas was again well treated by the Crown, partly as a reward for his services in connection with the king's Irish expedition. Thomas's promptness in setting aside properties for the foundation of Pleshey College from 1394 onwards indicates that he had recovered from the financial difficulties caused by the abortive Prussian and Irish expeditions. This recovery was probably assisted by the Stafford grant and by the royal remissions of debt. The unexpected reversion of Holderness in 1394 was a valuable windfall. Richard may have been annoyed and even alarmed that his uncle was flourishing— mainly as a result of the favour he considered it necessary to grant his formidable relative, who made ominously pointed remarks about the royal peace policy. In April 1395 Gloucester's ward William Stafford died at Pleshey, leaving his brother Edmund as heir. In June the duke was pardoned arrears owed for William's wardship and was granted that of Edmund's inheritance in Ireland and elsewhere, together with his marriage, without payment of rent. Edmund eventually married his sister-in-law, Countess Anne. According to Froissart, Gloucester, as the young man's guardian and kinsman, still maintained the feud with Huntingdon over the latter's killing of Edmund's brother in 1385. No more grants of consequence were made to Gloucester until 16 April 1397, when he was pardoned a number of debts owed to the Crown, totalling £1,074 1s 8¼d. Three months later the king had his uncle arrested. If the remissions were made in the expectation that the duke's property would soon be seized and as a means of lulling his suspicions (which certainly remained dormant), they were a clever and cynical move. But if they were the result of Gloucester's supplications, they provide another stimulus for his arrest: Richard and his councillors may have been infuriated at the need to give way once more to Thomas's financial pressure. Froissart heard it said at court in 1395–6 that the duke was continuously soliciting favours, although he could afford to spend 60,000 crowns (£10,000) annually—undoubtedly a gross exaggeration.[9] But the remark graphically illustrates the effects of the duke's lifelong dependence on Crown grants, which required constant pressure at court and on councillors to secure certain assignment, prompt payment and improvement of terms. The king's uncle, uncertain of his nephew's favour, had to compete with a host of eager gentlemen, ready to destroy the reputation of a magnate with a dubious past, who ostentatiously absented himself from court. Historians have stressed the unfortunate political consequences for the Crown of the endowment of princes with appanages. But in the case of Gloucester, tension resulted in Richard's reign from Edward's failure to endow his youngest son with sufficient income.

Some information about Gloucester's household and estate administration in the 1390s is available. In 1394 he had a chancellor, Thomas Feriby, and in 1395 his and his wife's wardrobes were at Pleshey. Their clerks of the wardrobe were respectively Robert Wade and Thomas Whitehed. The latter was the duchess's treasurer 1396–7. John Upton was then the duke's treasurer and Robert Fulmer had preceded him in office. Pleshey Castle was the centre of administration, where the household customarily resided. The Lordships of Huntington in the March of Wales and Holderness in Yorkshire had their local officials, supervised by and accountable to the duke's principal officers. The receiver of Holderness paid his profits to the clerk of the duke's wardrobe and to his treasurer. Throughout Gloucester's tenure of the lordship two of his leading estate officials, William Nafferton and John Lightfoot, acted as chief steward and auditor of accounts. There and in a number of Gloucester's manors the demesne was rented in 1397—at Wheatenhurst (Gloucs.), Cleton (Yorks.), Kelling and Salthouse (Norfolk), Long Bennington (Lincs.) and Kneeshall (Notts.). At the last two manors the tenants were said to be farming the demesne. In Essex Berwick, a part of High Easter, was in the hands of a farmer, but at High Easter and Waltham crops were still being grown on demesne for the lord. At High Easter and at Fulmodeston (Norfolk) the duke possessed cattle and sheep. In 1398–9 Wix (Essex) was held by a farmer and at High Easter a considerable amount of land was then leased.[10]

There is no evidence that Thomas of Woodstock was lavish, like Mowbray, in alienating manorial revenue for life to his servants and retainers. In November 1383 Thomas was licensed to grant John Torell esquire (who had served in his St Malo expedition in 1378) two-thirds of Arnall (Notts.), in return for his remaining with the earl for life. Torell was still holding this grant in 1397. Some time after 13 November 1387 Gloucester assigned a sum from the issues of Kneeshall (Notts.) to Sir John Clifton as part of his life annuity. The text of one of Gloucester's indentures for service in peace and war is contained in Chancery enrolment. On 30 September 1395 the duke retained William Cheyne esquire for life, with a fee of £16 *p.a.*, to be taken from the Lordship of Holderness. The indenture laid down the conditions of Cheyne's service:

> *bouche de court* for himself and a yeoman his chamberlain, and livery for three horses in time of war, and in time of peace, when he shall be in the duke's country [*sic*], such livery as others of his condition have had. With regard to prisoners and other profits of war taken by him or his the duke shall have the third part, and if any royal person captain or lieutenant of war shall be taken, the duke, if he please, shall have the prisoners, making compensation. Also, the said William shall make muster of his company whenever required.[11]

Many of the duke's servants were from families with properties in Essex, where he had a concentration of estates and most frequently resided. A relic of his presence in Essex is to be found in a window of Waltham church, which contains seven late fourteenth-century shields, three of the Bohun earls' arms, one of the royal arms and one of the bishopric of Ely's (Thomas Arundel's see). Many of his servants were from families which had a tradition of serving the Bohuns, who in Edward III's reign had been well rewarded by the Crown and active on military expeditions. One Essex man who became important in ducal service was John Boys of Tolleshunt (d. 1419), who was to be pardoned for his adherence to the Appellants. He was on Thomas of Woodstock's expedition in 1377 and in his military retinue in 1378; in 1383 he was a feoffee with Countess Joan of Hereford. In 1386 Boys was received into the St Albans confraternity together with the duchess of Gloucester. He was much involved in the property trans- actions of the Essex gentry. Consequently he may have been able to influence local opinion on the duke's behalf. In 1383 he was a feoffee with the latter's Essex friend Lord FitzWalter. In January 1388 he was among those appointed to search Queenborough Castle in the Isle of Sheppey for royal goods said to be hidden there. Its constable, the duke of Ireland, had just fled abroad from the castle.[12]

Gloucester's fall and forfeiture did not break up his household and estate organization, for many of his properties, especially in Essex, were held in right of his wife. Escheators were ordered to hand them into Eleanor's keeping in November 1397 and March 1398. Boys remained on in her service. He was one of the feoffees to whom she granted a moiety of Wethersfield (Essex) and the advowson there, together with two-thirds of Arnall (Notts.) and the reversion of the other third, held in dower by her mother, Countess Joan. In 1400 the trustees were licensed to grant Arnall to Sibyl Beauchamp, who had been a member of the duchess's household. Among the latter's trustees were Bishop Braybrooke, Thomas Percy Earl of Worcester, Glou- cester's old campaigning comrade, and the duke's former servants, Nicholas Myles, clerk, John Doreward of Bocking, Ralph Chamber- lain (possibly a Suffolk man) and John Lightfoot, probably of Essex. Myles, described as a chaplain, was one of the 'divers menial persons' whom Rickhill remembered as having been attendant on the duke at Calais Castle in September 1397. The others whose names he recalled were Thomas Whythed, chaplain, Reynald Rumbold and Robert Wade, clerks, and John Cok esquire. During the financial year 1398-9 Boys visited the duchess's manor of Wix (Essex) with Chamberlain and Lightfoot, to sell wood from the manor, and on 9 August 1399 the duchess appointed Boys as one of her executors, describing him as steward of her household.[13]

Continuity of services rendered to the duke and to his widow are likely to have made the king suspicious of the Essex gentry. Froissart describes how, after Gloucester's arrest, he had one of his knights called Cerber (Corbet?) executed. Another of the duke's knights, Sir John Laquingay, who knew his master's confidential affairs and encouraged his criticisms of the king's francophile policy, prudently left the duchess's service, despite her reliance on his advice. In the second 1397 parliament the lieges of Essex and Hertfordshire petitioned for the remission of excessive payments in their joint sheriffs' farm. After the first session a commission of leading Essex gentlemen was appointed to negotiate with the shire community for payment of a £2,000 fine, Hertfordshire also being fined. The communities of the two shires had petitioned at the same time to be pardoned for treasons committed. In 1398 London and other counties sued out pardons. The prior punishment of Essex in 1397-8 may have been a reflection of Gloucester's success, in 1387 as well as 1397, in attaching to himself traditional Bohun influence there. Three important servants of his who were probably Essex men were John Bray, Thomas Heveningham (both of whom took out pardons in 1398 for their support of the Appellants) and Lightfoot. Bray was in Thomas's military retinue in 1378 and, described as an esquire, he was in his service in 1384. Bray was among his executors in 1391, his feoffee in Sussex reversions in 1394 and attorney in 1395. The following year he witnessed the grant of South Fambridge by the duke and duchess to Pleshey College, as did John Doreward and two members of the Essex family of Coggeshall, Sir William and Thomas, the latter of whom was an adherent of the Appellants.[14]

Thomas Heveningham may have been identical with a younger son of Sir John, who held Little Totham (Essex) and acquired by marriage Gissing (Norfolk). Thomas was in the duchess's retinue when she visited St Albans in 1386 and was probably the 'Thomas Henknyng'm'' (Gough's transcription) who witnessed the South Fambridge grant of 1396. Heveningham was Constable of Pleshey Castle in the year 1397-8 and was granted an annuity of £10 by the duchess in letters patent dated Bristol, 10 April 1398.[15] John Lightfoot was among those who, on his master's behalf, told the Pleshey parishioners about the plans for a new church. In an inquisition of 1397 Lightfoot was described as the duke's auditor of accounts and in 1397–8 he was a receiver of the duchess's manor of Great Waltham (Essex). Lightfoot had travelled on her service from Wales to London, where he stayed eight days to have talks with the duke's executors. He made several visits to Wix—for instance, to make a final concord with the duchess's farmer there, Richard Gest. By June 1400 Countess Joan of Hereford had been granted the wardship of the duchess's daughter Isabel de Gloucestre. Her fellow guardians were Thomas Feriby, clerk, the leading Essex landowner Sir William Marny of Layer Marney, and Lightfoot.[16]

Feriby was one of Gloucester's principal officials. He had been in October 1377 the principal receiver of sums paid to Thomas to finance his first naval expedition. In June 1388 he was appointed to levy, on the wool subsidy in the port of London, a part of the £20,000 indemnity granted in parliament to the Appellants. In that year Feriby was rewarded with a canonry at Beverley Minster and the archdeaconry of Ely. In July 1389 Feriby was one of the feoffees who received Berner's forfeited manors on Gloucester's behalf and in 1391 he was appointed an executor. In 1394 the duke described Feriby as his chancellor, when ordaining that his obit should be celebrated at the collegiate church of Pleshey.[17] In the crisis period of 1386–8, Feriby probably acted as an influential advocate of his lord's policies among his extensive acquaintance, especially in Essex and London. In July 1387 the London fishmonger Thomas Spain granted properties in Essex to Feriby, besides Sir John Gildsburgh and John Corbet. Gildsburgh was a distinguished Essex landowner who had served in Hereford's and Thomas's military retinues, the former having granted him Nuthamstead (Herts.) for life. In March 1388 Gildsburgh was appointed to take oaths from the Essex gentry to uphold the convictions secured in the 'Merciless Parliament'. Corbet may also have been of an Essex family: he was an esquire of Gloucester in 1393–4, possibly related to the Agnes Corbet who was among the duchess's *domicellae* in 1386. Corbet's importance in the duke's service is reflected by the fact that he and Feriby went surety on Gloucester's behalf to Lancaster in 1394. Perhaps he was the mysterious Cerber whose execution was alleged by Froissart.[18]

Thus Spain's 1387 feoffees, Feriby, Gildsburgh and Corbet, were all at some time closely connected with Thomas of Woodstock. The witnesses to Spain's grant included Essex landowners with Bohun and Gloucester connections. Among them was John Doreward, attorney of the duke in 1395 and witness to the South Fambridge grant in 1396.

In 1399 Doreward's sympathies lay with Henry. He was Speaker of the Commons in the first Lancastrian parliament and was appointed to be of the king's council.[19] On 3 February 1389, soon before the Appellants lost control of government, Feriby was among the feoffees to whom Gildsburgh granted Essex properties. Included among his fellow feoffees were the Appellant supporter Thomas Coggeshall, another of the duke's attorneys in 1395. The group was headed by Sir Richard Waldegrave, a wealthy Suffolk landowner who possessed some Essex properties. He had been a military retainer and crusading companion of the Bohun earls and as Speaker of the Commons in 1381 had voiced criticisms of the manner in which Richard's household was run. In May 1388 Waldegrave was granted a wardship by John Corbet, which the latter had just received from the Crown. Possibly the grant of it to Waldegrave was intended by Gloucester to reward or buy his support. In November 1397 Sir Richard was pardoned for all offences committed against the Crown, including treasons. Feriby was also in trouble in 1397, perhaps because he had supported the Appellants conspicuously or because his influence was feared by the council. Between September and December 1397 orders were made for his arrest, imprisonment and appearance before the council. But Feriby speedily managed to ingratiate himself with Richard, taking the realistic attitude common among officials in the period, however partisan their private sentiments may have been. On 1 February 1398 his benefices were confirmed, including the canonry and prebend of Apesthorpe at York and prebends in the collegiate churches of Beverley (Yorks.) and St John, Chester. In April 1399 he was styled the king's clerk and it was said that he had been provided to a canonry in Lichfield Cathedral. However, Feriby is likely to have welcomed Henry's usurpation, for the new king immediately appointed him third Baron of the Exchequer. In 1400–1 Feriby appears as a leading official of Countess Joan of Hereford.[20]

Little is known of Gloucester's relations with the distinguished soldier Sir John Harleston, whom he singled out, in the foundation statutes of Pleshey College, as one of those whose spiritual welfare the priests were intended to promote—he was one of the few whose anniversaries were prescribed in the 22nd statute. Harleston may have held some Essex properties. He was already a knight when granted a royal annuity of 40 *m.* in 1365, and was Captain of Guines in the March of Calais from July 1370 until at least 6 November 1376 and Captain of Cherbourg for part of the year 1379. In both commands he was fortunate to procure valuable prisoners whose ransoms he sold. Sir John was one of Thomas's captains in France, Brittany and Essex (1380–1). In 1393 he was granted a royal annuity of 100 *m.* for life, in place of his previous annuity of £40 and in 1395 he was among those to whom Gloucester granted his Stafford and Moleyns wardships. On 10 October 1397, when the council ordered Feriby to be released from the Tower, his sureties for appearance before the council were Harleston, Sir Gerald Braybrooke the younger and the Stafford official Nicholas Bradshawe. Harleston may have been one of the veteran campaigners in whose interest Gloucester would have liked to see the war with France recommenced.[21]

Like Feriby, and in contrast to Gildsburgh, Waldegrave and Harleston, Sir William Castleacre, an adherent of the Appellants, is known to have been one of Gloucester's officials. He was a well-connected Cambridgeshire landowner who, through his involvement in administering the see of Ely's properties, had a link with Bishop Arundel. Castleacre was a professional administrator who probably had legal training. In 1379 and 1381 he was Lancaster's steward at Hertford and he was in Buckingham's service in May 1379 when he appeared as his attorney in Chancery. In 1382 Sir William was appointed on a commission to enquire as to what lands the earl of Hereford had held and in 1384 on one to determine who had assaulted Sampson Greenwich, a Kentish esquire of Buckingham who saw service on his military expeditions. In March 1388 Castleacre was granted the wardship of Cambridgeshire properties, probably as a reward for supporting the Appellants. In the same year he went surety with Feriby for Gloucester, when the latter was granted part of Egremont, and was appointed to enquire into defects in the royal castle of St Briavels (Gloucs.), in the Constableship of which the duke held a reversionary interest. In November 1388 Sir William was commissioned to enquire into Burley's former properties, in 1391 he was one of the duke's executors and in 1397 was said to have recently been one of his stewards. On 8 September 1397 his arrest and the seizure of his goods were ordered. But by early December he and his possessions had been released. Other arrests carried out at the same time as his suggest that Castleacre was involved in Cambridgeshire disturbances. The council is likely to have been sensitive about local troubles in which former adherents and officials of the Appellants were involved.[22]

Castleacre's influence in Cambridgeshire and Huntingdonshire probably contributed to the support which the Appellants received in the region. Both counties were fined in 1398. Recruits from the locality and from East Anglia may have joined during the Huntingdon conference. Gloucester had other connections with the local gentry. Hugh la Zouche, Lord of Fulbourn (Cambs.), an Appellant supporter, had sailed with him in 1377 and in 1380–1 served under his command. In March 1388 Zouche was appointed to administer the oath to maintain the Appellant cause in Cambridgeshire.[23] Sir John Lakenheath, who was influential in Cambridgeshire and Huntingdonshire, was probably one of the duke's councillors in the period of intense opposition to Richard. He had been a captain at Brest when Thomas arrived there in 1378. In June 1388 he was granted the forfeited De la Pole manor of Benhale (Suffolk), his sureties being John Corbet, probably then active in ducal service, and Thomas Bataill, an Essex man who knew some of the duke's servants. In October Lakenheath was appointed by Gloucester as his deputy to hear a case in the Court of Chivalry and in November pardons were granted at his supplication. In February 1389 Sir John was granted another former De la Pole manor, Lowestoft in Suffolk. He was probably alive on 9 November 1395, but died before 29 October 1396. This makes it difficult to identify him with the Sir John Laquingay who, Froissart says, was intimidated after the duke's arrest and who had listened sympathetically to the duke's recent diatribes against his royal nephew. However, it is possible that the biographies of two Lakenheaths have been conflated in the above account. A Sir Thomas Lakigleythe was among the duchess's travelling attendants in 1386, a Sir John Lakyngheth contracted to go to Ireland in the duke's retinue in 1392 and Edmund Lakyngheth was pardoned in 1398 for adherence to the Appellants.[24]

In East Anglia there appear to have been few landowners who were ducal officials, but several influential ones who were friends of Thomas of Woodstock and who may have supported or refrained from opposing his policies. The Norfolk landowner Thomas Lord Morley succeeded to his inheritance in his mid-twenties, after the death of his father in 1379. In 1380 he was knighted by Thomas, in 1391 he intended to go to Prussia in his company, he was pardoned for supporting the Appellants and in Henry's first parliament he accused Salisbury in connection with Gloucester's death. He died in 1416, having given good service to the Lancastrians. Related to Lord Morley was the Norfolk landowner Thomas, son and heir of Lord Bardolf, whose physique was exceptional. He appears to have been aged about nine when he served in Thomas of Woodstock's military retinue in 1378, in company with his kinsman Richard Moleyns. Thomas Lord Bardolf, in marked contrast to Morley, involved himself in plots against Henry IV, resulting in his death in 1408. Another important Norfolk landowner, Robert Lord Scales (*c.* 1372–1402), contracted to serve Gloucester in Ireland in 1392. Bardolf and Scales deserted Richard's cause in Wales in 1399, joining Henry at Shrewsbury.[25]

Some of Gloucester's officials, Lakenheath, Heveningham and Chamberlain, may have been of families which possessed Suffolk properties. Waldegrave of Bures St Mary (Suffolk) had, as has been seen, important connections with the duke. Another Suffolk landowner, Sir George Felbrigg (d. 1408), was among those for whose soul the duke provided in the Pleshey College statutes. He was head of a junior branch of the Norfolk Felbrigg family and had been retained by Edward III in 1361. Like Harleston, Sir George may have known and influenced Thomas when the latter was a boy in Edward's household. Richard kept Felbrigg in his service. In September 1385 he was granted an annuity of £40, which was doubled in 1395, after Felbrigg had served in the royal retinue in Ireland. On 18 May 1387, at a time when Gloucester's influence in council is likely to have been great, Sir George was appointed to negotiate an alliance against France with the duke of Guelders. In 1390 licence was granted, at Gloucester's request, for Sir William Arundel, Sir Simon Felbrigg and Robert Tey of Marks Tey (Essex) to travel and in 1395 Sir George was one of those to whom Gloucester granted the Stafford and Moleyns custodies. Apart from his connections with the Crown and Gloucester, Sir George had a long-standing connection with the earls of March. In July 1397 Roger Mortimer nominated him as one of his attorneys, with Sir Richard Waldegrave. The following day March granted Sir George £20 from his Lordship of Clare (Suffolk) for good service. In October 1398 Sir George was licensed to be of Norfolk's council during his exile and in November 1399 his annuities were confirmed by Henry IV. The little known about Felbrigg suggests that he was an influential and able man whose friendship and services were courted by kings and magnates: a gentleman who avoided political ruin by prudence and integrity.[26]

Some important servants of Gloucester had roots in counties not far from Essex—in Hertfordshire, Bedfordshire and Buckinghamshire, counties which were all to be mulcted for their alleged support of the Appellants. John Westwycombe was a Hertfordshire esquire who had served in Hereford's military retinues in 1371-2 and in Thomas's in 1377, 1378 and 1380. Like Thomas he was probably well known to the monks of St Albans, for in 1381, after the Peasants' Revolt, he was appointed on a commission to enquire into the services which were due to the abbot and convent. In 1385 Westwycombe was described as a member of the earl's household and his standard-bearer and the following year he was in the duchess's retinue when she visited the abbey. His services may have been politically useful to Gloucester in the next few years—in March 1387 he was appointed on a Hertfordshire commission to enquire whether a royal servant had paid no rent for a Crown wardship and had committed waste in the property.[27]

At Colmworth, not far south of Huntingdon, and elsewhere in northern Bedfordshire lay the principal estates of the well-endowed Braybrooke family, sympathizers with Gloucester in 1387-8. In November 1394 Sir Gerard Braybrooke the younger was appointed Gloucester's feoffee and in 1399 the duchess named him as one of her executors. After her death he became (if he was not already) one of the principal councillors of her mother Joan, Countess of Hereford. The Braybrooke family had some connections and influence in the neighbouring county of Buckinghamshire, where they held the manor of Horsenden. They were probably well acquainted with two of the leading Buckinghamshire families, the Aylesburys of Milton Keynes and the Moleyns of Stoke Poges. Thomas Aylesbury and Richard Moleyns were both knighted in 1378, when they were serving in Thomas of Woodstock's military retinue. Aylesbury's father, Sir John, was appointed to take the 1388 oaths in Buckinghamshire to support the Appellants. It may have been of logistic importance to the Appellants' army in 1387 that Gloucester, through his possession of the Moleyns wardship, controlled a number of Buckinghamshire villages in the Thames valley. He also held the important strategic centre of Henley-on-Thames (Oxon.), another Moleyns manor. One of the Moleyns family's trusted officials, William Nafferton, may have entered the duke's service. In February 1393 he was a guardian of the duke's widowed daughter, Anne, Countess of Stafford, and he was his steward in the Lordship of Holderness throughout Gloucester's tenure (1394-7).[28]

Thomas of Woodstock was endowed by marriage into a noble family, an expedient which had been frequently employed by English kings to set up their younger children. The Bohun possessions which he acquired were supplemented by large comital and ducal annuities in 1377 and 1385. For most of his adult life Thomas depended on court favour to secure sure assignment of a large part of his income. A son, Humphrey, was born in 1381, probably giving him an incentive to procure conversion of his annuities into landed grants entailed on his heirs male.[29] Once Lancaster had left England in 1386, Thomas probably considered that to enhance such family interests he needed to increase his influence at court. In the 1390s his continued need for such favour may have worsened his relations with the king.

There is some evidence to suggest that the duke was falling into considerable debt in the early 1390s, a situation likely to have increased his importunity. However, by his acquisition of the Stafford wardship and the Lordship of Holderness he added considerably to his wealth and territorial influence—developments likely to have pleased Richard as little as his importunity. In the 1390s Gloucester plunged into costly undertakings, notably his collegiate foundation. His hankering for the option of war with France may have been motivated partly by the desire to keep open another possible avenue of gain. He was determined to keep a princely estate and it was galling to have to do so in dependence on court intrigue and with incomes partially insecure.

six

The Wealthy Appellant:
Richard, Earl of Arundel

Dr M. E. Aston, in her study of Thomas Arundel's career up to
1397, has noted that his elder brother Earl Richard was honest to the
point of tactlessness.[1] The earl's outspoken criticisms of the king's
government in the royal presence at Salisbury in 1384 and his pointed
attack on Lancaster in the 1394 parliament were unsupported, at
least publicly, by his fellow peers. In the second 1397 parliament
Richard and the duke (with whom Arundel had ties early in his
career) displayed particular aversion to the earl. Unlike Warwick
and Gloucester, Arundel did not in 1397 attempt to excuse his opposition to the Crown, but assumed a defiant attitude, citing his pardons.
His notorious tactlessness may have resulted in his failure ever to be
appointed on an embassy. Though he was one of the leaders of
opposition to Richard in the 1386 parliament, it was his brother the
bishop of Ely who was sent as a delegate to the king. The bishop's
support of the earl's policies in the years 1386–9 rankled with Richard,
but he still felt able to be gracious with Thomas, his Chancellor in the
years 1391–6. The earl and his brother Sir John Arundel (d. 1379)
may have grown arrogant when they were youthful favourites at the
court of their father's friend, Edward III.

Sir John had a dazzling if brief military career, which the earl
probably hoped to emulate. The earl's martial interests were reflected
by the fine collection of battle and tournament armour probably
stored at Arundel Castle in 1397—some of it possibly captured during
his expeditions of 1387–8. Many of the pieces were from Flemish
workshops—there were also choice Milanese and Westphalian suits.
It would be rash to dismiss Arundel as a boorish fighter. He was
literate, as the text of a letter written in his own hand to Thomas
Arundel shows.[2] But like Warwick he seems to have had conventional
noble tastes and not much literary interest. In his will of 1392 he
mentioned books left by his father, kept in the chapel at Arundel
Castle. Family heirlooms which he had inherited and passed on as
perpetual possessions of the lords of Arundel were a coronet, a Bible

in two volumes, *Decretals* in French, jewels and relics. The will was drafted out at his 'Castle Philipp', a residence luxuriously fitted out in 1396. This was Shrawardine Castle in Shropshire: Arundel renamed it in honour of his second wife, Philippa Hastings, whom he married in 1390. The will is full of concern and devotion for the girl recently wedded by this middle-aged man: 'my dear wife gave me at our marriage a red vestment, etc., I will that my said wife retain the said vestment for her life, if she particularly wishes to have it': 'to my said wife Philippa her own cup called Bealchier, two salt cellars of silver which she gave me for my new years gift at Castle Philipp . . . the apparel for the heads of ladies as well of pearls as of other attire, which I gave my said dear wife'. He described a set of wall hangings of some magnificence at Castle Philipp, recently woven for him in London: they were blue, embroidered with red roses and the arms of his three sons-in-law—Nottingham, Lord Charlton of Powis and Warwick's brother Sir William Beauchamp. The will bears witness to some of his other noble connections—with two members of the council set up in the 1386 parliament, Lords Cobham and Richard Scrope, with his sisters, the countesses of Hereford and Kent and with his niece, the duchess of Gloucester. It shows his affection for his brother Thomas. In the 1390s the earl, besides keeping up old noble connections, made some new ones. As a result of the marriage to Philippa, he became a greater landowner than he had been when an Appellant, and the brother-in-law of the king's young heir-general, Roger Mortimer, Earl of March.

Arundel's will is pervaded by strong religious emotions. In contrast to Warwick's provision for lavish funeral entertainments, he decreed that he was to be buried quietly in the Cluniac priory of St Pancras at Lewes, of which he was patron: 'I forbid any hearse, armed men, or other pomp, being allowed at my burial.' This provision, like others in his will, was a reflection of filial piety, for the elder Earl Richard had willed, concerning his intended burial in the chapter-house at Lewes, 'I desire . . . that no men at arms, horses, hearse, or other pomp, be used at my funeral, but only five torches, with their morters, as was about the corpse of my wife, be allowed.' His son made provision in 1392 in case he died abroad, an indication that he still cherished hopes of going on pilgrimage or crusade overseas. It is a pity that he failed to go, for such voluntary exile might have mollified the king.[3]

Attractive sides of the earl's character—family feeling and piety—

are seen in the care and expense he lavished on the Arundel religious foundations. In 1345 his father had petitioned the papal curia for a dissolution of his marriage to Isabella, daughter of Hugh Despenser. One of the conditions on which he obtained it was that he should endow three chaplaincies in the parish church of his main residence. This was followed by permission to endow them in the chapel of Arundel Castle. In 1354 papal licence was granted for the conversion of the chapel into a college. But the earl apparently neglected to fulfil these grander aspirations for over twenty years, until shortly before his death. In 1375 royal licence was received to alienate Sussex properties to endow the chantry and in his will the elder Earl Richard ordered endowments for six chaplains and three boys to serve the chapel in a tower of Arundel Castle.[4] The earl's heir took trouble to fulfil his intention, and indeed to make a more distinguished foundation. One reason for his concern may have been his awareness of the obligation imposed by the papal dissolution, to which he owed his legitimacy and inheritance. In 1377 there survived a son by his father's first marriage, Sir Edmund Arundel, who, backed by his kinsman Bishop Despenser of Norwich, troubled the new earl by attacking some of his Essex properties. In 1378 Arundel received royal licence to alienate Sussex rents worth 95 *m.* to augment the chaplains whom his father had been licensed to establish. Next year Richard Northampton, herald, arranged to visit the Norman abbey of Séez, mother-house of Arundel Priory, situated just below the castle walls, in order to negotiate the transference of the chantry to its premises. The earl and his father's other executors felt that the permanence of the foundation was jeopardized by its location within the castle, which might be destroyed in a siege. The Franco-Castilian raids had emphasized the vulnerability of Sussex. The negotiations with Séez were concluded satisfactorily. In May 1380 Arundel made a £1,000 obligation to the Crown, to guarantee that he would grant the king an advowson worth £20 *p.a.*, as equivalent to the patronage of the alien priory of Arundel, in the Crown's hands for the duration of the war. The earl was released from the obligation in 1383, as he had granted the king Sevenhampton manor (Gloucs.), valued at 20 *m.*, instead of the promised advowson.[5] In August 1381 he had been licensed to alienate various properties to the master and chaplains of the chantry, by then established in the former priory, and styled Holy Trinity College. He temporarily endowed it with Sussex rents of 107 *m.* and 95 *m.* The first master, Adam Ertham, died before

1383, for in that year William Whyte (d. 1385) gave a surviving collection of sermons to the new college (B.M., Royal MS. 10 A xi). In the former collegiate church can be seen paintings of the Seven Deadly Sins and the Seven Corporal Works of Mercy, which E. W. Tristram dated as *c.* 1390. The formal completion of the foundation took place on 1 December 1387, when its statutes were confirmed by the diocesan, Bishop Russhook of Chichester.[6]

Arundel fulfilled other pious intentions of his father. The latter had wished to found a hospice attached to his chantry. In 1395 Arundel obtained licence to alienate property to the college, to endow the Hospital or *Maison Dieu* founded in honour of the Holy Trinity, which was to house twenty poor men, aged and infirm, with preference being given to the earl's retired servants or tenants. The Arundel family had the patronage of the house of Augustinian canons at Tortington (Sussex). The elder Earl Richard bequeathed the priory 200 *m.*, so that it should provide lodging for any chaplain of his chantry disabled by illness. In 1379 his heir was licensed to grant to the priory estates in St Swithun's parish, *Candelwekstrete*, London, in aid of the canons' maintenance. The elder Arundel had intended to alienate it to the canons, but died before he effected the grant. His son's care in carrying out these intentions and in establishing an impressive college show his care in performing religious duties.[7]

His father had been a highly prosperous magnate. Towards the end of his life he made a loan to the Crown of £20,000 and bequests amounting to a little over 19,000 *m.* An inventory of the money in hand at his death gives a total of 90,359 *m.* Walsingham commented on the wealth which his son inherited. The latter seems to have prospered in the 1380s. He offered to take soldiers overseas at his own cost, probably planned an overseas pilgrimage, raised a force in rebellion and alienated rents and manors for Arundel College. He was the greatest landowner in Sussex, especially in the south-west of the county: one set of inquisitions drawn up after seizure of his estates in 1397 lists over 50 properties in the county, including Arundel and Lewes, the heads of two of his southern lordships (Reigate, in his earldom of Surrey was the third). Much of this represented a recent growth of magnate power in south-east England, based on the royal favour and possibly the profits of war enjoyed by his father. The elder Earl Richard bought some twenty manors, besides other properties, in Sussex, investing in arable and pasture of high quality.

Inventories drawn up for the Crown in 1397 and a private one, analysed by L. F. Salzman, list grain, livestock and implements belonging to the lord on Arundel manors in East and West Sussex. 'On fifteen manors in the west there were, in round figures, some 250 oxen, 300 cows, and 6,600 sheep. On the same number of manors in the east, 200 oxen, 100 cows, and 8,750 sheep.' In 1397 the earl's largest flock in the county was at Patcham, 2,493 strong. Wool was one of the staples of his prosperity. At the time of his father's death the wool from the estates in the Marches, Surrey and Sussex had realized 3,062 m.: this was the amount due for sales after deduction of a quarter as the fee of the agent, the leading London merchant John Philpot. In March 1381 Chichester customs officials were ordered if need be to proceed to Lewes, weigh and cocket 60 sacks of wool, allowing the earl to lade them and, after payment of customs, ship them to Calais. In April 1381 he was assigned 500 m. on the Chichester customs, to be deducted primarily from dues on the wool he was exporting. In February 1389 Egbert Ludykesone of Kampen in Holland made a recognizance of £500 to the earl, possibly in connection with a wool sale. It was payable at the latter's London 'hostiel' of Pulteneys. Another reference to Arundel's wools is found in 1397. In August, after his arrest, a commission was appointed to receive a bond due to the earl for wool sold, valued at £100. The commissioners were also to take possession of all his wools in Lewes Castle. There was a weigh-beam in the castle, which was delivered to the royal weighing-officer in Sussex.[8]

It is probable that Arundel was one of the principal wool-exporters among the landowners of south-east England; if so, he must have been concerned about the closures of the Flemish markets resulting from the Flemish civil war (1379–85) and from Philip of Burgundy's policy of war with England. This concern helps to explain why Arundel gave support to the 'way of Flanders' in 1383 rather than to Lancaster's 'way of Spain' and why he attacked Flanders in 1387. Arundel was probably anxious to force Philip to negotiate, with a view to reopening the Flemish markets. Richard's failure to put Anglo-Flemish relations on a satisfactory basis in the 1380s, either by upholding Ghent or by coming to terms with the duke of Burgundy, may have been one cause of Arundel's dissatisfaction with the court. The invasion threats of 1385–6 put some of his most prosperous manors into the front line. Thus Richard's policies placed Arundel's economic interests in peril.

In 1377 and 1380, according to Walsingham, the inhabitants of Sussex blamed Arundel for failing to defend them against enemy raids. The fact that they looked to him to provide defence shows how dominant his position was in the county. The extent of this power is reflected by some of the reactions it provoked. In 1337 Edward III granted the elder Earl Richard the privilege of holding court and the sheriff's tourn in the liberty of Arundel. In the 1376 parliament, soon after his death, the lieges of Surrey and Sussex petitioned against his exercise of this jurisdiction. They said that the late earl had been granted sheriff's tourns in the rapes of Chichester and Arundel, valued at £10 p.a. (for which he paid 76s. to the Crown) and a rent called 'Shereveyeld' amounting to £14 19s. 1d. from the two rapes. On the authority of the grant he had set up a new court called a shire-court at Arundel, where pleas which should have been heard at Chichester were terminated, yielding him an annual profit of £30. They petitioned that either the tourns and rent should be rejoined to the county, in accordance with the provisions of the 1328 statute, or that the sheriff's farm should be adjusted. They wanted the novel court at Arundel to be abolished. In the second 1380 parliament the counties of Surrey and Sussex petitioned that their sheriffs should be in some way discharged from payment of the £15 accruing from the hundreds in the rape of Arundel, which the earl held as a result of Edward's grant to his father. In 1385 the Sussex lieges petitioned in parliament that the hundreds, wapentakes and the rent called 'Shereves-yeld' be rejoined to the county administration, or else that the sheriffs receive an allowance on their farm. The difficulty which sheriffs experienced in accounting seems to have been the root of the grievance, rather than the exercise of a novel baronial jurisdiction.[9] Nevertheless, Arundel power provoked some local violence. In 1373 a commission was appointed on the elder earl's complaint that many individuals had poached in a number of his Sussex properties. In 1377 another commission was appointed on his son's petition that a large group had entered his chaces and warrens and assaulted his men in the county. During the Peasants' Revolt some of his tenants were troublesome: on 2 July 1381 Edward St John, Edward Dallingridge and the sheriff were appointed to arrest those who refused to perform services for the earl. In May 1382, with his consent, the Crown established a felons' gaol in his castle at Lewes, to be delivered by the king's justices. Less than a year later, in February 1383, Robert

Bealknap, Edward St John, and John Fawsley were among those appointed to hold enquiry, on Arundel's petition that

> William Grete of Lewes, William Wodelond of Cliffe by Lewes and other insurgents in Sussex, came armed to Lewes, broke his closes and the gates, doors and windows of his castle there, threw down his buildings, consumed and destroyed ten casks of wine, value £100 and burned his rolls, rentals and other muniments.

The destruction of documents suggests that tenants were rising in protest against services. The castle, which Arundel had left undefended against the French in 1377, does not seem to have been secure in 1383, though in use as a woolhouse and gaol. The large amount of building materials stored there in 1397 suggests that it was in need of considerable repairs, perhaps as a result of the 1383 assault.[10] By then it had long gone out of use as a residence. In south-east England Arundel's finest residences are likely to have been Arundel Castle and Pulteneys Inn in London, the latter acquired in exchange for the advowson of Napton (Warcs.), which the earl granted away in February 1385. In the sixteenth century this splendid house, known as Cold Harbour, had an arched entry gate over which was built the steeple and choir of the parish church of All Hallows the Less.[11]

Outside of Surrey and Sussex, Arundel had few inherited properties in southern England. The revenue from some of them was granted out to his servants. In 1378 he granted tenements in Oving (Sussex) for life to Stephen Holt of Lewes, who in 1388 was appointed to collect profits bestowed on the Appellants in the ports of Southampton and Chichester. Holt's annuity was confirmed and soon afterwards revoked by the Crown in 1397.[12] In 1380 the earl, at his manor of Cuckfield (Sussex), granted a rent of £20 in survivorship from Gatton manor (Surrey) to Philip Broun and Avice his wife, for the former's services as constable of Reigate Castle. In Hampshire Arundel possessed property in Hambledon which was rented by his villeins in 1397; Finchdean hundred, held by John Yattere for life in 1397; property in Portsmouth worth 40s., granted for life to Walter Rotherfield and an estate worth 5 m. near Selborne, of which Richard Ferour had a life grant in recompense for good service. In Wiltshire Arundel inherited the manors of Keevil, Bulkington and Knighton. In 1386 the earl was licensed to grant life rents of £20 from Keevil to John Dauntsey and to John Chiselden esquire. In 1343 Keevil and Bulkington had produced a net revenue of about £150, but in 1397 the valuations set on them totalled only about £100. By 1394 demesne farming had entirely ceased at Keevil. The demesne at Knighton was rented for 11 *m.* in 1397.[13] In Buckinghamshire the earl held Wing where shields in the church's glass commemorate the ownership of the manor by the Warenne earls of Surrey. He granted Wing to Mowbray as part of his daughter's dowry in 1384. Arundel had one Middlesex property, Tyburn manor, which he granted for good services, past and future to Stephen Hyndercle *alias* Clerk, yeoman of his chamber, for life. In Essex there were several properties. By an indenture dated at London, October 1379, Arundel granted his life retainer William Rees the manor of Househam for life: William agreed to serve him in time of peace with a yeoman and two horses, like the earl's other esquires, and in war with a yeoman, a groom and three horses. In August and October 1387 Arundel was licensed to make life grants of Margaretting and Wolston to Richard Alderton and John Cocking respectively. He used High Roding for retaining purposes. In March 1378 a life annuity from it was granted to John Bonham esquire, which was cancelled before June 1383. In March 1388 Sir Edward Dallingridge was pardoned for receiving Roding for life without licence. In 1395–6 this valuable manor was granted by the earl to Gloucester's Essex retainer, John Doreward.[14] In Norfolk the Appellant inherited Mileham and Beeston manors, a quarter of Longham, the hundreds of Launditch and South Greenhow and property in Castleacre. In May 1388 Sir Payn Tiptoft was pardoned for acquiring Beeston for life without licence.[15]

Arundel's second marriage in 1390 gave him control of a considerable amount of Hastings property, including Ashendon (Bucks.), Towcester (Northants.), Barwell (Leics.), Filongley (Worcs.), a manor in Great Shelford (Cambs.), Saxthorpe, Runcton, Gooderstone and Sutton in Norfolk. Most valuable was a third of the Lordship of Abergavenny in the March of Wales. Apart from the Sussex estates, the bulk of Arundel's properties lay in the northern Marches; he was also a leading Shropshire landowner. His valuable lordships, with their large rent-rolls and their profitable palatine jurisdiction, drove a wedge between Chester and the Principality to the north and stretched southwards between the

Principality and Shropshire. The Lordship of Bromfield and Yale, protected by Holt Castle, lay adjacent to the county palatine of Chester. Further south were Chirk Castle and Chirkland, Oswestry Castle and Lordship and Clun Castle and Clunsland. Arundel had to guard his Marcher interest vigilantly. In 1380 the king's half-brother, Sir John Holand, was granted the Lordship of Hope and Hopedale, near Arundel's towns of Holt and Wrexham. In 1381 Holand was appointed Justice of Chester and before July 1384, in his court of Flint, Arundel's townships of Llay, Burton, Huncley and a moiety of Trevalyn, which were part of the Lordship of Bromfield, were adjudged as held of the Lordship of Hope, confiscated and by letters patent dated 30 June 1384 granted to Holand. This may have been one reason for Arundel's discontent during the recent Salisbury parliament. When Holand's properties were confiscated in 1385, Arundel on petitioning was restored in possession.[16] In 1387 Arundel's men are found raiding in Cheshire. In November the constable at Holt, David Eyton, with a force of twenty-eight, carried out abductions at Shocklach Oviatt (Cheshire), less than four miles south of Holt. This raid took place not long before the defeat of the duke of Ireland's Cheshiremen in the Midlands by Arundel and his fellow Appellants: whether Eyton's foray had any connection with this is unknown. He and his companions went by night to the house of Lln' Gogh at Shocklach and took him and Edn' ap David ap Ken to Arundel's castle at Oswestry, imprisoning Lln' there 'contrary to the franchise of the county'—thus flouting Ireland's authority as Justice of Chester. In March 1389 Eyton was pardoned. After the Cheshiremen had risen in 1393 Arundel garrisoned Holt Castle with a large retinue. Dr J. G. Bellamy has surmised that he was taking precautions against forays into his lordships by Cheshiremen. An undated petition presented by Arundel (or possibly by his father) to King, Lords and Commons illustrates the difficulties of protecting Yale and Bromfield from incursions. According to the petition, Cheshiremen in defiance of royal injunctions had committed outrages, invading the lordship and robbing the earl's officials and tenants. On his council's advice he had complained to the king, but the misdoers had treated Privy Seal letters summoning them to appear before the royal council with contempt. It was asserted that 'the said malefactors cannot be punished by any law nor for the said contempts except by the ordinance of you our said Lord the Lords and commons'; in conclusion, reflections were made on offences committed daily by

Cheshiremen in the neighbouring lordships. The royal reply promised remedy and contained a proviso safeguarding the Cheshire franchise.[17] It is not surprising that Arundel's Marcher castles were well stocked with arms in 1397. Arundel's power to stop raids from neighbouring franchises and to punish his own meddlesome tenants made him a natural leader in the northern marches. He was on good terms with some neighbouring magnates—with his son-in-law Lord Charlton of Powis, with Lord Grey of Ruthin, probably with Lord Lestrange of Knockin, influential in Shropshire, with the important Welsh landowner Owain Glyn Dŵr, and possibly with the Shropshire landowner Hugh Lord Burnell, who may have had friendly relations with Gloucester and Warwick too. Charlton, who came of age in 1382, was appointed Justice of North Wales in March 1388, when the Appellants were in control, and Arundel made him a Chirkland feoffee in 1395.[18]

At the valuations quoted in 1397, Arundel's income totalled £3,700, and this excluded his income from wool sales, likely to have been a substantial addition. In Sussex Arundel may still have found it profitable to cultivate some valuable demesne. His Marcher income (mainly in rents and profits of lordship) was alone sufficient to maintain a magnate—over £2,000. From English counties (exclusive of Sussex) he received less than £900. His wife's Hastings lands, too, had added £450 to his income. If the profits Gloucester drew from wardships are discounted, Arundel was throughout his life the wealthiest of the senior Appellants. At court he is likely to have sought Crown appointments and grants to conduct military expeditions, rather than as the necessary supplements to inherited income needed by Thomas of Woodstock and Mowbray. Arundel's wealth helps to explain why Richard continued to fear him after 1389—and why he coveted his Marcher lordships. In 1387 Arundel's wealth may have enabled him to make an important contribution to the Appellants' military power—it was his retinue which Richard forbade the Londoners to supply, and the Westminster Chronicler's account of the subsequent campaign suggests that Arundel's force was sufficiently large to operate independently in Oxfordshire.

A number of Arundel's servants were of Sussex origin and through their activities and relationships his influence in the county was probably on the whole strengthened. One important friend was Sir Edward St John, a prominent landowner in the county and elsewhere in south-eastern England. When Arundel's father made a settlement of his inheritance in 1366, St John was one of the feoffees and when he died, St John owed him 60 *m*. Sir Edward's connection with the future Appellant appears in 1372, when they were fellow feoffees. He was a retainer of the Black Prince, after whose death in 1376 the king confirmed his annuity. In December 1376 St John was granted for life the keepership of a manor in addition to Woolmer and Alice Holt Forests (Hants).[19] The following year he was a choheir of John Brocas, with Sir Edmund FitzHerbert. The latter went surety for Arundel in 1381, witnessed a grant by him in 1385 and served in his naval retinue in 1387: he was well known in Hampshire and in Dorset.[20] In 1378 the great council had confirmed the Black Prince's annuity to St John. In 1379 he witnessed a quitclaim to Arundel of Knighton (Wilts.) and in 1381 the earl appointed him a Chirkland feoffee. Sir Edward died before 10 March 1385. His widow willed to be buried beside him in Lewes Priory, bequeathing a great gilt covered cup embellished with her father's arms to the earl of Arundel and a matins book to his eldest son Richard.[21]

Another distinguished landowner who had long Arundel connections was Sir Edward Dallingridge. He was born *c*. 1346 and so belonged to the same generation as the Appellant Earl. In 1386, giving evidence in the *Scrope v. Grosvenor* suit, Sir Edward said that in his youth he had been with the elder Earl Richard. He recalled remarks which that earl had made about Scrope's forbears. Sir Edward was frequently appointed on Sussex commissions. In November 1378 he was at Cherbourg in the company of its captain, Sir John Arundel. His reputation was such that he was one of the few shire knights appointed on the commission to examine royal expenditure in the first 1380 parliament. Between 1379 and 1388 he represented Sussex in ten parliaments. In 1381 Dallingridge acted as a surety for Arundel and was appointed a Chirkland feoffee. The following year he was keeper of Lancaster's Ashdown Forest in Sussex. But he later fell out with the duke. On 26 July 1384 the sheriff of Sussex was ordered to set Sir Edward free, after his conviction for offences probably against John of Gaunt. Arundel may have procured a pardon for Dallingridge when the king came to Arundel Castle that summer. But in October the sheriff was ordered to arrest Dallingridge, convicted at Lancaster's suit. It is possible that the knight's activities contributed to the enmity developing between Lancaster and Arundel.[22]

But the invasion threat of 1385–6 may have made Dallingridge hostile to the court, for his properties, like Arundel's, were directly threatened. By 1377 he had married Elizabeth, heir of a Northamptonshire landowner, John Wardieu or Wardedien. The marriage gave Sir Edward possession of Bodiam in Sussex. In October 1385 licence was granted to him to crenellate his manor there 'and to make a castle thereof in defence of the adjacent country against the king's enemies'. In March 1386, when invasion was again feared, he was appointed to head a commission whose task was to wall, repair and fortify the Cinque Port of Rye. He was eminent in Arundel's service, for in March 1387 he was listed fourth among the earl's knights taking part in the naval expedition and on 8 June 1388 Arundel received one of the sums to finance his second expedition by the hands of Sir Edward and Thomas Wysbech. It is very probable that Dallingridge was a member of Arundel's military retinue in the civil war of 1387. In 1398 he was described as 'an adherent of Thomas, Duke of Gloucester in the tenth year'. Arundel's life grant to him, before 17 March 1388, of High Roding may have been in part a reward for his services during the rising. In 1388–9 Dallingridge was Arundel's lieutenant as Captain of Brest.[23]

The outstanding change in Dallingridge's career was his adherence to the king's service in 1389, after the earl had lost his influence and place as a councillor. On 24 August Sir Edward was granted, for life or until further notice, with custody of the alien priory at Wilmington (Sussex), its rent of 100 m. per annum, as his fee on being retained by the king. He had originally been granted the custody in January, when the Appellants were in control, at the same rent, and had since offered 10 m. more to keep it. Sir Edward sought the patronage of a lord in favour at court, Huntingdon, whose deputy at Brest he was in October 1389. His talents were certainly appreciated by the king, for in February 1390 he was a royal councillor and in 1392, when the king suspended the government of London, he was appointed *custos* of the city. In February of that year he had been granted two annual tuns of red Gascon wine 'for good service, in continually attending the king's council in London'. Sir Edward did not continue long as *custos*, for Richard considered that he was too lenient with the Londoners. Before 10 March 1394 Dallingridge died.[24]

His son and heir, John, who had been in Arundel's naval retinue in 1387, prudently attached himself in the 1390s to lords more in favour at court. He went on crusade with Derby and in April 1399 was preparing to go to Ireland in the retinue of Huntingdon (then duke of Exeter). The previous year Sir John Dallingridge had paid a fine of 500 *m.* for remission of any claim which the king might have on Bodiam Castle and on his father's Sussex and other properties, consequent on the latter's adherence in rebellion to Gloucester. Sir John died in 1408, having performed good service for Henry IV. He had willed to be buried beside the tomb of his parents, in Roberts-bridge Abbey (Sussex), a house to which the Appellant Arundel had made a bequest.[25]

Another prominent gentleman connected with Arundel who had Sussex properties was John Lord Fawsley of Fawsley (Northants.), born 1345-6, and thus, like Dallingridge, a contemporary of the earl. In 1381 Fawsley was a Chirkland feoffee. The following year he married Elizabeth, sister and heir of John de Say, a marriage which brought him manors in a number of counties, including Buxted, Street, Sedgwick and Bidlington in Sussex. As a result of his acquisi-- tions he was summoned personally to parliaments. It is very likely that Fawsley gave support to Arundel's political activities in the period 1386-9. In March 1387 he was the knight listed second in Arundel's retinue for naval service. The previous month he had been licensed to grant Fawsley manor to John Waltham (appointed Keeper of the Privy Seal in the 1386 parliament) and Robert Publow, a cleric high in Arundel's service. In January 1388 he was licensed to grant five manors to Bishop Arundel, for his wife's jointure, and in the same month he was ordered to survey the defences of London. In August 1388 he was appointed on a Sussex commission of array. The earl and abbot of Battle were named before him and Sir Thomas Poynings, Sir William Percy and Walter Dallingridge were also among the commissioners.[26]

On 15 February 1392 Lord Fawsley was present at the great council when Richard and the magnates swore mutual oaths. He made his will the following September and died before 25 November 1393, by which date his widow had married another landowner connected with Arundel, Sir William Heron. He was very probably one of the Herons of Ford (Northumberland) and Croydon (Cambs.). Heron served at sea under Arundel in March 1387 and was to be pardoned for adherence to the Appellants. In June 1388 order was made for the repair of his ship, *la Marie* of Sandwich, which was to serve under Arundel, the Captain of Brest. Heron led a retinue on the earl's expedition which set off that month and was one of his servants who appeared before the Cambridge parliament to answer questions about the conduct of the expedition. According to his 1404 will, he had profited from his military service to Arundel, Richard II and Northumberland:

> Also having been a soldier with the Earl of Arundel, and peradventure received more than I was worthy of, I desire my executors to pay £10 to the executors of that Earl, or to the poorest men to whom they may know of any debt being owed by the said Earl.

By 1394 Heron had sought military service elsewhere than in the earl's retinue. In a letter from Ireland dated 5 March 1395 Rutland referred to 'lord William Heroun' as having received the submission of a captain of Munster.[27]

Besides possibly losing Heron's services by 1394, in the period 1385-93 Arundel lost those of three important Sussex landowners— St John, Dallingridge and Fawsley. But there were others who had continued connections with him. The pardon accorded in 1382 to Sir William Percy (or Percehay) for escapes during his shrievalty of Surrey and Sussex was granted at the earl's supplication. In 1383 Percy witnessed a quitclaim which Arundel made and in 1385 a grant. In 1392 Arundel willed him a bequest and in 1395 appointed him a Chirkland feoffee. In 1399 Richard II's councillors hoped that they could rely on Percy's loyalty during the king's absence in Ireland, for on 3 July he was appointed among those ordered to besiege the ancient Lancastrian fortress at Pevensey, which Lady Pelham was holding for Henry.[28] Sir Thomas Poynings of St John Basing was a Hampshire and Sussex landowner active on commissions in the two counties from 1377 until his death in 1429. He led a retinue of seventy-six on the earl's 1387 naval expedition and was to marry his widow Philippa.[29] Thomas Lord Camoys (d. 1419), who succeeded to his inheritance in 1372, had been licensed to grant a reversion to Sir John Arundel in 1370, with remainder to Sir Richard Arundel. The earl and Camoys (who had been knighted by Buckingham in 1380) were fellow feoffees in 1397. Camoys was to give good service to the Lancastrians, advertised by his brass at Trotton in Sussex, where his armoured figure, holding hands with his wife, is shown wearing the SS collar and he is described as 'providus consul regis et regni Anglie ac strenuus miles de gartero'.[30]

A number of Sussex men probably of less exalted origin served Arundel. One such was John Cocking, described as 'squyer' in 1387,

who may have come from the Sussex manor of Cocking acquired by
the earl's father. In 1372 Exchequer prests were delivered to Sir
Richard and Sir John Arundel by John Cocking. In 1381 he was one
of the Chirkland feoffees, remaining so until 1395. In his 1392 will
Arundel appointed Cocking an executor.[31] John Warburton may have
come from the Sussex village of Warbleton (a manor of Sir Thomas
Poynings). In October 1379 John de Warbourton had a grant of
legal protection, as he was going overseas in Sir John Arundel's
company. In November 1387 Exchequer payment was made to John
Warburton, described as Arundel's esquire, for the repair of the
fortifications at Rye. His appointment on commissions connected with
Rye in 1386-7 suggests that he had property in or near the port.[32]
His service may have been of political use to Arundel in 1387, when
Burley tried to muster the Cinque Ports in the king's cause. Another
Sussex servant of Arundel was John Stevens or Estevenes. In September 1388 he went surety for Arundel, when the earl received the
marriage of Robert Poynings, which gave him interest in an important
Sussex inheritance. Robert's father, Richard Lord Poynings, had
been in Sir John Arundel's military retinue in 1377, a Chirkland
feoffee in 1381 and had died serving Lancaster in Castile in 1387. In
1389 Stevens was appointed to enquire into who had abducted Martin
le Grant of Spain, a prisoner in the earl's custody at Southampton.[33]

An important Arundel retainer from another part of southern
England was the Cambridgeshire landowner Sir Payn Tiptoft, whose
connections with the earl were not severed by the latter's political
reverses in the 1390s. He was in the earl's naval retinue in March 1387,
in 1388 was holding a manor granted to him for life by Arundel and
in 1397 was his feoffee. In September 1397 a sergeant-at-arms was
ordered to arrest Tiptoft and bring him before the king and council,
perhaps in connection with the support he had given to the Appellants,
for which he was to sue out a pardon. He sat for Cambridgeshire in
Henry IV's first parliament, in which the Commons' Speaker was John
Doreward of Bocking (Essex), who had been Arundel's retainer.[34]
Some of the earl's servants were drawn from the west of England.
Sir John Dauntsey, a Wiltshire landowner, was party to a deed in
1373 which Sir Richard Arundel witnessed. In 1386 Arundel was
licensed to grant Dauntsey an annuity and in 1387 he was in the
earl's naval retinue.[35] The cleric Robert Publow may have come from
Publow, Somerset. In 1388 his services received reward—he was
granted by the Crown the prebend of Highley in Chichester Cathedral.

In April 1388 Publow was given the first instalment of subsidy for Arundel's naval expedition. In 1392 the earl appointed him an executor and in 1395 he was the only original Chirkland feoffee of 1381 to be appointed in the new group. Publow appears to have weathered Arundel's fall with some success, for in January 1399 his estate as parson of Westbourne (Sussex) was confirmed.[36]

In the Marches Arundel's lordships each had their own officials: stewards, receivers, bailiffs, constables of castles and their lieutenants, keepers of parks and studs where Arundel kept and bred numerous horses. Most of the subordinate officials in 1396–7 were Welsh. At this time the financial officials in these and Arundel's other lordships were subordinate to a receiver-general, Thomas Harlyng, clerk. He may have been the Thomas Harlyng (d. 1423), canon of Chichester and rector of Ringwood (Hants.) and of Pulborough (Sussex), whose brass is to be seen in Pulborough church.[37] One of Arundel's servants who may have originated in the Marches or adjacent counties was Sir William Herdewyke. In 1376 he was a receiver of the elder Earl Richard, in 1381 a Chirkland feoffee and in 1382 a fellow feoffee of the earl, when he was parson at the latter's manor of Cound (Salop.). In August 1388, a canon of Hereford, he was appointed to enquire into the value of property forfeited by Burley.[38] Another cleric possibly from the same regions was Alan Thorpe, parson of Marchwiel, near Arundel's town of Wrexham (1382). He was then a feoffee with Arundel, Publow and Herdewyke. In February 1387, when Arundel had influence on the council, Thorpe was appointed by the Crown to the living of Llanarmon Dyffryn Ceiriog, west of Oswestry. In October 1397 the Crown confirmed his estate as parson of Arundel's former living of Clungunford, in the March adjacent to Shropshire; he was a receiver of Chirkland, 1399–1400.[39]

An important Marcher gentleman retained by Arundel was the Cheshire knight Hugh Browe, to whom he granted for life in March 1388 the manors of Trofford and Dunham in the county palatine of Chester. Browe was one of the many Cheshiremen who had made a name for himself in the French wars. When examined in 1386 in the *Scrope v. Grosvenor* suit, in St John's church, Chester, Browe said that he was aged forty and had been employed in garrison duty in France, but never on great expeditions. He was in the retinue which March intended to take to Brittany in 1374 and contracted to go on Buckingham's 1380 expedition. He may have been the nephew of Sir Robert Knolles, 'Sir Hues Broes', who, Froissart says, was at the siege of St Malo in 1378 and, like his uncle, ravaged the surrounding country which the pair knew well. In March 1387 Browe was in Arundel's naval retinue: the earl may have been anxious to retain an experienced soldier whose services the duke of Ireland might try to gain. In December 1390 some prominent Cheshiremen went surety that Browe would abide Arundel's award in a local dispute. In September 1394 Browe was granted legal protection, as he was going to Ireland in the company of Arundel's kinsman Richard Lord Talbot and in May 1399 he was preparing to go there on the king's second expedition. He probably died in or before the early months of 1403: his property was forfeited as he 'had grievously offended against the king and prince' (Henry Prince of Wales).[40]

The skilled soldiers whom Arundel had attracted into his service were tending to look elsewhere for chivalrous employment in the 1390s. Arundel wanted to emulate the military achievements of his father. He lacked opportunities in Edward III's last years and, unlike his brother Sir John, failed to make much impression in Richard's minority. Only in 1387–8 did he succeed decisively in warfare. The inept handling of the war with France in the early 1380s by Richard's councillors may have been a factor in turning Arundel into an implacable critic of the court—his valuable Sussex manors were threatened with devastation and the profits from his wool exports almost certainly followed the general downward trend. From 1389 onwards Richard tried to isolate this dangerous and resourceful opponent, cutting him off from court favour and influence. Arundel had not been the man to accept such neglect in the past. However, in the 1390s increasing age and a happy marriage may have lessened his political activity, though he voiced harsh criticisms of royal and Lancastrian policies. In 1393 Arundel once more showed ability to array a military retinue speedily, at Holt. His concentrations of propertied wealth near London and the Principality of Wales continued to threaten royal control in vital regions—he even exercised influence in the king's cherished county of Chester. If Arundel stayed often at Shrawardine with his wife, Richard may have been disquieted rather than reassured, viewing the earl as a malignant spirit in the part of the realm where he most sought support. Richard's determination not to buy Arundel off with favours and offices in the 1390s was a threat to the compromise settlement of 1389, for it was a coldness which no king could expect a powerful kinsman to bask in contentedly.

seven

The Expeditions of Thomas of Woodstock and the Earl of Arundel (1377–95)

Thomas of Woodstock and the earl of Arundel had their first experiences of high command as a result of the revival of war with France and Castile in July 1377. In August Buckingham was at Dover with the constable of the castle, his brother Cambridge. The forces they drew up deterred the cruising Franco-Castilian force from attempting another landing, such as that which Arundel's brother Sir John had just frustrated at Southampton. Authorized by a writ of Privy Seal dated 29 September, Buckingham prepared to lead a naval expedition whose forces were mustered at London and in other ports. The fleet embarked early in November with about 4,000 soldiers on board, its probable objective being to attack the Franco-Castilian ships then docked at Sluis. The August loan from the Londoners may have provided finance for the expedition; the House of Commons' hopes for its success help to account for their failure to make a concerted outcry about recent raids. Buckingham's retinue consisted of 2 bannerets, 15 knights, 180 esquires and 200 archers. Also commanding retinues were Jean de Montfort, Duke of Brittany, Lords Latimer and FitzWalter, Sir Michael de la Pole, Admiral of the North, and Sir John Arundel. A great storm dispersed the ships before they could attack Sluis. Only in December was the fleet re-constituted, sailing to relieve Brest, an objective which was attained by 9 January 1378. The duke of Brittany delivered the port into English keeping. Also leading retinues to the relief of Brest were John Lord Cobham and the earl of Northumberland's brother Sir Thomas Percy. Buckingham's kinsman, Edward Courtenay, Earl of Devon, had joined his retinue. The fleet's subsequent operations were not sufficiently well co-ordinated to damage Franco-Castilian naval power decisively. Buckingham and FitzWalter captured eight Castilian ships off Brest and Percy scored successes too. The earl and his retinue arrived at Southampton on 25 January.[1]

There were plans for more expeditions in 1378, facilitated by the second 1377 parliament's generous grant of subsidies. An opportunity for exploitation was provided by Charles V's attack on the possessions of Charles II of Navarre: the latter leased the important port of Cherbourg to Richard II. In April a fleet embarked to implement the Anglo-Navarrese treaty, commanded by the well-reputed soldier, William Montague, Earl of Salisbury, and his son's father-in-law, the earl of Arundel, whose retinue was mustered at Gravesend on 7 April. The earls arrived off Harfleur, hoping to force the Rille estuary and to relieve the Navarrese castle of Pont-Audemer. But local levies repulsed the attack which Arundel led on the port and galleys successfully blockaded the estuary. The earls withdrew and headed for Cherbourg, which they occupied. When reinforcements had arrived from England to garrison it, they re-embarked, but according to French sources their fleet suffered severely in an engagement off Cherbourg.[2] In June 1378 arrayers were appointed to organize contingents for the main expedition of the year, under Lancaster's command. Apparently he hoped to destroy the enemy's naval forces, since Buckingham and Arundel had failed to do so, though they had succeeded in consolidating enclaves in Brittany and France. Thomas of Woodstock was an arrayer and he and Arundel were among the distinguished lords and knights who led retinues. The muster roll of Buckingham's retinue gives the dates of its service as from 15 June until 17 September: he had one banneret, 7 knights and 42 esquires in his company. The force set out in July from Sandwich, but failed to engage the Franco-Castilian ships which retreated up the Seine estuary. Lancaster then sailed to besiege St Malo. His failure, according to Walsingham, was his own fault, but Froissart fixed the blame on Arundel's lapse in neglecting to ensure the adequate night guard of a mine, for which he was reprimanded by Lancaster and Cambridge. This episode may have contributed to Arundel's inability to get a high command until 1386, when he received one as the reward for his alliance with Gloucester. Before then the two of them do not seem to have been linked militarily, though Buckingham had sailed in 1377–8 with Arundel's brother Sir John, his colleague as Marshal of the Realm. Sir John Arundel's martial reputation far outshone his elder brother's: he was appointed to lead retinues to Brittany in 1379 and it was the dispersion of his fleet and his death in December which necessitated the formation of a new and impressive expedition under Buckingham's command. This was to be the earl's great chance to emulate the achievements of his father and brothers overseas. A subsidy for the expedition was granted in the parliament which met in January 1380, in which one of the earl's retainers, Sir John Gildsburgh, was Speaker of the Commons. The Lords approved Buckingham's appointment, which had probably been canvassed by his elder brothers. Lancaster may have had self-interested motives for wishing his brother abroad, but the choice was a politic one. Thomas, since he was inexperienced in land warfare, would have to defer to the opinions of the veterans with whom he had already served at sea: his royal blood enabled him to co-operate on equal terms with the duke of Brittany. His status and his office as Constable might help impose discipline on the retinues, a frequent problem for English commanders in this period.[3]

The earl's indenture was sealed on 3 May 1380 and those of other captains a few days later, all undertaking to serve for a year. The expedition attracted an impressive array of talent, though few magnates participated. Among the captains were Lords Basset of Drayton, Bourchier, FitzWalter and Latimer, the renowned knights Hugh Calveley and Robert Knolles, the veterans Sir John Harleston (for whom Buckingham was to display an especial affection) and his successor as Captain of Cherbourg, Sir William Windsor, Sir Thomas Percy and the successful defender of Carisbrooke Castle, Sir Hugh Tyrell. Bourchier, like FitzWalter, was an Essex neighbour of Buckingham's: both lords and Percy had served under the earl in the relief of Brest. Only two of his fellow earls served with him in 1380 and then only as members of his retinue—Devon and the young Robert de Vere, Earl of Oxford.[4] The leadership of the 1380–1 expedition cannot be easily condemned, though the outcome was negative. Failure was due primarily to diplomatic and military factors handicapping all English offensive operations in France. In an army whose captains included many veterans, and in which numerous well-born novices were serving, discipline held through a long and circuitous summer march, an autumn siege in adverse conditions and a harsh Breton winter without proper quarters. There had not been enough shipping available to transport the army direct to Brittany, so it was ferried piecemeal from Dover and Sandwich to Calais, the operation being completed by 19 July. The force was about 5,200 strong: Buckingham had in his retinue 2 earls, 7 bannerets, 84 knights, 1,121 esquires and 1,340 archers, one of the largest retinues which an individual led overseas in Richard's reign.[5]

At Ardres and near St Omer Buckingham dubbed knights, including Devon, the Norfolk landowner Lord Morley and Walter Fitz-Walter, son and heir of the marshal of the army. Decisions on the march were taken with the counsel of the captains, who enforced good discipline and promoted daring forays. Relentless destruction of the countryside was carried out, increased in volume by the circuitous route taken. The army pivoted north of Paris into Champagne, where Philip of Burgundy lay in its path with his forces. But he refused to sally out of Troyes to fight, and lack of supplies forced Buckingham to withdraw eastwards towards Brittany. Bold and dangerous crossings of the Sarthe and Mayenne were undertaken, opportunities which the pursuing French failed to exploit. On the day the Sarthe was crossed (16 September) French affairs were thrown into confusion by the death of Charles V. The succession of his son Charles, a minor, made the regency government anxious to make terms with the duke of Brittany, as a means of warding off the English threat. Duke John was inclined to take up a neutral position in the Anglo-French conflict, as a means of securing fuller control of his duchy. After Buckingham and his army had arrived there, he for long postponed meeting the earl, his former campaigning colleague. Thomas repeated Lancaster's move in 1378, by undertaking the siege of a great port—Nantes. The late Charles V had garrisoned it strongly, and without the support of the Bretons Buckingham lacked the requisite siege equipment and shipping to stop supplies reaching the garrison up the Loire estuary. After two disheartening months, in which *mêlées* caused heavy losses, Buckingham abandoned the siege and marched to the duke's residence at Vannes. There he and Duke John agreed that the English should remain in the locality until the spring of 1381, when the Bretons would join them. This was cold comfort, as the towns refused to allow billets to the English soldiers. The army maintained itself with difficulty throughout the winter, supplies being sent from Cornwall, the Channel Islands and the Isle of Wight. Buckingham and his council planned an invasion of France in 1381. He would first march into Normandy, to link up with reinforcements ferried across the Channel to Cherbourg. Between 22 February and 7 May 1381 letters of protection were granted to men preparing to go to Brittany in the company of the Gloucestershire landowner, Thomas Lord Berkeley. Meanwhile the royal council tried to make good Buckingham's deficiencies in specialized personnel. In March Henry Yevele was appointed to select for service in Brittany 30 masons; 50 carpenters and 8 smiths were also to be impressed.

But these preparations were too late. By 15 January John de Montfort had come to terms with the French Crown and peace was ratified on 6 April. Buckingham and his council, apparently taken by surprise, and deprived at a stroke of their only ally and base, decided on total withdrawal. Thomas had an angry personal exchange with the duke and on 11 April the army left Vannes for the coast. He embarked on 28 April and, after a bad crossing, reached Falmouth on 2 May. According to French sources, the English lost all their horses and suffered many casualties on the expedition through sickness. English chroniclers expressed disappointment. Buckingham felt cheated. The experience may have generated the intense suspicion of French diplomacy which he later exhibited. In middle age he was to be complacent about his achievement in 1380:

> I remembre me of the last iourney that I made into Fraunce. I thynke I had in my company but two thousande speares and eyght thousande archers, and so passed the see, and entred in to the realme of Fraunce fro Calayes, and so went a longe in to the realme, and founde none to with stande me, nor none that durst fyght with me . . .

Thus he never lost the impressions of France gained on the expedition —of its riches and the ease with which an army could traverse the land. *Amour-propre* and fading memory had drawn a veil over the unpleasant lessons of the last fourteenth-century *chevauchée* through France.[6]

In 1381 Buckingham was not to campaign in France, as anticipated, but, unexpectedly, in England. On 10 July he was appointed to assemble and array the Essex lieges for an assault on the rebellious peasants defiantly encamped at Rettendon. His fellow commissioners included Oxford, FitzWalter, Bourchier, Sir Thomas Mandeville and Sir John Harleston, all of whom had just served with him in France. Buckingham and Percy drove the rebels from their forest encampment, but they reassembled and retreated to Colchester. Failing to arouse the townsmen in their support, they fell back towards Sudbury and were ambushed and finally crushed by FitzWalter and Harleston. This rapid success against hardened rebels, taking refuge in difficult country, was no mean achievement.[7] In the next few years Buckingham—and Arundel—had few opportunities for military employment, as the tempo of the war momentarily slackened, though there were occasions when they believed that their services would be required. Crises in 1382 made it likely that a royal expedition would have to be mounted against the Scots or French. In 1383 the council was prepared to back Arundel's proffer of his service with a retinue as lieutenant to Bishop Despenser, on crusade in Flanders—but the bishop replied that he did not want Arundel's help, doubtless to the latter's chagrin. In August Lancaster and Buckingham moved to the Kent coast with retinues, to counter the threat which the assembly of Charles VI's army at Arras presented to the English in Flanders and Picardy. However, John of Gaunt was reluctant to go to the assistance of Despenser, taking over the bishop's command only when the military position of the English army in Flanders had become hopeless. For both Buckingham and Arundel 1383 was a year of dashed military hopes.[8] Nor is the former likely to have derived much satisfaction from the very brief campaign which Lancaster and he carried out in the Eastern Lowlands of Scotland (March–April 1384).[9] The duke was more concerned to negotiate than to fight with the Scots— a policy whose failure was marked by the arrival in Scotland of a considerable French force in May 1385. Richard II's tenants-in-chief were summoned to assemble in his company at Newcastle on 14 July, but his army in fact left York only on 20 July, arriving at Berwick at the end of the month. Buckingham and Nottingham (who had been granted the office of Marshal in June) commanded the vanguard with Lancaster, and Arundel and Warwick were in the central 'battle' under the king's command. Of the four future Appellants leading retinues (Derby was presumably a member of his father's), Buckingham mustered the largest force, 400 men-at-arms and 800 archers: Arundel and Nottingham both mustered 99 men-at-arms and 150 archers, being slightly outnumbered by Warwick with 120 men-at-arms and 160 archers. Altogether these future allies mustered 1,978 soldiers—a total far outnumbered by Lancaster's retinue of 3,000. Buckingham (created duke of Gloucester on 6 August) was probably annoyed like other lords by the king's acceptance of Oxford's counsel, after the capture of Edinburgh, against extending the campaign north of the Forth, the strategy which Lancaster urged. What may have made the king's preference more galling to Thomas was that Oxford's only previous military experience had been as a member of his own retinue on the 1380–1 expedition.[10]

Nevertheless, in Lancaster's absence in Spain from July 1386 onwards, it was apparently Robert de Vere, together with the veterans Suffolk and Burley, who had the major share in determining measures to counter the French invasion threat from Flanders and Brittany. Gloucester and Arundel seem to have been merely among the heads of county commissions of array until the end of September. By then it had proved necessary to summon them and other magnates to bring retinues for the defence of London. Derby, controlling the Lancastrian resources, brought 249 men-at-arms and 314 archers: Arundel had 95 men-at-arms and 341 archers.[11] The need for finance to pay magnates' retinues and garrisons put Richard's government at the mercy of a highly disgruntled House of Commons. Their anger at the prolonged invasion threat and the stern defence measures Richard had instituted was probably shared by Gloucester and Arundel. It was incumbent on the councillors whose appointment the king was forced to accept during the 1386 parliament to initiate more aggressive action against the enemy. The decision may have been taken that Gloucester should stay in England to help implement and safeguard the parliamentary settlement, so that Arundel received the opportunity to command. On 10 December 1386 he was appointed Admiral of the West and North, a combination of commands giving him control over a large amount of shipping. Parliamentary subsidies were earmarked for his expedition. On 8 March 1387 two councillors, York and Cobham, together with the earl of Kent, were appointed to muster his force of nearly 2,500 soldiers. Arundel's retinue included 4 bannerets, 32 knights, 127 esquires and 217 archers. There were at least 26 other retinues engaged including ones captained by the earl of Devon, who had campaigned with Thomas of Woodstock, by Lord Beaumont, a friend of the king related to Arundel, and by Sir Thomas Mortimer, the earl of March's uncle.[12]

This force put to sea in March and anchored in Margate roads, hoping to intercept a predominantly Flemish fleet sailing from La Rochelle laden with wine. The ambush was successful—most of the ships, including French and Castilian ones, were captured. Some broke away and ran for Sluis, but Arundel's ships beat them to it and forced them on to Cadsand, making further captures. English seamanship seems to have been as deft then as it was to be when pitted against the Armada. The date of the victory (25 March) and the name of the great ship captured, *Mews colman*, commanded by the Admiral of Flanders, Sire Jean de Bucq, were long remembered by London citizens. It was probably gratifying to Arundel that his fleet scored successes at Sluis, where his father had played an important part as admiral in the victory over the French fleet in 1340. The earl now landed soldiers near the port, presumably to render the hinterland untenable as an invasion base and to plunder. The Zwin estuary was blockaded and ships bound for Sluis were captured. Early in April Arundel returned to England, putting in at Orwell, laden with more than 8,000 tuns of wines of Poitou and Saintonge. Soon afterwards he set out with reinforcements for the garrison at Brest, which Jean de Montfort was besieging. A force was landed which went on foray. About 24 June Arundel's fleet finally came back. Knighton says that on its expeditions about 160 ships were taken. This was the greatest naval success since 1356: Englishmen, so recently fearful of invasion, could toast the earl in the captured wine glutting the market.

Arundel's abilities must not be overrated. His strategy of blocking the route to Flanders was copied from that which Richard II's admirals, Lord Darcy and Sir Thomas Trivet, had applied success-fully with much smaller forces in the summer of 1386. The size of the fleet which the earl intercepted may have been swollen because the previous admirals had blockaded the Channel. Indeed, one of Arundel's retinue captains, Richard Cryse, esquire of Devon, may have served under him in a Castilian ship captured by Darcy and Trivet, *la Seint Marieship* of Santander, which had been granted to Cryse in January 1387. A necessary condition for Arundel's success was the previous enfeeblement of Franco-Castilian naval power, one cause of which was the Portuguese alliance, promoted by the expeditions of Cambridge and Lancaster to the Peninsula. Richard's councillors had exploited the enfeeblement in 1386 by their naval action. Arundel merely copied their strategy, backed by larger finan-cial resources: he and Gloucester were no more prepared than Richard to risk the expensive gamble of an invasion of France or Flanders. Instead he and they initiated the strategy of naval pressure against the Flemings, one which was to have its advocates in the fifteenth century. One criticism can be made against Arundel's execution of his command, if Froissart is to be relied on: he missed a golden oppor-tunity of capturing Sluis.[13]

The most important campaign which Gloucester and Arundel under-took was the brief civil war of November–December 1387. The rapidity with which they armed and moved their retinues was an important factor in the success of the Appellants: an example is Arundel's night march in November from Reigate to join Gloucester and Warwick at Harringay Park. J. N. L. Myres, in his reconstruction from the chroniclers' accounts, showed how the Appellants, by con-verging movements, trapped the duke of Ireland's army at Radcot Bridge. Little is known of the Appellants' army—or its movements.

According to the Westminster Chronicler, Warwick was a persuasive advocate of the strategy adopted—to march into the Midlands and to block Ireland's lines of approach to London. Surviving references to the campaign, though making the application of the Appellants' strategy broadly clear, fail to clarify their tactics. According to the Westminster Chronicler, the duke of Ireland marching on Witney encountered Arundel and his retinue. Arundel parleyed and the allies came up, trapping Ireland's army. The duke then fled to Radcot Bridge. But the Worcester Cathedral register cited by M. E. Aston relates that Gloucester, based at Moreton in Marsh (a long way north-west of Witney), intercepted and defeated Ireland's army between Blockley and Bourton-on-the-Hill. Knighton says that Ireland found his passage barred at Radcot Bridge by Derby and that Gloucester threatened his rear. The continuator of the *Eulogium's* account suggests that the retinues of Gloucester and the Earl Marshal were both drawn up within sight of Ireland's company at one point. Gloucester gave the order that one of the Thames bridges, at Lechlade, should be broken down. After the battle, Adam of Usk saw the Appellants march through Oxford on the way to London and gives their battle order as they passed through the town: Warwick and Derby had the van, Gloucester commanded the main 'battle' and Arundel and his son-in-law the Earl Marshal led the rearward. Whereas the Westminster Chronicler suggests that Warwick, whose military experience dated back to 1355, advocated the strategy that won the campaign, the hints of the chroniclers about its conduct contain a few indications that Gloucester was the field commander. This would have been consonant with his princely dignity and with English practice.[14]

In 1388 the Appellants may have stressed the threat from France, in order to suggest their indispensability to the realm and to gain subsidies necessary to seek profits of war. French invasion preparations had ceased after the duke of Brittany had arrested the Constable de Clisson in 1387. Brittany's ally, Burgundy, who controlled French policy, and whose secure possession of Flanders was jeopardized by English attacks, wrote to Gloucester suggesting a renewal of negotiations. When the 'Merciless Parliament' met in February 1388, the Chancellor, Bishop Arundel, announced that among the causes of summons were the French threat at sea and pressure in Gascony. On 24 March Arundel indented to hold the admiralties for five years: on 7 April, according to Froissart, the council (with York and Gloucester present) decided that he should lead another expedition.

The chronicler says that it was intended for his force to land in Brittany or Normandy: on 9 April he was appointed Captain of Brest and Lieutenant in Brittany and on 12 May Admiral and Lieutenant at Sea. Two days later a commission was appointed to muster his forces, headed by the Earl Marshal and two royal retainers, Sir Bernard Brocas and Sir Nicholas Sharnsfield. At Southampton on 10 June embarkation took place in sparkling summer weather, a month later than when the earl had contracted to set off: there were nearly 3,500 soldiers on board. Arundel's retinue consisted of 4 bannerets, 27 knights, 138 esquires and 193 archers. There were 40 other retinues, among the captains of which were the Earl Marshal and the earl of Devon. A large number of retinues were commanded by a captain or captains not of knightly rank—whereas there were 9 such captains on the 1387 expedition, there were 19 in 1388. The increase in the number of retinues and of non-knightly leaders perhaps reflects the popularity and repute that Arundel had gained among the lesser property-holders as a naval leader.

The fleet included a number of shallow-draught vessels, useful for inshore work, but no horses were taken. It may have been the intention either to rely on Jean de Montfort for the provision of horses, or to confine activities to the sea and coasts. After cruising off the Norman and Breton shores, Arundel's forces seized as a base for a month the Ile de Brehat which was ideally placed for intervention in northern Brittany. There news was received that Duke Jean had gone to Blois to negotiate with his rebellious nobles, through the mediation of the dukes of Burgundy and Berry. He may have been able to make the same kind of diplomatic capital out of the presence of an English army as he had in 1381—but this time the English force, based on naval power, was not so dependent on his co-operation. Arundel and his captains decided to sail for Poitou, to concert their attacks with the activities of *routiers* who still held out in Limousin and Auvergne in the name of Richard II. The *routier* Perrot le Béarnois, having received dispatches overland from Arundel, rode with his men towards Berry. The earl's fleet doubled round Brittany, probably pillaging the western Ile d'Ouessant on their way. They sailed down the Poitevin coast and anchored off the Serre estuary, up which light craft were sent. The soldiers occupied and pillaged the small town of Marans. The rest of the force (minus a guard for the ships) was brought up in support. The capture of Marans threatened the land communications of the great port of La Rochelle—only

local levies were available for its defence. Perhaps, with more bold-
ness, Arundel's forces could have burst their way into La Rochelle.
On the contrary, it was the French levies who proceeded to surprise
Arundel, attacking his camp near Marans. But they lacked the tactical
ability to exploit their success. The experienced English soon held
firm and the earl with 400 men-at-arms pursued the Rochellois back
to their gates, but were driven off. The army stayed at Marans for a
fortnight, failing to tempt the defenders out again. They lived well
off the countryside, carrying out raids as far inland as Thouars. If
the earl had landed horses and been able to co-ordinate the attacks
of the *routiers* with his own, he might have posed a serious challenge
to the French Crown in Aquitaine, even though his force was small.
A remarkable feature of this phase of the expedition is the apparent
absence of help from John of Gaunt, the new lieutenant in Aquitaine,
who was trying to bring fighting to a stop, as a corollary to his peace
with Castile, and was therefore working against the interests of
Arundel's expedition, just as he had ditched those of the Breton
expedition in 1375.

Lacking a secure base, mobility and allies, the army had to embark.
The fleet was scattered by bad weather and Arundel's ship with
several others narrowly escaped capture whilst sheltering near La
Rochelle. The ships managed to run to the haven of the Gironde.
With the fleet reassembled, Arundel returned to the Channel, calling
at the English base of Cherbourg. On 26 July commissioners were
appointed by Lancaster to conclude with Berry's representatives a
truce south of the Loire, operative from 18 August. Arundel cruised
down the Norman coast, landing with a plundering force near Carentan
and moving inland south of St-Lo to sack Torigny. He then circled
back to the outskirts of Bayeux and retired through the Cotentin,
embarking at Cherbourg. According to an Exchequer account, the
earl and his retinue arrived at Winchelsea on 3 September. Walsingham credited his force with the capture or destruction of 80 ships and
the burning or levying of a number of islands, including the large
ones of Ré and Oléron off La Rochelle. Arundel vindicated his great
naval reputation: in 1389 the inhabitants of North Sea ports from
Scarborough southwards were eager to hire his services for their
protection at sea.[15] But the failure of the senior Appellants to retain
power resulted in the loss of his commands. It was a measure of the
coolness between himself and Richard that he never received another.
Arundel was not a member of the Irish expedition in 1394–5 and his

name is not mentioned in connection with the ventures projected at court in the 1390s. Rustication must have embittered the man who had won military fame in 1387.

Gloucester too suffered a military eclipse, though he was better placed at court to gain support for military undertakings. Among those who prepared to go on his Prussian expedition were the earl of Stafford, Lord Morley, whom he had knighted in France in 1380, and Sir Michael de la Pole, Stafford's brother-in-law.[16] Among those who contracted in 1392 to serve him in Ireland were Lord FitzWalter, whom he had also knighted in 1380, Robert Lord Scales of Newcells (Norfolk) and Philip Lord Darcy, the successful admiral of 1386. On 10 August 1394 Gloucester indented to serve the king in Ireland for six months with 100 men-at-arms and 300 archers. Near the end of October, having crossed the Irish Sea with his retinue, he joined the royal army before the wood of Leighlin, Art MacMurrough's fortress, and took part in the successful assault on it. Presumably the duke also went on Richard's Leinster campaign.[17]

When the war with France and Castile was renewed in 1377, adverse strategic and diplomatic factors hampered English success. Thomas of Woodstock and the earl of Arundel, experiencing high command for the first time, failed to strike decisively. From the 1380s onwards younger men, enjoying greater favour, tended to exclude them from commands. But opportunities for martial action, which the two of them exploited well, came their way during the brief civil war of 1387. The ability of Gloucester and Arundel to take the field quickly in November 1387 may have resulted from the retaining and recruiting capacity which they had developed to meet the military needs of the Crown—particularly in Arundel's case, since his retinues for naval service had been dismissed only in June. As a commander, Thomas of Woodstock appears to have been sound and conventional. He was friendly with veterans of Edward III's French wars and in the 1390s, according to Froissart, represented the belligerent aspirations of many knights and esquires. The cautious strategy of Charles V in face of English invasion in 1380 was not imitated. In 1382, 1383, 1385 and 1386 French armies had risked a confrontation with the English on the field of battle. Long before Agincourt the French, made confident by their victory at Roosebeke, were forgetting the lessons of Crécy and Poitiers. Gloucester may have appreciated this: he is purported to have said to his knight Laquingay ' . . . it has never been so good for fighting in France as today, for, if one goes there, one will be opposed.'[18] Arundel's expeditions of 1387-8 had shown that French defences were not as efficient as they had been a decade before —La Rochelle had nearly fallen to the earl and the reactions to his raiding in Poitou and Normandy had been slow. But if, as Gloucester and Arundel would have liked, there had been war with France in the 1390s, it is likely that they would have encountered further frustrations. Huntingdon, Nottingham, Rutland and other friends of the king would have striven to keep the best commands for themselves, as in Ireland in 1394-5.

The earl of Arundel seems to have been more erratic as a commander than Thomas of Woodstock, though he was not without flair. In 1387-8 he developed techniques of coastal and naval warfare copied from the strategy of Franco-Castilian fleets and of the English admirals in 1386. The overseas expeditions of Gloucester and Arundel, though somewhat barren of results, gave them experience in command and made them popular. Gloucester emerged as the principal spokesman for soldiers who wished to reverse the defeats of the 1370s, Arundel enforced the strong naval pressure needed as a result of the Anglo-Flemish confrontation. Like a pamphleteer of the 1430s, like Warwick the Kingmaker at Calais, Arundel wanted to raid the shipping lanes of Western Europe, the arteries of Flanders. Whilst the Lords Appellant were in control of royal policy, he succeeded at sea: the 1389 truces with France and Flanders ended his naval policy and set in train a diplomatic process which thwarted his and Gloucester's military aspirations.

eight

The Eldest Appellant: Thomas Beauchamp, Earl of Warwick

Thomas Beauchamp, Earl of Warwick, endured the ignominy of losing in old age the good repute which he had previously enjoyed. Two leading chroniclers of Richard's reign bear witness to his erstwhile high reputation. According to Walsingham during the first 1380 parliament the earl was appointed as the king's governor, at the instance of the Commons, because of his outstanding character. This incident is probably apocryphal, but nevertheless significant. The Westminster Chronicler relates how in November 1387 Richard refused to countenance Suffolk's suggestion that Warwick should be killed. The king demurred on the grounds of Warwick's eminence. If the chronicler's account of this and of following incidents is to be believed, it was lucky for the king that he refused, as Warwick argued decisively with his fellow Lords Apellant against deposition—and, incidentally, settled their political and military strategy. The fact that Richard spared Warwick's life in 1397 probably indicates that he felt less vindictive about the role that the earl had played in 1387–8 than about the parts of Gloucester and Arundel. In 1395 Richard had been expected to visit Warwick Castle.[1]

If Suffolk did make his extreme suggestion, one reason was probably the earl's significance as the principal lay magnate encouraging Gloucester and Arundel to defy the king. Warwick, with his high status and noble family connections, may have persuaded important men to refrain from hostility towards the king's opponents. The marriages of some of his sisters had forged ties of kinship. Maud Beauchamp had married the leading Cumberland landowner, Roger Lord Clifford (d. 1389), who did not take up arms in support of Richard, despite the favour which his son and heir Sir Thomas enjoyed at court. Philippa Beauchamp had married Hugh Earl of Stafford (d. 1386), whose niece Elizabeth, a member of the important Yorkshire family of Ros, married Sir Thomas Clifford. Warwick's deceased sister Joan had been the first wife of Ralph Lord Basset of Drayton, who refused to fight for Richard in 1387.[2]

At that time Warwick was one of the two senior earls, having inherited his earldom eighteen years before. The appearance of such an eminent peer, prudent by repute, in arms at Harringay Park is likely to have had a profound effect on public opinion. Warwick's participation as a Lord Appellant has been characterized by Dr G. A. Holmes as 'half-hearted'. This is certainly the impression given by Adam of Usk, when describing the earl's pitiful reaction to the Appeal of Treason in 1397:

> And like a wretched old woman he made confession of all contained therein, wailing and weeping and whining that he had done all, traitor that he was; submitting himself in all things to the king's grace, and bewailing that he had ever been an ally of the appellees.

But this description of Warwick in 1397 must be contrasted with the impression given by the Westminster Chronicler of his decisive leadership in 1387. Moreover, in the first 1388 parliament Warwick appears to have been associated with Gloucester and Arundel in pressing for harsh measures against the former household knights, especially against Burley. It must be remembered too that the inflexible Gloucester confessed contritely in 1397.[3]

Warwick was then nearing the age of sixty, and his health, like Gloucester's, may have sometimes been indifferent. In a petition presented during the 1394 parliament, Warwick referred to the 'great maladies' which often afflicted him, and which made it distressing for him to travel long distances. In the context of the petition, these allegations seem tendentious. But since the state of health of a great noble was open to wide observation, it may have been difficult for him to make totally spurious claims on the subject. Bad health may have been a reason for the less vigorous part which Warwick took in public affairs from 1389 onwards. But his retirement must not be exaggerated: he was possibly present at the Stamford great council in May 1392 and he stood surety for the earl of Arundel at Lambeth in 1394. He was well enough to accept the king's fateful invitation to dinner in July 1397 and survived imprisonment in Cornwall and the Isle of Man.[4]

Adam of Usk's vivid cameo of a great lord who had broken down and lost his self-respect has probably harmed the 'image' of a chivalrous knight and crusader who had been a vigorous if not outstanding campaigner in his youth. The earl was intensely conscious of his rank and rights, brusque and high-handed in defending his interests. In November 1377 commissions were appointed in Warwickshire and Northamptonshire

> on complaint by Juliana late wife of Sir Richard Vernon that after taking a vow of chastity before Robert Bishop of Coventry and Lichfield, and after receiving the mantle and ring according to custom, she had come to Westminster by writ of the late king, and was returning home when William Bagot . . . and others assaulted her at Potterespirie [Potterspury a Northamptonshire manor belonging to Warwick], took her prisoner to Warwick Castle, carried away her goods, and assaulted her servants.

In 1382 and 1386 writs directed the earl to relinquish Bishopston manor in his Lordship of Gower, which was said to pertain to the bishopric of Llandaff.[5] In the 1390s Warwick conducted a virulent dispute. In August 1392 a commission was sent to the keepers of the peace in Cornwall, to determine a complaint by the earl, who alleged that when David and John Tregoz were being escorted to trial, a large crowd had threatened his servants. The Tregoz family took legal measures to counter-attack. On 24 November following a writ was issued from Chancery releasing the earl's lands and goods: he and a group from the West Country had arrested David Tregoz. In May 1393 he was ordered by writ to release John Tregoz, as the latter's petition showed that

> he and all his ancestors time out of mind were free men, but that the earl had caused him to be taken on the Thames near Westminster Palace, brought to Warwick Castle and there imprisoned in close custody, laying upon him that he is the earl's neif,* and shows that he is ready to declare his freedom as the law demands.

John produced an impressive array of West Country sureties in Chancery, who pledged that he would sue the matter. In the 1394 parliament Warwick petitioned concerning David Tregoz, whom he styled his villein, claiming that David had sued out a writ *de homine replegiando* against himself and others, directed to the sheriff of Cornwall. The plea had been heard in the King's Bench before Walter Clopton and other justices and a jury of the county was empanelled. In Trinity term 1393 they set out to appear before

* *Neif*, serf.

justices of assize at Derby, but, according to the earl, they did not get far out of Cornwall, as they were intercepted by David's son John with many others arrayed for war at Crediton (Devon), and forced to return home. David then obtained a writ *nisi prius* against the earl, which was produced before a justice at Saltash, where the earl or his attorney found it difficult to put in an appearance. Subsequently, a Cornish jury travelled up to the King's Bench, after the postponement of the suit, but the inquest was again delayed by David Tregoz, who intended to get it held in Cornwall—where, it may be presumed, he rather than Warwick was in a position to put pressure on the jurors. Warwick's determination to assert, by force or process, his rights over a family whom he claimed as serfs shows an obstinate side to a man whom chroniclers tended to characterize as politically moderate or even pusillanimous. Many landowners were sympathetic to attempts by their fellows to secure evading serfs. But the Tregoz family were clearly not in the usual category of such villeins. They had wealth and local connections, with which they were able to retaliate vigorously against the earl. It was somewhat undignified for a leading peer to confess that alleged serfs had thwarted him so persistently. Warwick's petition shows that he had little influence in Cornwall, where he possessed few properties. The Tregoz family was able to bring local pressure on the operation of the law, a sort of influence which was often the subject of complaint against magnates.[6]

Warwick appears to have been a conventionally religious layman. He was particularly interested in making benefactions to foundations at Warwick. His grants bear witness to lifelong associations with his brother Sir William Beauchamp. In March 1383 a group of Warwick burgesses was licensed by the Crown to acquire property in mortmain, in their capacity as masters and brethren of the gild of Holy Trinity and St Mary in the dominating collegiate parish church of St Mary, Warwick. It had been endowed as a college by Warwick's predecessors in the twelfth century: he possessed the right of collation to its deanery and five of its canonries. Royal permission to establish the gild had been granted at the petition of the earl and Sir William. The obits of the two brothers were to be celebrated, as were those of their parents and of the earl's recently born son Richard. In 1385 Warwick was licensed to alienate to the collegiate church Haselor manor (Cambs.) and advowsons. The valuation set on these properties was 80 *m.* per annum: Sir William alienated two advowsons worth

65 *m*. These endowments were to provide for masses. The earl had bought Haselor manor *c*. 1384 and granted it to St Mary's in 1395. By 1391, according to Sir William Dugdale, he had completed the choir of the church, which his father had begun, and by 1393 had completed the 'whole body' of the church.[7]

In the will which the earl made at Warwick Castle on 1 April 1400, he left instructions for a very large number of masses to be offered for his soul, and for his burial in the collegiate church. With a genial touch indicative of a hospitable nature, he ordered that all his friends attending the funeral were to be well entertained. It was unusual to leave explicit instructions about the provision of supper on the night of one's burial and of dinner next day. Among the earl's culinary tastes may have been a fondness for green ginger. But he does not seem to have been a book-lover, if conclusions can be drawn from the negative testimony of the inventories compiled in 1397. A few missals are mentioned as being at Warwick Castle, one of them a former possession of an earl of Stafford. But the castle contained a splendid collection of tapestries. Among the subjects depicted were the histories of King Alexander (also the theme of one of Gloucester's tapestries at Pleshey), John the Baptist, and, as might be expected, the mythical family hero celebrated in epic, Guy of Warwick. The pieces of this last set are likely to have been of especial magnificence, for in 1398 Richard granted them to his nephew the duke of Surrey. In his will Warwick bequeathed heirlooms supposed to have belonged to Guy to his heir Richard: there was his sword, coat of mail, harness and ragged staves. The ancient coats of mail which the fifteenth-century antiquary Rous depicted so accurately may have been supposed memorials of Guy preserved at the castle. The Beauchamp family had unique reasons for pride of ancestry. Warwick's elder brother was named after the mythical hero and his younger brother Reynbrun after the latter's son, also the hero of a romance.

The earl had many other luxurious possessions at Warwick besides the tapestries, some glittering with the golden bear and silver staff. He left Henry IV, who had delivered him from prison and restored his honours and possessions, an image of the Virgin, with two gold and silver cruets shaped like angels. He possessed a cross with a silver and gilt pedestal and images of the Passion, which he left to St Mary's at Warwick. In 1397 he had a bed with fine hangings and other precious possessions in the Hospital of St John there. Warwick's cultural interests and tastes (in so far as conclusions can be formed from the scanty evidence) were somewhat conventional, perhaps a little old-fashioned and provincial. The scale of his religious patronage was certainly munificent, but there is no evidence that he was deeply involved in the intense lay devotional movement of the period, reflected in the interests, pious and literary, of the ducal household at Pleshey. His funeral arrangements were pompous, not strikingly simple and austere like those favoured by the earls of Arundel. But Warwick, like his father, built on a grand scale: Caesar's and Guy's Towers at the castle still command admiration. According to Dugdale, the rakishly bold Guy's Tower cost him £395 5s. 2d. and was completed in the regnal year 1393–4.[8]

The earl's principal manors lay in Warwickshire. They were listed in 1397 as the castle and manor of Warwick, the manors of Haselor, Claverdon, Haseley, Tanworth, Sutton, Budbrooke, Berkswell, Brailes, Lighthorne, Moreton Morrell and Ashorne, Wedgenock Park, a messuage in Stratford-on-Avon and two shops in Coventry. He also possessed a large amount of property in the neighbouring county of Worcester, of which the earls of Warwick were hereditary sheriffs. Listed in 1397 were the castle and manor of Elmley Castle, the manors of Comberton, Wadborough, Earls Croome, Grafton Flyford, Abberley, Salwarp, Shrawley, Ribbesford, Elmley Lovett, Ficken-appletree, Beoley, Yardley, Wyre Piddle, Hadzor and Wick. He also took £18 from rents in Worcester, the profits of the shrievalty and a valuable income from saltworks. In December 1376 the earl granted to a syndicate all his saltworks 'situate in Upwyche, and his bullary of fourteen leads of brine there, rendering yearly to the exchequer of Wyche the services and customs for the same'. The charter received royal confirmation in 1383. There was mentioned in 1397 a saltwork in Wick, worth £10 p.a., called 'Shirriefsele' and containing eight boileries of brine, besides a rent from twenty-five boileries there.

At the time of his forfeiture, Warwick was holding the Worcester-shire manor of Holt (valued at £32 11s. 2d.), in right of his ward John Beauchamp, son and heir of the Steward of the Household executed in 1388. The Beauchamps of Holt (a fourteenth-century tower of whose Holt Castle survives) were kinsmen of the earls of Warwick and their feudal tenants. In 1389 Earl Thomas procured grants of the wardships and marriage of John Beauchamp. Possibly relations between the young man and the guardian who had helped to cause his father's death were strained. Whilst still a minor John married Isabel, sister of William Ferrers, Lord of Groby, a niece of the countess of Warwick. The earl alleged that he had married without his permission, which the young man denied. Lord Ferrers negotiated a settlement, according to which Warwick was to hold John's manors of Holt and Shotteswell (Warcs.) until he had levied 250 *m.* as an indemnification.[9]

In 1397 Warwick owned manors in many counties of central and eastern England. In Northamptonshire he had five manors— Buckby, Moulton, Preston Capes, Cosgrave and Potterspury. Buckby and Moulton, together with Walsall (Staffs.) and Olney (Bucks.) had, as part of a marriage settlement, been granted in remainder to Ralph Basset of Drayton and the future Appellant Thomas Beauchamp's sister Joan, with reversion in default of heirs to Thomas. Basset died without issue in 1390 and his second wife, Joan de Montfort, granted to Warwick the entailed manors, together with Drayton Bassett and Pattingham (Staffs.), in return for an annuity of 200 *m.* But the earl did not enjoy undisputed possession of this second significant addition since 1388 to the properties in his hands. Henry Grey Lord of Wilton occupied part of Olney and the earl of Derby disseised him of another part. In November 1394 a plea concerning Buckby was pending between the earls, but Derby failed to win it.

Warwick also possessed Uppingham, Preston, Greetham and Barrowden (Rutland), Kibworth (Leics.), Necton, Little Cressingham, Saham Tony, Panceworth and the hundreds of Wayland and Grimshoe (Norfolk). Further south there were the manors of Walthamstow (Essex), Flamstead (Herts.) and Hanslope, Shenley and Quarrendon (Bucks.).[10] Flamstead was not far from St Albans Abbey, with which the earl had ties. In the chancel floor of Flamstead church is the brass of a rector, John Oudeby, presented by Warwick or his son to the living. Oudeby (d. 1414) had been appointed by the Appellant to the Beauchamp Chamberlainship of the Exchequer in 1396. He weathered the crises of 1397–9, being confirmed in office by the Crown on 27 September 1397 and again in April 1401, during the short minority of Warwick's son and heir. In Hanslope church can be seen a painting of a bear and ragged staff, a memorial of Warwick ownership.[11]

In northern England Warwick was not a great territorial lord, though he held valuable properties in the bishopric of Durham and, as has been mentioned, had family connections in the region. The lordship was Castle Barnard (the fine remains of whose castle still stand) and the manors were Gainford, Piercebridge and Long Newton. In the West Country there were a number of properties, including Chedworth (Gloucs.) and Cherhill (Wilts.), where the manor-house was in good repair in 1397.[12] In Devon the earl then held the manor and hundred of South Tawton, the manor, hundred and borough of Okehampton and the lordship and borough of South Zeal; in Cornwall the manors of Blisland, Carnanton and Helston and the town of Tywarnhail. Warwick was a considerable landowner in the Welsh Marches, holding Swansea Castle and the Lordship of Gower, which he lost to Mowbray in 1397, and the Lordship of Pain's Castle (or Maud's Castle) in Elfael, besides Cydelegh and Aberedw.[13]

At the valuations set down in 1397, Warwick's annual income, minus customary manorial expenses, would have been over £2,900. This did not include Gower, from which the receiver-general received £200 in 1395. Before the loss, his annual income may have been in the same bracket as Gloucester's, but less than Arundel's. Warwick may have been better off, as far as revenue from estates was concerned, than his son, whose estimated income in 1420–1 (including a considerable number of dower properties) amounted to £2,612. In 1397 Warwick's estimated income from his Warwickshire properties was £676, property in Warwick producing over £300. His most valuable manor elsewhere in the county was Brailes (£70 $p.a.$). In Worcestershire he had an estimated income of £529, over £260 of which was drawn from the manors of Abberley, Elmley Castle, Salwarp, Wadborough, Ribbesford and Beoley. His estates in other English counties were said to yield £1,580, and the lordship of Pain's Castle £171.[14]

On the available evidence it is difficult to be certain whether Warwick's income sufficed to cover the costs of noble living. Expenses recorded by the receiver-general in an account of 1395 totalled £648 15s. 10d., leaving a large surplus from receipts (£1,064 7s. 5d.). The earl, on his departure from Warwick to London about Easter 1397, had various silver vessels brought before him, including ten 'chargeours', twenty-two dishes and a salt-cellar. These were among the items which Thomas Aldebury, his former receiver, sold in London after the earl's arrest, perhaps in accordance with his master's original intentions. Before the Easter departure, the earl had raised cash by pledging a basin and three silver candlesticks to William Whitchurch of Coventry. But this penury was probably more apparent than real, the result of seasonal factors. Though Earl Thomas was not a notable recipient of royal favours, in the 1380s and early 1390s he undertook a number of expensive projects, such as the endowment of St Mary's at Warwick and the completion of building works at the church and castle. In 1397 materials were stacked for the building of a lodge in the park at Drayton Basset, though this may not have been an expensive undertaking. In 1389 the earl had paid 1,200 *m.* at the Exchequer for a grant of estates in Astley and Kidderminster (Worcs.), former Beauchamp of Holt properties, to his feoffees.[15]

The 1397 commissioners took note of a few manors and annuities which Warwick had granted. Ashorne manor (Warcs.) had been given by him to John Daniel for life and was valued at £13 6s. 8d. *p.a.*: he was an esquire of the earl who had received it in September 1377 'for his good service'. In 1397 Peter Holt esquire was holding a life annuity from Beoley (Worcs.), of £10, which he was granted in March 1378. Holt had been in Warwick's retinue in 1377 when he was at St Albans Abbey and in May 1388, described as of Warwickshire, he went surety for the earl. At the time of the royal confiscation, Sir Nicholas Lilling was enjoying a life grant of Hadzor, worth £8 *p.a.*, which he had been granted by November 1387, and Warwick's illegitimate brother, John Atherston, was receiving £4 8s. from Wyre Piddle, which the earl had granted him in March 1381. It was probably at the earl's request that Atherston was appointed captain of Poil Castle in the March of Calais (July 1387). Poil fell to the French the following March.[16]

Record of several other grants made by Warwick to his servants remains. In March 1383, by indenture dated at Warwick Castle, he granted £20 in peace and £40 in war from Chedworth (Gloucs.) to Sir John Russell, and Walter Power was granted from the same manor £5 in peace and £20 in war. In September 1392 Power was granted sums assigned on the Warwickshire manors of Budbrooke, Haseley and Grove Park. In 1394 this grant was confirmed by the Crown. In September 1385 the earl's esquire Nicholas Trimenel was granted for life 10 *m.* per annum assigned on properties in and near Warwick: this received Crown confirmation in 1391. In December 1396, at Warwick, the earl demised to his esquire Robert Hugford a rent of £10 from Pattingham (Staffs.), one of the manors acquired from Lady Basset. The fewness of these grants gives the impression that Warwick, like Gloucester and Arundel, alienated property for life sparingly.[17]

Dr Holmes has indicated that in the second half of the fourteenth century the Beauchamps lost the interest they had displayed in the first half in adding numerous parcels of land to their property, except in Warwick itself. This loss of interest is paralleled in the contrast between Arundel's and his father's acquisitions. As Holmes points out, Warwick's failure to add to the inheritance is unlikely to have been the result of comparative penury, as he spent highly on building works. Moreover, he was certainly interested in acquiring the wardship and reversion of whole manors. In Warwick itself he bought property after November 1387 valued in 1397 at £140 *p.a.* Two manorial acquisitions in the county were properties in Erdington and Tanworth. In 1395–6 Panceworth (Norfolk) was leased to the earl's feoffees.[18]

This decline of interest in the improvement of manors by adding parcels may have resulted from the tendency in the later fourteenth century to lease demesnes. Professor Hilton has shown that the Warwickshire manor of Tanworth was farmed out in 1381. An account for the valuable manor of Brailes (April to September 1401) indicates that the demesne was leased then for a rent in the form of part of the crop, and Erdington was leased in 1408. As early as 1375 a lease of the demesne had been made at Flamstead (Herts.). In the 1397 valuations compiled for the Crown, some demesne at Warwick and the demesne at Blisland and Carnanton (Cornwall) was said to have been farmed. Farmers were mentioned at Brailes, Claverdon and Tanworth (Warcs.), Shenley (Bucks.) and South Tawton (Devon).[19]

But in 1397 Flamstead was producing crops for the earl, who was still owed considerable work services there. His bailiff and receiver in the manor was a leading Beauchamp estate official, Thomas Aldebury, parson of Flamstead. He had been one of the Appellants' deputies in 1388 to levy instalments of their parliamentary indemnity, being appointed their collector at Hull. In 1397 Aldebury sold wheat and barley sown on 80 acres at Flamstead and oats sown on 60 acres. On a number of other manors Warwick owned cattle, sheep, crops and farm implements in 1397. At Rhulen manor (co. Radnor) he had 537 sheep and at the grange of Cabalva (co. Radnor) 251 sheep. In both properties he had crops and implements stored. He was leasing Cabalva and another grange of Cwmhir Abbey at a yearly rent of 26 quarters of wheat.[20]

The Beauchamps relied particularly on the services of Warwickshire and Worcestershire families and individuals. One probable example was Richard Piryton, who may have come from the village of Piryton (Worcs.). His epitaph in Old St Paul's described him as having been an archdeacon of Colchester and canon residentiary of the cathedral, and gave the date of his death as 26 August 1387. He was buried on the south side of the nave, next to Warwick's uncle, John Lord Beauchamp, K.G. (d. 1360). Thus a man of simple origin, such as Piryton probably was, could by skill in administrative service attain posthumous equality with the great. In 1356 and 1361-2 he was acting as feoffee of the Appellant's father and in 1367 was appointed as the future earl's attorney. In 1369 he was an executor of the elder Earl Thomas and in 1371 rented Blounts manor in Essex with his heir. The following year Piryton and other Warwick servants made a recognizance to the earl of Arundel. The cleric was one of the feoffees holding Warwick's manors in 1373, probably for the whole duration of his service overseas with Lancaster. In September of that year Bishop Sudbury of London presented Piryton to the archdeaconry of Colchester, in an exchange with those to whom Warwick had granted his rights of presentation in his absence. In 1383 Piryton was party to a plea over property near Colchester, jointly with the earls of Stafford and Warwick. Piryton's death in 1387 may have been a blow to Warwick, depriving him of an experienced administrator who was an important figure in London and Essex, at a crucial time when his services, in particular his counsel, may have been especially needed.[21]

An important Warwickshire landowner who took a leading part in the earl's affairs after his father's death was Sir Henry Arderne of Curdworth, whose family had long been established in the county and who sat twice for it in parliament, and once for Worcestershire. In 1371 Ardene went surety in Chancery for the good conduct abroad of the earl's chaplain Thomas Visshawe, going to Rome on his business. Together with Sir William Beauchamp, he was a feoffee in the dower property of Alice (a sister of Sir William and the earl), widow of John Beauchamp of Hatch (Somerset). In 1372 Sir Henry, like Piryton, was among those to whom the earl granted manors as a feoffee. In 1375 he was acting as one of the earl's council, concerned with the farming of a manor. At an inquisition held in Oxfordshire in 1381, it was said that since the death of Giles Arderne in November 1376, Sir Henry had occupied two-thirds of Drayton and received the profits, by grant of the earl of Warwick, and that the latter had granted the wardship of Giles's coheirs to him. In

September 1383 Sir Henry, his wife Eleanor and his son Thomas were received into the St Albans confraternity, in the company of the countess of Warwick.[22]

Arderne had been in 1377 one of the witnesses to the earl's grant of Ashorne to his esquire John Daniel. It is likely that Daniel was an especially trusted member of Warwick's household. He was in the latter's retinue in 1377 at St Albans Abbey and a 'John Danielservant' was an abductor of Lady Vernon. Daniel was among the feoffees to whom Lady Basset demised properties to the earl's use and in 1395 he was closely concerned in the earl's various financial transactions. In 1397 he was described as having been Warwick's chamberlain, and he again received the office after the Beauchamp restoration of 1399. The loyalty of the Daniel family is shown by the fact that John Daniel the younger went with the earl to his prison at Tintagel in 1397, taking with him a case of razors and scissors to trim his master's beard and hair.[23]

Like Arderne, some of the other witnesses to the 1377 Daniel grant, and their connections, provide evidence for the earl's links in Warwickshire and Worcestershire. These were Sir Richard Harthill, Sir William Breton and William Spernore. Harthill had married an illegitimate half-sister of Warwick: in 1379 he was holding Warwickshire property in Poley and Kings Newton and he then acquired Baddesley Ensor for life.[24] Breton, a landowner in the county, probably went surety in 1371 with Arderne for Warwick's chaplain.[25] Spernore (whose name probably derived from Spernall, Warcs.) was appointed in 1390 on a commission to enquire into concealments of Beauchamp of Holt goods and was to be one of the earl's feoffees in property demised by Lady Basset. In 1397 order was made for his goods to be arrested with Warwick's, doubtless because it was thought that some of the latter's might be in his keeping. It was found by inquest that he had eight of his master's horses at Salwarp.[26]

It was at Salwarp, in March 1383, that the earl enfeoffed Spernore and William Cocksey, described as his esquires, in several of his Worcestershire properties. Other feoffees were the clerks Roger Tangley and Richard Bromley. In the same year Cocksey was received into the St Albans confraternity at the earl's instance. In May 1388, described as of Worcestershire, he received with Warwick the wardship of the late Sir John Talbot's properties. Tangley may have been an executor of Warwick's mother in 1369 and was received at St Albans Abbey with the countess in 1378: he and Bromley were feoffees in Basset properties in the 1390s.[27] Bromley was also among the trustees appointed in 1382 to hold in reversion, on behalf of the earl, the properties which Philippa, widow of his elder brother Sir Guy, had as dower. In 1395 Warwick granted his Devon and Cornwall manors to Bromley, among others: the cleric was his receiver then at Castle Barnard and journeyed to Pain's Castle with Sir Nicholas Lilling and John More and to Norfolk with More and the earl's receiver-general, Thomas Knyght, on his business. In 1397 Bromley was one of the attorneys appointed to deliver properties of the earl to feoffees.[28] In that year he received revenues from Warwick's Durham lordships and was holding a loan raised for him in Coventry. Bromley's close connections with the earl may have almost lost him the prebend in St Mary's, Warwick, which the latter had probably bestowed on him. On 8 October 1397 it was granted to a king's clerk, but on 6 December Bromley's title received royal ratification.[29]

Two laymen who entered the earl's service, both probably of Warwickshire families, deserve mention. These were the esquires Walter Power and Robert Hugford, respectively retained by the earl in 1383 and 1396. Power may have entered Warwick's service through Sir Henry Arderne's patronage, for his wife Margaret had previously been married to an Arderne. In October 1398 he was granted a royal annuity of £10, because he was retained to stay with the king for life and this was confirmed by Henry IV. It is possible that he re-entered Warwick's service after the restoration, for in 1401 he granted a manor to St Mary's, Warwick, on condition that his and his wife Mary's obits should be celebrated. In 1407 the church possessed 'a coupe of sylver and wyth ynne a peece of sylver, and a boiste of gold of Watkyn Powers gift' and also his gift of 'a new canape with the crownes and a belle of silver and gilt'. Hugford was a receiver of sums from Beauchamp manors in 1395, Warwick's receiver-general in the last year of his life and knight of the shire for Warwickshire in 1403. His son Thomas enjoyed a distinguished career in Beauchamp service.[30]

Two men who were probably connected with Warwick played minor but significant parts in royal administration, in the period when Warwick and his allies dominated the council: Sir John Say and John Hermesthorp, clerk, appointed Beauchamp Chamberlain of the Exchequer. Say was appointed in 1382 as one of the earl's feoffees in the reversion of Philippa Beauchamp's dower and in February 1387, described as of Warwickshire, he went surety when the earl and others received the wardship of the Stafford inheritance. In 1397 it was said that Say had enfeoffed the earl and countess jointly in possession of Kibworth (Leics.). He may have been identical with the John Say who in December 1387 was appointed by the council to receive part of Jean de Blois' ransom and in May 1388 as an envoy to negotiate with Flanders.[31] Hermesthorp had been commissioned in May 1387, with Gloucester's friend Sir George Felbrigg, to negotiate an alliance with the duke of Guelders, and in August to help take the muster of forces going to the relief of Brest under Sir Henry Percy. In 1389 he was appointed to sell off lands forfeited by the traitors and was one of the feoffees who received Beauchamp of Holt's former property to Warwick's use. In 1395–6 he was granted Panceworth (Norfolk) to Warwick's use, together with Lord Cobham and William Wynter.[32]

A Warwickshire servant of the earl who almost certainly gave him political and military support in the years 1387–8 was Sir William Bagot of Baginton, whose career was outlined by T. F. Tout. On 1 March 1398, when high in Richard's favour, he was pardoned for all 'treasons felonies, trespasses and misprisions' committed. On 2 February 1388, in Bishop Braybrooke's London hostel, Gloucester had presented to an advowson in an exchange of livings made at Bagot's request. Bagot had been a fellow feoffee of Warwick's councillor Arderne in 1375–6, and in 1377 a member of the earl's travelling retinue and an abductor on his behalf of Lady Vernon. As shire knight for Warwickshire in the 'Merciless Parliament' of 1388, he was possibly conspicuous in supporting the Commons' impeachments, being appointed to take oaths in the shire on behalf of the Appellants. He impressed the junior Appellants—the Earl Marshal granted him a manor and in May 1390 he sent ten valets to Calais, probably as a contribution to Derby's proposed expedition on the Tunis Crusade.[33] Besides serving the king and Mowbray notably in the 1390s, Bagot kept up some links with his first great patron, Warwick. In 1397 he owed the earl £35, seven years' rent for a manor in Tanworth (Warcs.), and he was stabling a horse at the earl's Worcestershire manor of Beoley. After Warwick's arrest Bagot was appointed to seize his goods and those of Sir Nicholas Lilling, John Catesby, William Spernore and Robert Walden of Warwick. On 9 October 1397 Bagot was granted custody of property without rent, 'in consideration of his recent great expenses, labours and diligence in the king's service'. According to an anonymous versifier Warwick, the 'bereward' (bear-keeper) had made a 'bag' of this 'rag' (Bagot), but through him was brought down. In May 1398 Bagot was appointed for life as steward and surveyor of the former Arundel lordships in the Marches and in September, the night before the Coventry duel, the king may have slept at Baginton Castle. In the last year of the reign, Sir William was one of Richard's trusted councillors: in March 1399, 'because retained to be of the king's continuous council during pleasure', he was granted £100 *p.a.* at the Exchequer, in addition to his existing fees.[34] During Bolingbroke's invasion Bagot, luckier than some of his no more notorious colleagues, escaped summary execution. He was eager to tell Henry what he knew about Richard's recent policies. His evidence when on trial in the 1399 parliament produced moments of drama. He pointed out bluntly that he was only one of the many present who had collaborated in Richard's policies, coolly related how Norfolk, of all people, had vindicated Henry's right to the succession in Richard's presence, and blamed Surrey, Exeter and above all Aumale for Gloucester's death. It was he who named Halle, then locked up in Newgate, as the key witness in that business. In conclusion, Bagot cited his charters of pardon. Henry had good reason for gratitude—after his evidence, magnate feeling against Richard's noble favourites was at fever-pitch. The next House of Commons, in 1401, instead of wanting Bagot's blood, petitioned for the restoration of his confiscated estates. In Baginton church his brass still proclaims this belated Lancastrian's suddenly discovered sympathies: Sir William and his wife wear the Lancastrian collar of SS.[35]

Of those whose goods Bagot was ordered to arrest in 1397 with the earl's, the most interesting is Sir Nicholas Lilling, who sat for Worcestershire in the 1386 parliament and the 'Merciless Parliament'. He was named third in the list of those who accompanied Warwick to St Albans Abbey in 1377: in 1383 his wife Isabella joined the confraternity, in company with the countess's *domicella*, Alice Russell. In 1386 feoffees in Lilling's Northamptonshire properties were licensed to grant them to him and his wife. They included some leading Essex landowners—Gloucester's friend Lord FitzWalter (d. 1387), Sir Robert Swynbourne of Little Horkesley and Sir Richard Waldegrave. In 1390 Lilling was appointed on the commission to enquire into concealments of Beauchamp of Holt goods and in September of that year he was enfeoffed with Warwick's servant Thomas Aldebury in the Beauchamp of Holt manor at Kidderminster (Worcs.) by a group probably acting on the earl's behalf, including

the clerics Hermesthorp and William Wenlock and the laymen Henry
Bruyn and Robert Borguyllon. In 1392 Lilling was Warwick's chief
steward and he was probably acting as such in 1394–5.[36] On
28 October 1399 the newly restored earl granted Castle Barnard to
his son; Lilling was the third witness, named after William
Beauchamp, Lord Abergavenny and Hugh Lord Burnell. In his will,
drafted the following April, Warwick made a bequest to Lilling and
in 1406, at the supplication of Earl Richard of Warwick, he was
granted the privilege that no royal officials should exercise the right of
purveyance over him or his tenants against their will.[37] On 14 October
1399 his parkership of Moulton (Northants.) received royal confirmation and in December he was appointed on a commission of array in
the county, together with Sir Giles Malory of Litchborough, who had
been Warwick's steward in 1397. Lilling's appointment on key commissions in Northamptonshire during the next few years indicate that
Henry regarded him as one of the gentlemen in the county on whose
weighty support he could count.[38]

Lilling was prominent in Worcestershire incidents of the 1390s, one
of whose causes may have been some local opposition to the influence
which Warwick could exercise in the county. The disputes reveal how
successfully Warwick's steward could apply pressure there, in marked
contrast to the earl's efforts against the Tregoz family in Cornwall
during the same period. Lilling's leading opponent was Sir John
Russell of Strensham (Worcs.). The Russell family had a tradition of
service to the Beauchamps. The Robert Russell, Lord of Strensham
(not far from Elmley Castle), whose brass is in Strensham church
may be identical with the man of that name to whom the earl granted
Wickwar manor (Gloucs.) in 1376, together with Edmund de Brugge
and Richard Bromley. Sir John Russell was retained by Warwick in
1383. But in 1387 the king detached him from Warwick's service:
on 25 November, described as the king's knight, he was granted a
royal annuity, to date from 16 August 1387. The grant recited that the
king had retained him to be of his household, 'whereby he lost fees
which he was wont to receive from his lord, with whom he stayed'.
In February 1388 Russell was licensed to crenellate his Worcestershire
manors at Strensham and Dormston and in July 1389, after the
dismissal of the senior Appellants, he was granted custody of the
valuable alien priory at Deerhurst (Gloucs.).[39]

In the Winchester parliament of January 1393, Russell impeached
Lilling, who as a result of his failure to answer the accusations was

sentenced to imprisonment. Russell alleged that he had come into the fields of Defford, accompanied by 500 men armed with bows, 60 of them placed in ambush. Russell challenged Lilling as to why he came armed and arrayed and asked how he was to get to his own house. Lilling told him to go another way. Russell also accused Sir Nicholas and a justice of the peace of failing in their duty, as they had not arrested a group who had murdered Russell's bailiff at Pershore. A third accusation was that when Sir John Blount seized three of Warwick's bondmen in Worcestershire and took them to Lancaster's castle at Tutbury (Staffs.), Lilling caused Blount's son and a priest to be forcibly taken from their Worcestershire house and held in Wales until the bondmen were released. Sir Nicholas Lilling was pardoned for his non-appearance at Winchester in May 1393. Though the accusations are unreliable as evidence, they suggest that Warwick maintained his interests among the Worcestershire property-holders in a high-handed manner. Russell may have had a grievance against his former lord over a property claim. On 28 September 1397 he was granted Worcestershire lands in fee simple, in place of the 25 m. which Richard had promised him in addition to his £50 annuity. The grant included former Beauchamp property, but was vacated, and Russell received other property which the earl possessed there before his forfeiture to which, according to the patent, Russell had asserted just title. This grant was also vacated.

In 1394 Russell had taken part in the Irish expedition. The favour which he was to enjoy at court is reflected by the endorsement of two petitions considered by the council, one from Bayonne dated 2 December 1398, the other from the county of Lancaster. On the dorse of the first Russell's presence is noted among the eight councillors who considered it, and on the dorse of the second with four other councillors. Sir John was a member of the council on which Richard relied to guard the realm during his second Irish expedition—which explains why he nearly lost his life after Henry landed. The 'Religieux de St-Denys' says that Russell only managed to survive by feigning madness. The story receives some corroboration from a grant of Deerhurst Priory dated 29 August 1399. The patent recites that it was made because the priory's possessions had been dissipated and its services neglected 'on account of the infirmities of Sir John Russell, farmer of the priory'. He was appointed, despite these timely ailments, on the Worcestershire commissions of peace in November 1399 and June 1400. His narrow escape, like Bagot's, seems to have deterred him from plotting in favour of Richard's restoration. Russell was not reappointed on commissions issued in May and July 1401. According to the inscription on his brass at Strensham, he died in 1405.[40]

In Richard's reign Thomas Beauchamp was for the most part content to stay in the background of national politics. Stately and proud, possibly the dispenser of lavish hospitality, he was heir to a great name and family, well connected with fellow nobles, the inheritor of wealth and established influence—sometimes overbearing influence, particularly in the Midlands. Warwick is unlikely to have approved Commons' criticisms of the manner in which magnates maintained their interests in the localities. In the late 1380s he was one of the few surviving magnates who had been of political and military importance in Edward III's reign—he was looked on as an elder statesman, a reputation which may have allowed him to play a decisive role in 1387. Warwick's career does not support the view that the social and financial needs of magnates were then leading them to put intolerable pressure on the Crown. Like his contemporaries and kinsmen, March, Stafford and Suffolk, he had probably become concerned from the late 1370s about the decline of good government. When older he may have reflected that their deaths in the 1380s happily delivered them from the personal and political dilemmas of a more troubled period. They died with their good repute intact.

nine

The Junior Appellants: Bolingbroke and Mowbray

Henry, the eldest son of John of Gaunt and Blanche of Lancaster, was born at the Lancastrian castle of Bolingbroke (Lincs.) in 1366. Not a great deal is known of his political and personal activities before he joined the Appellants at Huntingdon in December 1387. Like Mowbray he was then only just of age. In the campaign against the duke of Ireland he seems to have been allotted the less hazardous and more passive task of guarding Radcot Bridge. However, in the Appellants' debates about the deposition proposal he probably made his weight felt with his elders by representing his father's viewpoint. The remark which Usk attributed to Arundel in the second 1397 parliament, that Lancaster when overseas knew as much of that treason as himself, might have been meant to imply that Henry was acting under paternal instructions in 1387.[1]

Henry was among the young nobles knighted with Richard by Edward III at Windsor in April 1377 and in December he visited St Albans Abbey in the company of his royal cousin and of Robert de Vere, Earl of Oxford. Henry was then styled by one of his father's titles, earl of Derby.[2] By 1380-1, as Sir Robert Somerville has shown, Derby had his own household, with his wardrobe in Coleman Street, London, where there was a yeoman of the chamber, two clerks, esquires and a keeper of the palfrey. Hugh Waterton had been in charge of Henry's financial and household arrangements in his youth: he disbursed for Henry's wardrobe expenses in 1376-7, accounted for his expenses in 1380-1 and was acting as his chamberlain in 1386 and 1393. He visited St Albans Abbey with the earl in 1377. The young Henry received grants for his expenses from his father: in May 1380 the receiver in Norfolk was ordered to continue disbursing to him 250 *m*. per annum. In March 1384 the duke had it noted that he had granted Soham (Cambs.) to his heir. In December 1384 Henry and his wife Mary received her moiety of the Bohun inheritance—the Lordships of Brecon and Hay, lands in Wiltshire, Gloucestershire, Herefordshire and elsewhere, ten advowsons, mostly in Wales, and the fees of the earldoms of Hereford and Northampton. The partition did not include the lands of Bronllys and Cantref Selyf, appurtenant to the Lordship of Brecon, over which there was a long dispute with Gloucester. A valuation of the Bohun lands drawn up between 1385 and 1397, cited by Dr Holmes, assesses the parts held by Derby as worth just over £900 *p.a.* By 1394–5 his father had granted him various manors—Sutton (Beds.), Hallaton (Leics.), Grandborough (Warcs.), Kilburn (Yorks.), Soham (Cambs.), Daventry and Passenham (Northants.). The increase in properties explains his ability to go on crusade and pilgrimage in the 1390s.[3]

By the 1390s, as Somerville has shown, Derby had a well-developed household and estate organization. From 1390 onwards, if not before, he had a receiver-general and general attorney, John Leventhorpe, who had been appointed the Appellants' deputy to collect instalments of their grant at Boston in 1388.[4] Among those who achieved prominence in Derby's service were the Yorkshireman Sir Peter Buckton, Chaucer's friend, steward of the earl's household 1390–1; Sir John Bromwich, a Herefordshire landowner, surveyor and governor of his lands 1385–9; Simon Bache, clerk, treasurer of his household from 1385 onwards, and William Loveney, clerk of the wardrobe 1390–8. The indispensable Waterton was granted by Derby for life the constableships of the Bohun castles at Brecon and Hay, by letters patent dated June 1387, at the Lancastrian castle of Kenilworth (Warcs.), where some of his father's magnificent building works can be seen. Waterton supported the Appellants.[5]

Derby, apart from his adherence to the Appellants in 1387–8, is a somewhat enigmatic figure politically until the end of Richard's reign. Perhaps his interest in English politics was rather perfunctory. To discern the high-minded and adventurous young man it is necessary to forget the grim and careworn figure he presented as king, racked with ill-health—corpulent and somewhat hunched in effigy at Canterbury. Henry was a devoted son, as Froissart emphasizes. Even the hostile French apologist for Richard acknowledged the genuine quality of Henry's grief when he visited his father's tomb in St Paul's Cathedral for the first time. John of Gaunt had tirelessly promoted his son's interests—by procuring his marriage to Mary de Bohun, by helping to finance his 1390 crusade to Prussia and by attempting to found a hereditary principality in Aquitaine. It was probably due in part to Lancaster's influence that Derby was *persona grata* at court in the 1390s. The earl's prolonged absences overseas may have helped in this too, keeping him from becoming involved in court intrigues. In 1398 Richard had good reason to believe that his cousin would spend his exile harmlessly in knight errantry. If Froissart's account is reliable, Henry certainly needed good advice on how to forward his English interests during exile. Lancaster restrained him from visiting a congenial warlike cousin in Hainault, the count of Ostrevant, pointing out that he would be better placed at the French court. On first hearing of Boucicaut's proposed expedition against the Turks, Henry was eager to participate. A letter from his father advised against this, advice reinforced by its bearer, who doubtless emphasized that, since the duke was very ill, it would not be wise to dash off to Hungary. The scheme for the return to England in 1399 was instigated not by Henry but by the former archbishop, Thomas Arundel, according to Froissart.[6]

In the 1390s Derby had apparently been in favour with Richard and some of the leading English magnates. After Mary de Bohun's death in 1394, the king promoted princely marriages abroad for the earl. In the period 1395–8 Derby was friendly with his sister Elizabeth, wife of the favourite Huntingdon, as gifts recorded in his household accounts show. In 1399 Huntingdon (duke of Exeter) was well received by his brother-in-law, as was another of Richard's favourites, Henry's cousin Aumale. Norfolk (whose son and heir had married Derby's niece, Constance Holand) seems to have thought in December 1397 that Henry would treat his dangerous utterances confidentially. But in the 1390s Derby had been on good terms with the duke and duchess of Gloucester. In 1395 Derby appeared as the duke's ally at the Eltham great council and probably in the same year attended a tournament at Pleshey. In 1396 he sent his uncle an image of John the Baptist as a New Year's gift. These relations between Derby and Gloucester help to explain why the former denounced Mowbray, popularly reputed the duke's murderer, so bitterly in 1398.[7]

Despite Henry's well-known deceptions when confronting Richard in 1399, he seems to have possessed in eminent measure the knightly qualities, before they were dulled by closer political involvement. Froissart says that he was an amiable knight, courteous and pleasant to all. He had been eager to abandon the posture of a rebel in 1387, showing himself loyally disposed towards the king. He thought himself one of the most loyal knights in the world, according to Froissart.[8] He spent longer abroad on crusade and pilgrimage than any other noble of Richard's court, acquiring a fine collection of tournament armour. On his travels he had mingled with and impressed the nobility of western Christendom. Giangaleazzo Visconti provided him with armour for the Coventry duel in 1398; Charles VI, his uncle of Berry and brother of Orleans were charmed by Henry in 1398-9; Henry's kinsman the duke of Brittany had an affection for him. When Burgundy said that Henry must be a traitor—because of Richard's attitude to him—his world collapsed. Froissart's detailed version implies that, more than any other slight, it was the blow to Henry's chivalrous reputation which turned him into a determined plotter and rebel.[9]

Derby was well educated and cultivated. His great love was music, in the study of which he showed talent and expertise. He may have been the 'Roy Henry' whose compositions survive in the Old Hall MS. As befitted the son of John of Gaunt and the father of Humphrey of Gloucester, he was interested in literature. When in Italy he paid homage at the tombs of St Augustine, which he clasped with enthusiastic reverence, and Boethius. In 1392-3 John Gower rededicated his poem 'Confessio Amantis' to the earl and in 1393 Derby ordered payment to be made for a new collar which had been given to Gower. The poet's effigy at Southwark wears the SS. collar of Lancaster's livery. Chaucer was a retainer of the earl in 1395-6. In the range of buildings erected at Eltham Palace when Henry was king, he had a study built for himself, with figures of saints in its seven windows, and furnished with two desks, the larger of which was divided into two stages 'to keep the king's books in'.[10] Doubtless he was unable to retire to this oasis of scholarly calm as much as he wished. Instead he had to deal with subjects in rebellion, who unbearably branded him as a Ganelon, a traitor to his lord.

Henry of Bolingbroke, regular in features and short in stature, as depicted by the effigy at Canterbury, was a moderate, cultivated and amiable noble, orthodox and pious, a devoted son and father. He was not keenly impelled, as were probably Gloucester, Arundel and Nottingham, to contend and intrigue for Crown patronage, as a means of consolidating inheritances and winning military commands. As a politician, Henry was cushioned by his father's status and achievements, until John of Gaunt died, and Richard denied to the exile, whose popularity and potential influence he feared, his good name and inheritance. Then Henry had to assume novel and uncomfortable roles.

Thomas Mowbray was born on 22 March 1366. He was a great-grand-son of Thomas of Brotherton, Earl of Norfolk and Marshal of England, a brother of Edward II, and was eventually to inherit the lands of the baronial houses of Mowbray and Segrave. Thomas was the younger son of John Lord Mowbray, who was killed by Saracens when on pilgrimage or crusade, at the age of twenty-eight. Attention in the early years was focused on John, the heir to the Mowbray inheritance and that of his mother, Elizabeth Segrave. In May 1369 the custody of the Isle of Axholme (Lincs.) and other properties of John's inheritance had been granted to Ralph Lord Basset of Drayton, whose interest in the wardship was held by the earl of Northumberland from October 1377 onwards. John Mowbray was one of the young nobles knighted in April of that year with Prince Richard by the ailing Edward III. At Richard's Coronation he was created earl of Nottingham. In 1380 Northumberland granted his interest in the earl's lands to a group including the latter and headed by Lancaster. Commissions appointed in 1377 and 1380 found that Basset and other former guardians had neglected and plundered many of the Mowbray properties. The young earl of Nottingham died unmarried on 8 February 1383.[11]

Before this hardly anything is known about his brother and heir Thomas. In October 1382 he was a royal retainer; about the same age as the king, he was clearly a favourite companion. He was created earl of Nottingham within a few days of his brother's death. He was granted custody of his inheritance almost immediately, though he was not due to come of age until 1387, and also granted his own marriage, without rent. Richard purchased for his favourite from Lancaster the marriage of John Lestrange of Blackmere's daughter Elizabeth—a purchase which had cost the Crown 1,000 *m.* by May 1383, with the promise of further compensation for the duke worth between 600 and 1,000 *m.* Mowbray's expensive bride died in August 1383.[12]

Thomas seems to have been an intensely ambitious young man with a taste for intrigue. According to Froissart, he was notable among the courtiers of the 1390s for his pride and presumption. He plotted against Lancaster in 1385, against Richard in 1387, probably against the senior Appellants in 1389 and 1397, and in December 1397 he may have been trying to involve Hereford in manœuvres against rivals at court. When Norfolk was imprisoned in the Wardrobe in London in April 1398, pending proceedings on Hereford's accusations, elaborate precautions were taken to prevent him from escaping.

Mowbray was a direct descendant, albeit through two females, of

Edward I. His aspirations were rewarded by the two comital titles which Richard bestowed on him (earl of Nottingham 1383, Earl Marshal 1386), besides the later ducal one and a stream of more tangible benefits. Nevertheless, the earl's inheritance does not seem to have sufficed to sustain his considerable pretensions. Mowbray, like his rival, fleeting ally and judicial colleague, Thomas of Woodstock, was cursed with the need for court favour, for the bestowal of wardships, custodies and financially lucrative offices, to maintain rank. It may have been characteristic of his need to create a fine impression, that when breakfasting with John Northampton in 1384, the day before the anniversary of his brother's death, he persuaded Northampton to assemble the London gilds for a procession to the earl's tomb at the Carmelite Friars in Fleet Street.[13]

The Earl Marshal certainly did not lack ability, though as a politician he was inclined to be rash and unheeding. In the years 1394–7 the king relied particularly on his diplomatic services in Ireland, France and Germany. He was eager to hold military commands and to take part in expeditions, distinguishing himself in international tournaments in 1390. Mowbray was orthodox in religion, one of the court patrons of a proposed crusading order in 1395 and benevolent towards monks, especially the Carthusians.[14] In 1385 a royal favour was granted at his supplication to the abbot of the Premonstratensian house at Croxton (Leics.); in 1395 he alienated land at Findon (Sussex), with the advowson, to Rochester Priory and the following year a favour was received by the alien prior and convent of Sele (Sussex) at his petition. He was patron of the house—one of the prior's servants had supported his opposition to the Crown in 1387, perhaps in arms.[15] Norfolk founded one of the few new monasteries in fourteenth-century England, a Charterhouse at his manor of Epworth in the Isle of Axholme (Lincs.). Royal licences for amortization were granted in 1395–6. Mowbray made the foundation to the honour of God, the Blessed Virgin Mary, St John the Evangelist, Edward, King and Confessor, and to the object of his special devotion, the newly instituted Feast of the Visitation of the Mother of God. St John and St Edward were especially revered by Richard II. The Carthusians were to celebrate and pray 'for the health of the king and the earl while they shall live and for their souls after death, the souls of their forefathers and heirs and of all the faithful departed'. Mowbray was somewhat dilatory in carrying out the foundation in the eyes of some contemporary Carthusians, but his close relations with the Order may be also indicated by the fact that on the morning of the day appointed for the duel at Coventry he heard three masses at the Coventry Charterhouse. When sentenced to exile the earl chose to go on pilgrimage—perhaps he felt some remorse at his implication in Gloucester's mysterious but almost certainly shameful and unknightly death.[16]

The principal Mowbray lordships inherited by Thomas were those of Axholme (Lincs.) and Bramber (Sussex). Included in the Lordship of Bramber were the hundreds of Brightford, Steyning, Grinstead and Burbeach and the half hundreds of Easwrith, Fishergate and Wyndham. There were the towns of Bramber and Shoreham, the manors of Beeding, King's Barn, Findon, Washington, Knepp and Grinstead, the town of Horsham, the park of Bewbush and the chace of St Leonard's. Other Mowbray properties were Stotfold, Haynes and Willington manors (Beds.) and the site of Bedford Castle, Linslade (Bucks.), Melton Mowbray (Leics.), property in Ickleton (Cambs.), Thirsk, Burton in Lonsdale, Hovingham and Kirby Malzeard (Yorks.). Properties of the Segrave inheritance were West Hatch (Wilts.), Caludon and Great Kington (Warcs.), Chalcombe manor and Barton Seagrave Castle (Northants.), Alconbury (Hunts.) and two-thirds of Lodden (Norfolk). By his marriage to Arundel's daughter Elizabeth Montague in 1384, Mowbray acquired Wing (Bucks.), Prittlewell (Essex) and Kenninghall with Guiltcross hundred (Norfolk).[17] In 1394 the king granted him the Irish Lordship of Carlow and in 1397 he made good his claim to Warwick's Lordship of Gower. The estimated income from the properties confiscated in 1398 (which did not include the Lordships of Axholme, Carlow and Gower or much of the Sussex property) totalled over £550, the duke being allowed to retain properties valued at £1,000 p.a. Even allowing for the possibility that the 1398 valuations were too low, Mowbray does not seem to have been well endowed as a leading magnate, discounting Gower and the forfeited properties showered on him in 1397. When he inherited, some of the properties may still have been recovering from dilapidation under his brother's guardians. Living a great deal at court, he neglected ancestral castles. The people in Sussex were distressed about the defenceless state of Bramber Castle in 1388; the earl granted Barton Seagrave Castle to Nicholas Colfox in 1394–5. A surviving fragment of Caludon Castle suggests that a fine hall had been built there in the mid-fourteenth century. By 1398 Mowbray had let the castle to Sir William Bagot. In January 1394, when intending to go overseas, he was granted the privilege that his executors might hold all his properties and his royal annuity of 200 *m*. for two years after his death, which suggests that he had substantial debts. He died leaving a large debt for spices—£86 6s. 4d. owing to a London spicer.[18]

Mowbray's burdensome pretensions and pressing need for royal favour are indicated by the large number of life annuities charged on his properties. Great Kington (Warcs.) was granted by him in September 1387 to Robert and Hugh Dalby for their lives; Crick manor was granted, probably in 1388, to Sir William Bagot. In 1391 Nottingham appointed Edward Clinton master forester in the Isle of Axholme for life, with £20 *p.a.* from the issues of Epworth.[19] In January 1394 Thomas Missenden was pardoned for having received with his wife Joan the earl's properties in West Hatch (Wilts.), without royal licence, for the term of their lives.[20] During and just before the month of February 1397 the earl was particularly lavish. On 10 February Hugh Dalby was granted, for the term of his life, £10 from Chalcombe (Northants.). Three days later the earl's yeoman John Tunstal received 40s. from Willington (Beds.), and William Wymondeswold esquire 20 *m*. from Thirsk (Yorks.) on similar terms. On 15 February William Rees was granted £10 from Hinton (Cambs.) and in October, described as an esquire, 20 *m*. from Willington.[21]

Other life grants which Mowbray made before 29 September 1397 (the date of his creation as duke of Norfolk) were of Weston by Cherrington (Warcs.) to Sir William Morrers and his wife, with reversion to Richard Burgh esquire; £20 for good service to Edward Perys, assigned on Haynes (Beds.), and £10 to Herman van Megre from the earl's Sussex revenues.[22] Granted probably after Mowbray's ducal elevation were life annuities of £20 to his esquire Robert Goushill (Willington manor) and £40 to his esquire John Hopcroue (Epworth).[23]

The Earl Marshal's servants were drawn from many counties, like their annuities. A number of them served under him in France in 1388—Sir John Peyto, William Rees, Thomas Missenden, John Lancaster and, as an archer, Nicholas Colfox. From Lincolnshire came Thomas Brunham, who was enfeoffed by the earl in September 1390 with Thomas Yokflete, clerk, in Alconbury (Hunts.). Yokflete was appointed in 1388 as receiver for the Lords Appellant in the ports of Lynn and Yarmouth. Subsequently his association with Mowbray may have assisted his career in royal service.[24] Yokflete and Brunham were involved in the releases made between Mowbray and Warwick in 1397, in connection with the transfer of Gower, together with Archbishop Arundel (uncle of Mowbray's wife), Rutland (the earl's colleague on recent diplomatic missions), the Treasurer Roger Walden, Rees, John Rome, clerk, Missenden and Hugh Dalby.[25]

Thomas Missenden, who was pardoned for the support he had given ten years before to the Appellants, had Lincolnshire connections. In 1390 he appeared in Chancery on behalf of Robert Goushill, who was receiving a pardon at Mowbray's supplication; possibly there to assist was the earl's esquire Richard Wade. Missenden probably attended the St-Inglevert tournament in Nottingham's retinue, for Froissart mentions the tilt of Thomelin Messiden, a young and well-armoured English esquire, eager to do well in the lists. In February 1396 Missenden was granted custody of Oye in the March of Calais, where Mowbray had been captain since 1391. Missenden, in his will of 1402, made at Healing (Lincs.) near Grimsby, left 40s. to celebrate for his late master's soul and appointed Brunham an executor.[26]

Robert Goushill, for whose pardon Mowbray petitioned in 1390 for outlawries and alleged felonies, was the son and heir of Sir Nicholas Goushill, Lord of Hoveringham (Notts.). Robert had supported the Appellants. In 1397 he was appointed with Mowbray's retainer Sir William Bagot to enquire into whose hands goods of Warwick and his servants had fallen. In September 1401 Mowbray's widow Elizabeth was pardoned for marrying Robert Goushill without royal licence: they were then allowed to have her valuable dower but were fined 2,000 m. Goushill fought for Henry IV in 1403 against the Percies. He was knighted before the battle of Shrewsbury and badly wounded in the encounter. As he lay abandoned, one of his household came across him. Goushill asked him to take a ring to his wife, the duchess, but the man killed and then robbed his master. In Hoveringham church are effigies supposed to be those of Goushill and the duchess. He wears armour and the Lancastrian SS. collar, and clasps his wife's hand.[27]

Sir William Bagot of Baginton (Warcs.) was one of Mowbray's servants connected with Warwickshire. In 1380 he was among those, headed by Lancaster, to whom Northumberland granted the wardship of Mowbray properties. According to a 1385 inquisition, Bagot, as guardian of Caludon (Warcs.), committed extensive damage in the manor, felling a great deal of timber, demolishing buildings and carrying away the materials, and even removing the bell from the chapel. But these activities did not permanently impair his relations with the Earl Marshal. Bagot may have been party to the plot to kill Lancaster in 1385, in which the former was probably a ringleader. As a retainer of Warwick, Bagot possibly helped to persuade Mowbray to join the Appellants in December 1387. Three other servants of Nottingham who had Warwickshire associations were Hugh Dalby, Sir John Peyto and Edward Clinton. Peyto went surety for the earl in November 1388 and was described as his knight in 1392. Edward Clinton and his elder brother William, sons of John Lord Clinton, owner of Maxstoke Castle, were supporters of the Lords Appellant.[28]

Two East Anglian servants of Mowbray were the Appellant supporter, William Rees esquire of Norfolk, who was probably the life retainer of Mowbray's father-in-law Arundel, and John Lancaster, whose career has been outlined by Professor Roskell. Lancaster took part in the St-Inglevert jousts and was high in the Earl Marshal's favour in the 1390s.[29] Another of his esquires involved, like Lancaster, in the circumstances of Gloucester's death, was Nicholas Colfox of Nantwich (Cheshire), whose notoriety was echoed in Chaucer's 'col-fox, ful of sly iniquitee'. Colfox, who was to serve Mowbray's son and heir, was pardoned in 1404 for his involvement in the Calais murder. Nottingham's life appointments in 1394 as Justice of Chester and North Wales had probably enabled him to extend his patronage and reward generously. In 1395 the Cheshire knight Robert de Legh was pardoned at his request, possibly for rebelling in 1393 against Gaunt and Gloucester.[30] Other great appointments which Notting-ham received from 1389 onwards, on the Scottish Borders and at Calais, placed lucrative offices in his gift. Captaincies in the March of Calais went during his tenure of the command to Lancaster (Marck, 1391) and Missenden (Oye, 1396). Sir Thomas Swynbourne of Little Horkesley (Essex), an able soldier, was the earl's lieutenant at Roxburgh in 1389 and was granted the custody of Calais Castle in 1394 and the reversion of the castle and lordship of Hammes in 1395.[31] Sir Thomas Grey of Heaton (Northumberland), who headed the councillors whom Norfolk was licensed in 1398 to retain during his exile, had been his lieutenant as Warden of the East March.[32]

The earl had other important knightly connections. Among the witnesses to the indenture he made with the Irish chief MacMurrough in 1395 were the royal retainers Sir John Golafre and Sir William

Faringdon. Another witness was Jean de Grailly, the Gascon lord who a few months later gave Froissart an account of English politics hostile to Gloucester. Among the councillors Norfolk was licensed to retain in October 1398 were the royal knights William Elmham and George Felbrigg. Elmham was one of the eighty or so gentlemen who took leave of Norfolk when he embarked at Lowestoft the same month to go into exile. Also present was Sir John Calveley and one of the witnesses to the MacMurrough indenture, Sir Nicholas Langeford.[33]

Norfolk may have derived some East Anglian connections from his grandmother Margaret Marshal, Countess of Norfolk, whose imposing residence, Framlingham Castle, and estates derived from the Bigod earls of Norfolk gave her influence in the region. Among those who served Mowbray in France in 1388 was Thomas Lord Bardolf of Wormegay (Norfolk), who had fought overseas under Buckingham. Like Mowbray's son and heir, he rebelled against Henry IV in 1405. The Norfolk landowner Lord Morley, who had strong feelings about Gloucester's death, was acting as Mowbray's lieutenant as Marshal in 1397 and as his deputy was responsible for arranging Arundel's execution. A leading Lincolnshire landowner connected with Mowbray was the chivalrous knight John Lord Welles, who married his sister Eleanor before May 1386 and served under him in France in 1388. He was present at Norfolk's embarkation in October 1398, but, unlike Mowbray's heir or Bardolf, avoided trouble in the next few years of political crisis.[34]

Thomas Mowbray has never had an apologist. He did not please defenders of Richard II's reputation, because of his disgrace in 1398. Pro-Lancastrian writers remembered him as Gloucester's executioner and Hereford's opponent. Mowbray was certainly ambitious and unscrupulous in politics. But he was probably an able diplomat and soldier and until 1397 he was reputed a chivalrous knight. There is little information about his personality. His patronage of the Carthusians indicates a discriminating appreciation of monastic virtues. He may have been fond of music; in 1395 he took trouble to get his minstrel, John Kirkeby, out of prison, in order to take him to France. Mowbray's part in the death of Gloucester may have been undertaken with reluctance, as a cruel necessity. The hostile Walsingham says that after his 1399 pilgrimage Norfolk returned to Venice shattered in spirit—a pitiable state of mind for a fourteenth-century noble who had just been to Jerusalem. Sir William Bagot was to recall

Norfolk's conversation with him as they had ridden down *Savey Strete* towards Westminster in October 1397:

> the same duke asked me whether I knew anything about the manner of the duke of Gloucester; and I said: 'nay by my Troth, But the people say that you have murdered him'. And he swore great oaths nay . . . swearing as he would answer before God that it was never his will that he should be killed but only for dread of the king, and eschewing of his own death.[35]

Conclusion

The military success of the Lords Appellant in 1387 and their political failure in 1389 were both swift and dramatic. To finance their rising, they had a concentration of lands in their possession in 1387, including an interest in the Mortimer and Stafford wardships. They, almost alone among later medieval rebels, based a successful rising partly on the support of the southern English communities, rather than on that of remote provincial communities. To confirm their victory, they harnessed the new assertiveness of the House of Commons in parliament.

In the long run, the support of public opinion, which the Lords Appellant won so brilliantly, proved an unstable foundation for the exercise of their influence over the Crown. The property-holders had no permanent ideological or material reasons for combining to impose a lasting restriction on royal authority. Moreover, personal tensions among the Appellants themselves undermined their coalition, appearing even before their victory and the problems which success entailed.

The rising of the Lords Appellant is to be closely related to the personal tensions at court and in the royal council chamber caused by the foolish behaviour of the king, a youth who proved incapable of wielding sensibly the considerable powers prematurely confided in him in the early 1380s. Was the Appellant rebellion the product of a *crise nobiliaire*? On many estates held by the Lords Appellant, the demesne was no longer farmed for the lord's profit, but rented. Their difficulties in increasing or even maintaining income may have led some of the Appellants to intensify their pressure to win Crown patronage. Gloucester, Arundel and Nottingham wanted to enjoy lucrative military and naval commands and to have opportunities for making profits of war. The Crown was being importuned by nobles at a time when its own financial problems were complicated by economic regression and the requirements of defence and warfare. A king's son, Thomas of Woodstock, and a king's favourite, Thomas Mowbray, were both elevated to earldoms, without being granted sufficient income from land to maintain their status. They contributed to the political restlessness of the period by their need to win favour at court for the improvement of their financial position.

Magnates required skilled administrators to run a stately and luxurious household and to exploit incomes fully, good neighbours to defend their propertied interests in the localities and experienced soldiers to fulfil large-scale military contracts with the Crown. These competitive needs led magnates to develop private governmental organizations and to build up an 'affinity' of livery-holders. The pardons sued out for adherence to the Appellants by their household and estate servants and by other retainers show how these organizations provided a ready-made nucleus of personnel to support and run the political movement. But it was necessary for the Lords Appellant to use persuasion as well as influence to gain support in the regions where they rose in arms. Gloucester in his country could not command obedience to the extent that the Percies and Nevilles could in the north. His environment helps to explain the style and limitations of his opposition to Richard II. Living at Pleshey, Thomas had to attune to the political opinions of London and the neighbouring counties. A magnate, albeit a king's son, was not so outstanding in that region: his servants and neighbours could easily seek the patronage of other lords, rich gentry and great merchants. Therefore, Thomas of Woodstock was the king's son who turned to court the gentry and the Londoners, who won the confidence of Houses of Commons—expedients which he may not have entirely relished. It is a measure of his political stature that he was able to build up support in this politically complex region and to use it to coerce a king.

But there were grave weaknesses in the political movement which Gloucester led in the period 1386–9. The lesser property-holders had no firm tradition of alliance with magnates against the Crown. Many were critical of the manner in which magnates' officials exercised rights and in which livery-holders abused noble protection. There was no recent respectable precedent for coercing an English king by force of arms, though there were theoretical justifications for resistance. But Gloucester's resort to the expedient produced mixed reactions. However, he created a precedent which may have helped Henry of Bolingbroke's rebellion to win acceptance speedily in 1399. In the fifteenth century many noble rebels staked all on winning the Crown, as Henry had done. The experiences of the Lords Appellant showed that rebellion aimed at coercing rather than replacing a king faced formidable theoretical and practical problems. As the terminology of the 1388 Appeal of Treason shows, Gloucester and his peers believed in a concept of royal prerogative. They were in a dilemma when the king behaved in a manner which they considered unjust and harmful to their interests. The duke wrote to Richard, in connection with jurisdiction over duels in the Court of Chivalry:

> to you and your right high and royal majesty belongs the sovereignty, jurisdiction and knowledge, as it should be governed by justice and equity to your honourable renown, in which all justice should dwell and be.*

* 'The Order of Battel in the Court of Chivalry', *The Black Book of the Admiralty*, ed. T. Twiss, i, 300–1.

Notes

Chapter 1

1 *C.P.*, xii, part ii, 372ff; *Test. Vet.*, i, 79–80; *Polychronicon Ranulphi Higden*, ed. J. R. Lumby, viii (R.S., 1882), 370; Thomas Walsingham, *Historia Anglicana*, ed. H. T. Riley, i (R.S., 1863), 308.

2 *Anonimalle Chronicle*, ed. V. H. Galbraith (Manchester, 1927), 3, 4, 6, 7, 34–6, 44; S. Armitage-Smith, *John of Gaunt* (London, 1904), 9–10; *C.P.R., 1358–61*, 369.

3 *C.P.*, xii, part ii, 375–6; *Chronica Johannis de Reading et Anonymi Cantuariensis*, ed. J. Tait (Manchester, 1914), 338ff; *Pageant of the Birth, Life and Death of Richard Beauchamp, Earl of Warwick*, ed. Viscount Dillon and W. H. St John Hope (London, 1914), 44.

4 J. W. Sherborne, 'Indentured Retinues and English Expeditions to France, 1369–1380', *E.H.R.*, lxxix (1964), 720, 722; *Chronicon Angliae*, ed. E. M. Thompson (R.S., 1874), 63–4; 'Continuatio Eulogii', in *Eulogium (historiarum sive temporis)*, ed. F. S. Haydon, iii (R.S., 1863), 336; *Anonimalle Chronicle*, 59–62; *The Brut or The Chronicles of England*, ed. F. W. D. Brie, ii (E.E.T.S., 1908), 321–2; *Polychronicon*, viii, 370.

5 *C.P.*, xii, part ii, 376; Armitage-Smith, *op. cit.*, 102ff; *C.P.R., 1367–70*, 443; *Chronicon Angliae*, 68; *C.P.*, xii, part i, 177–9; C. C. Bayley, 'The Campaign of 1375 and the Good Parliament', *E.H.R.*, lv (1940), 370ff; *C.P.*, viii, 445ff.

6 *Anonimalle Chronicle*, 79ff; *Chronicon Angliae*, 68ff. Warwick had married Suffolk's kinswoman Margaret Ferrers by 1378 ('Liber Benefactorum' of St Albans Abbey, B.M., Nero D. vii, fo. 131d; *C.P.*, xii, part ii, 377–8).

For the comital families which had received great favours from Edward III, see G. A. Holmes, *The Estates of the Higher Nobility in Fourteenth-Century England* (Cambridge, 1957), 7ff.

7 *C.P.*, i, 244–5, xii, part i, 512; M. A. Tierney, *The History and Antiquities of the Castle and Town of Arundel* (London, 1834), i, 225ff; E. Perroy, 'The Anglo-French Negotiations at Bruges 1374–1377', *Camden Miscellany XIX* (1952), no. xi.

8 *Life-Records of Chaucer*, iv, ed. R. E. G. Kirk (Chaucer Soc., 1900), 158–9, 162–3, 173; Sherborne, *op. cit.*, 721n.; G. F. Beltz, *Memorials of the Order of the Garter* (London, 1841), 303.

9 P.R.O., E. 101/31/15; *The Brut*, ii, 325; 'Continuatio Eulogii', 336;

Polychronicon, viii, 377; Perroy, *op. cit.,* p. x. In 1359 Arundel was licensed to entail on his son Richard and on Elizabeth a rent of £216 13s. 4d. *p.a.* from the Lordship of Chirkland, together with the manor of Medmenham (Bucks.), valued at £50 *p.a.* Richard Arundel's sister Alice married Thomas Holand in or by 1364 (*C.P.R., 1358–61,* 274; *ibid., 1361–4,* 480).

[10] *C.P.R., 1370–4,* 83, 364, 371, 150–1; *ibid., 1374–7,* 25, 243.

[11] *R.P.,* ii, 326–7; T. F. Tout, *Chapters in the Administrative History of Mediaeval England,* iii (Manchester, 1928), 298ff; *C.P.R., 1374–7,* 441.
For Arundel's links with Lord Latimer, see *C.P.,* vii, 474 and n.; *Test. Vet.,* i, 108.
In 1369 a group including Arundel's father and the earl of Hereford had been licensed to hold Lancaster's property and in 1372, by a bond dated at Arundel's castle of Reigate, the duke acknowledged a debt of 1,000 *m.* to Arundel (*C.P.R., 1367–70,* 212; *John of Gaunt's Register, 1372–76,* i, ed. S. Armitage-Smith, Camden Third Ser., xx, 1911, nos. 162, 167).

[12] *C.P.,* v, 719–20; *Chronicon Angliae,* 34, 40; *C.P.R., 1358–61,* 117; Account of Keeper of Wardrobe, E. 101/396/2, fo. 56; *Life-Records of Chaucer,* iv, 158–9, 162.

[13] *C.P.R., 1370–4,* 472; *ibid., 1374–7,* 210, 373, 407–8, 279, 337; *Chronicon Angliae,* 121ff; R. Bird, *The Turbulent London of Richard II* (London, 1949), 44 and n.

[14] *Œuvres de Froissart; Chroniques,* ed. Kervyn de Lettenhove, ix (Brussels, 1869), 244; *Anonimalle Chronicle,* 106; *R.P.,* iii, 12ff; *C.P.R., 1374–7,* 297–8.

[15] *Chronicon Angliae,* xvi–ii, xxvi–ii; V. H. Galbraith, 'Thomas Walsingham and the Saint Albans Chronicle, 1272–1422', *E.H.R.,* xlvii (1932), 12ff. The Anonimalle Chronicler mentions the earls present at the dinner held by the shire knights at the end of the 1376 parliament. He lists, besides Cambridge, March, Warwick, Suffolk, Salisbury and Stafford, the earl of 'Herford'—almost certainly meaning Thomas of Woodstock, on whom it may have been Edward's intention to confer the earldom (*Anonimalle Chronicle,* 94; *cf Cal. of . . . Papal Registers, Papal Letters, 1362–1404,* 138, 142).

[16] P. E. Russell, *The English Intervention in Spain and Portugal in the time of Edward III and Richard II* (Oxford, 1955), 238ff; *Chronicon Angliae,* 168–9; *C.P.R., 1377–81,* 19, 44; *R.P.,* iii, 5–7, 15–16; Tout, *op. cit.,* iii, 333ff. On 1 July 1377 Arundel was appointed to head the Surrey and Sussex commissions of array and in September he and Bishop Courtenay of London were given custody of royal jewels as security for repayment of a £10,000 loan to the Crown from the Londoners (*C.P.R., 1377–81,* 40, 24, 147).

[17] *Handbook of British Chronology,* ed. Sir F. M. Powicke and E. B. Fryde (London, 1961), 130; *R.P.,* iii, 34ff; Tout, *op. cit.,* iii, 342ff. For Arundel at St Malo, see above, 123.

[18] *Memorials of London and London Life,* ed. H. T. Riley (London, 1868), 424, 427–8.

[19] *R.P.*, iii, 55ff; Tout, *op. cit.*, iii, 346ff.

[20] Russell, *op. cit.*, 245; *C.P.R.*, *1381–5*, 425–6; *Chronicon Angliae*, 267ff; R. L. Storey, 'The Wardens of the Marches of England towards Scotland, 1377–1489', *E.H.R.*, lxxii (1957), 595.

[21] Tout, *op. cit.*, iii, 365ff; *Anonimalle Chronicle*, 133ff; *Chronicon Angliae*, 285ff; A. Steel, *Richard II* (Cambridge, 1941), 77; *C.C.R.*, *1381–5*, 84.

[22] *C.P.R.*, *1381–5*, 23, 72–3; *Gesta Abbatum*, ed. H. T. Riley, iii (R.S., 1869), 342–3; *C.P.R.*, *1381–5*, 71. On 1 August 1381 Buckingham was appointed to head an enquiry into treasons in Cambridgeshire and Huntingdonshire; on 14 September to head one appointed on the princess of Wales' complaint about damage to her Essex properties and on 8 October to deal with rebels from Kent who had entered Essex to stir up revolt (*C.P.R.*, *1381–5*, 76, 78–9).

[23] *R.P.*, iii, 100–1; Tout, *op. cit.*, iii, 379ff; *Chronicon Angliae*, 333, 353–4.

[24] *C.C.R.*, *1381–5*, 14; *C.F.R.*, *1377–83*, 270–1, 278; M. Aston, *Thomas Arundel* (Oxford, 1967), 151–2.

[25] *C.P.*, xii, part ii, 378 and n.; *C.P.R.*, *1381–5*, 263, 268; *C.C.R.*, *1381–5*, 249–50; *C.P.R.*, *1381–5*, 176. For Richard's grief at the death of Sir Ralph Stafford, see *Polychronicon*, ix (R.S., 1886), 61.

[26] Froissart, *Œuvres*, ix, 461; *Polychronicon*, ix, 26; Holmes, *op. cit.*, 18; *C.P.R.*, *1381–5*, 345; *R.P.*, iii, 155; *Polychronicon*, ix, 19–20.

[27] *Catalogue des rolles françois*, ed. T. Carte (London, 1743), 144–5; *Foedera*, vii (London, 1709), 412–14.

[28] *Polychronicon*, ix, 32ff; *Historia Anglicana*, ii, 114–15; *C.P.R.*, *1381–5*, 403, 407; Armitage-Smith, *John of Gaunt*, 287–8.

[29] *Polychronicon*, ix, 44; *C.P.*, xi, 391; *R.P.*, iii, 185; *Polychronicon*, ix, 55ff; *Chronicon Angliae*, 364; *Chronicque de la Traison et Mort Richart Deux*, ed. B. Williams (London, 1847), 148.

[30] *Polychronicon*, ix, 70ff; *R.P.*, iii, 213ff; *Chronicon Henrici Knighton*, ed. J. R. Lumby, ii (R.S., 1895), 213ff; *C.C.R.*, *1385–9*, 271; *R.P.*, iii, 350–1.

Nottingham was appointed Marshal in June 1385 and created Earl Marshal in January 1386 (J. H. Round, 'The Marshalship of England', in *The Commune of London*, London, 1899, 313ff).

Chapter 2

[1] Tout, *op. cit.*, iii, 418ff. For examples of grants made to members of the household in 1387, see *C.P.R.*, *1385–9*, 270, 275; for other royal grants of that year, *ibid.*, *passim*, and *C.F.R.*, *1383–91*, *passim*. A copy exists of a Privy Seal letter, dated Westminster 4 May 1387, directing the Chancellor to have drawn up letters assigning profits from the lands of two royal wards to household expenses (B.M., Harleian MS. 3988, fo. 36).

[2] *C.P.R.*, *1385–9*, 323; *Diplomatic Correspondence of Richard II*, ed. E. Perroy (Camden Third Ser., xlviii, 1933), p. 201; *Polychronicon*,

Notes

ix, 93. Among those who received robes for the 1387 Garter Feast were the dukes of York, Gloucester and Ireland, the earls of Derby, Kent, Warwick, Salisbury, Northumberland and Nottingham, and Lords Basset and Neville (Beltz, *op. cit.*, 250).

[3] *Polychronicon*, ix, 93; H. J. Mills, 'John of Northampton's Pardons', *E.H.R.*, lii (1937), 474ff; Bird, *op. cit.*, 88, 141; *Cal. of Select Pleas and Memoranda of the City of London, 1381-1412*, ed. A. H. Thomas (Cambridge, 1932), 109ff.

[4] *Polychronicon*, ix, 115-16; Carte, *op. cit.*, 155; *C.P.R., 1385-9*, 301. The Thomas Holand who headed Arundel's esquires mustered for naval service in 1387 may have been Kent's son and heir, who, by the time he succeeded his father in the earldom in 1397, was a strong supporter of the king. Also going to sea in 1387 under Arundel's command was his kinsman John Lord Beaumont, who in June 1388 acted as surety with Lord Cobham, a 1386 councillor, for Richard Lord Scrope, who spoke to the king in Westminster Hall on behalf of the Appellants (E. 101/40/33; *C.P.*, vii, 156ff, ii, 61; Aston, *op. cit.*, 155, 215; *C.P.R., 1385-9*, 476; *Polychronicon*, ix, 107-8).

[5] Knighton, *op. cit.*, ii, 233, 236; *R.P.*, iii, 233. For the careers of Russell, Dallingridge and Bagot, see above, 115ff, 148-9, 150ff, 161-2.

[6] S. B. Chrimes, 'Richard II's Questions to the Judges, 1387', *Law Quarterly Review*, lxxii (1956), 365ff; M. McKisack, *The Fourteenth Century* (Oxford, 1959), 448 and n.; *R.P.*, *iii*, 238-40; 'Continuatio Eulogii', 363-4; *C.C.R., 1385-9*, 388-9; P.R.O., Pardon Roll, C. 67/31, m. 12d; *C.P.R., 1385-9*, 459; *C.F.R., 1383-91*, 276-7. For Rickhill in 1397, see above, 68. The Appellants acquired a good source of information about the justices' consultations, for in December 1387 they detained one of those consulted, Sir John Holt of the Common Pleas (*Polychronicon*, ix, 110).

[7] *Chronicon Angliae*, 382-3; *Polychronicon*, ix, 69.

[8] *Historia Anglicana*, ii, 162; *R.P.*, iii, 242-3; Tout, *op. cit.*, iii, 421n.; *C.P.*, xii, part ii, 897; *C.P.R.*, 1385-9, 217.

[9] Mills, *op. cit.*, 478 and n.; *Cal. of Letter-Books . . . of the City of London, Letter-Book H*, ed. R. R. Sharpe (London, 1907), 314-15, 317; *C.C.R., 1385-9*, 444-5; *Polychronicon*, ix, 104ff.

[10] *Polychronicon*, ix, 104ff; *Historia Anglicana*, ii, 163ff; 'The Kirkstall Chronicle, 1355-1400', ed. M. V. Clarke and N. Denholm-Young, *Bulletin of the John Rylands Library*, 15 (1931), 126ff; 'Chronicle of Dieulacres Abbey, 1381-1403', ed. M. V. Clarke and V. H. Galbraith, *ibid.*, 14 (1930), 167-8.

[11] Knighton, *op. cit.*, ii, 244; *C.P.*, ii, 3ff; *C.F.R., 1383-91*, 173-4. For Lady Basset's connection with the duke of Gloucester, see above, 83.

[12] Knighton, *op. cit.*, ii, 250; *Historia Anglicana*, ii, 169; *V.C.H. Buckinghamshire*, iv, 12; Carte, *op. cit.*, 149, 157; Knighton, *op. cit.*, ii, 243-4.

[13] *C.P.R., 1381-5*, 535; *C.F.R., 1383-91*, 261-2; *C.C.R., 1389-92*, 501; E. 101/41/5; C. 67/30, m. 19; J. S. Roskell, *The Commons in the Parliament of 1422* (Manchester, 1954), 193-4.

14 *Polychronicon,* ix, 95; *Historia Anglicana,* ii, 160–1; *R.P.,* iii, 232. In March 1388, in response to a petition from the countess of Oxford (Vere's mother), the duchess of Ireland was granted for life lands forfeited by her husband, to be held to her use by Archbishop Courtenay, Bishops Braybrooke and Arundel, the duke of Gloucester and John Waltham, Keeper of the Privy Seal (*C.P.R., 1385–9,* 423–4).

15 Knighton, *op. cit.,* ii, 241ff; *Polychronicon,* ix, 107ff; *Historia Anglicana,* ii, 164ff; *R.P.,* iii, 376, 229; Thomas Favent, 'Historia . . . mirabilis parliamenti' (etc.), ed. M. McKisack, *Camden Miscellany,* xiv (1926), 8ff; C. 67/31, mm. 13, 12; C. 67/30, m. 19; Mills, *op. cit.,* 474ff; *The History of the King's Works,* ed. H. M. Colvin *et al.,* i (London, 1963), 544; *R.P.,* iii, 379, 235; *Letter-Book H,* 321; 'Continuatio Eulogii', 364ff. In November 1387 there was a rumour that Trivet and Bramber planned to ambush the Lords Appellant on their way to Westminster to present the Appeal, as they passed the Mews, of which Burley was keeper (*Historia Anglicana,* ii, 165; *C.P.R., 1377–81,* 78).

16 *Historia Anglicana,* ii, 167; Knighton, *op. cit.,* ii, 242; *Polychronicon,* ix, 109ff; *R.P.,* iii, 242; Favent, *op. cit.,* 11; R. Somerville, *History of the Duchy of Lancaster,* i (London, 1953), 120. For the division of the Bohun inheritance, see above, 89–90, 91n.

17 *R.P.,* iii, 376; *Chronicon Adae de Usk,* ed. E. M. Thompson (London, 1904), 158, 161; Knighton, *op. cit.,* ii, 243–4, 256, 296, 246; *Chronicon Angliae,* 376, 386–7; *R.P.,* iii, 234–5, 243. In January 1388 the council may have instituted a search for evidence of suspicious traffic between England and France since 20 November 1386 (*C.C.R., 1385–9,* 388).

18 *R.P.,* iii, 235; *Polychronicon,* ix, 110–11; C. 67/30, mm. 2, 3, 19; *V.C.H. Northamptonshire,* iv, 74; Aston, *op. cit.,* 342 and n.; J. N. L. Myres, 'The Campaign of Radcot Bridge in December 1387', *E.H.R.,* xlii (1927), 20ff.

For the campaign, see chapter vii. According to an article in Burley's impeachment, he brought the mayor of Dover to Richard at Sheen, with an offer of 1,000 men-at-arms from the Cinque Ports for his service (*R.P.,* iii, 242).

19 *C.P.R., 1385–9,* 409; *V.C.H. Gloucestershire,* ii, 125–6; C. 67/31, mm. 13, 12.

20 *Chronicon Angliae,* 386–7; *Polychronicon,* ix, 114ff; 'Kirkstall Chronicle', 126 and n.; M. V. Clarke, *Fourteenth Century Studies* (Oxford, 1937), 91ff; *R.P.,* iii, 379; *Historia Anglicana,* ii, 172. The commons in London were in favour of admitting the Appellants, and helped to force the city governors' hands (*Historia . . . Ricardi II,* 98). Knighton says that when Richard had conferred with the Appellants, Derby and Nottingham accepted his invitation, but that Gloucester excused himself (*op. cit.,* ii, 255ff).

21 *R.P.,* iii, 248; 'Continuatio Eulogii', 365; A. Goodman, 'Owain Glyndŵr before 1400', *Welsh History Review,* v (1970), 67ff; E. 101/40/33; E. 101/41/5; *C.P.,* v, 502, xii, part i, 615–17. For references to the Appellants' estates and connections, see appropriate chapters above.

Notes

[22] Holmes, *op. cit.*, 77; E. 101/40/33; *C.F.R.*, *1383–91*, 173–4; *C.P.R.*, *1381–5*, 442.

[23] Clarke, *op. cit.*, 104ff; J. S. Roskell, *The Commons and their Speakers in English Parliaments 1376–1523* (Manchester, 1965), 132ff; *C.P.R.*, *1396–9*, 331.

[24] C. M. Barron, 'The Tyranny of Richard II', *B.I.H.R.*, xli (1968), 9 and n.; C. 67/30, mm. 19, 4, 3; C. 67/31, mm. 13, 13d, 12, 4, 2; Knighton, *op. cit.*, ii, 252; Myres, *op. cit.*, 21. For Veretot's connection with Arundel, see *C.F.R.*, *1383–91*, 57. For references to the Appellants' servants and properties, see appropriate chapters above.

[25] *Polychronicon*, ix, 115ff; Tout, *op. cit.*, iii, 429, 288n; *Test. Vet.*, i, 13–15; E. Rickert, 'Thou Vache', *Modern Philology*, xi (1913–14), 209ff; *C.C.R.*, *1385–9*, 494–5; Carte, *op. cit.*, 157; *C.P.R.*, *1385–9*, 383.

[26] *C.C.R.*, *1385–9*, 494–5, 405–6; *C.P.*, ii, 44–5; B.M., Add. Charter 35,043; *C.P.R.*, *1370–4*, 93; *C.C.R.*, *1377–81*, 382; *C.P.R.*, *1385–9*, 60; *V.C.H. Bedfordshire*, iii, 339. For Gildsburgh, Coggeshall, the Braybrookes and Waldegrave, see chapter v: for the pardons, see the Pardon Rolls cited above in note 24, except for Waldegrave's which is calendared in *C.P.R.*, *1396–9*, 184.

[27] Somerville, *op. cit.*, 372, 374–5, 502; Tout, *op. cit.*, iii, 427n.

[28] *R.P.*, iii, 228ff; *Polychronicon*, ix, 118ff; Favent, *op. cit.*, 14ff; *Chronicque de la Traison*, 9–10; *R.P.*, iii, 376; Usk, *op. cit.*, 158; 'Kirkstall Chronicle', 127–8. Derby tried hard to prevent Burley's execution, quarrelling with Gloucester over the matter (*Historia . . . Ricardi II*, 102).

[29] Tout, *op. cit.*, iii, 435.

[30] *Polychronicon*, ix, 183, 157; *C.P.*, v, 195ff; *C.F.R.*, *1383–91*, 224, 244.

[31] *R.P.*, iii, 234; *Foedera*, vii, 583ff; Russell, *op. cit.*, 504ff, 512, 524 and n. For Lancaster's relations with the Burley family, see N. B. Lewis, 'Simon Burley and Baldwin of Raddington', *E.H.R.*, lii (1937), 662ff.

[32] *C.P.R.*, *1396–9*, 277; Storey, *op. cit.*, 600–1; Froissart, *Œuvres*, xiii (1871), 200; *Polychronicon*, ix, 185ff.

[33] Froissart, *Œuvres*, xii (1871), 159ff; *C.P.R.*, *1385–9*, 502–3; *Foedera*, vii, 610ff, 594; *Polychronicon*, ix, 187; *Rotuli Scotiae*, ii (Record Comm., 1819), 95.

[34] *Polychronicon*, ix, 202ff; Storey, *op. cit.*, 600–1, 612; *C.C.R.*, *1385–9*, 571. For 1388 grants of wardships to Warwick and Arundel, of a marriage to the latter and custody of De la Pole properties to Nottingham, see *C.F.R.*, *1383–91*, 233, 260; *C.P.R.*, *1385–9*, 501; *C.F.R.*, *1383–91*, 258–9. In June Gloucester was appointed justice of North Wales and Chester (*C.P.R.*, *1385–9*, 450).

[35] *Foedera*, vii, 616–19; Knighton, *op. cit.*, ii, 310–11; Tout, *op. cit.*, iii, 454ff; *Historia Anglicana*, ii, 181–2.

[36] *Rot. Scot.*, ii, 97; *Handbook of British Chronology*, 130 and n.

[37] Carte, *op. cit.*, 159; *Polychronicon*, ix, 211, 213, 215; *Foedera*, vii, 636ff;

173

C.P.R., *1388–92*, 98. The captaincy of Brest, which Arundel had received in April 1388, also went to Huntingdon (*Foedera*, vii, 578–9, 622).

Chapter 3

[1] *Proceedings and Ordinances of the Privy Council*, ed. Sir H. Nicolas, i (Record Comm., 1834), 11ff; Storey, *op. cit.*, 601–2.

[2] *Historia Anglicana*, ii, 193ff; *Polychronicon*, ix, 218ff; Armitage-Smith, *op. cit.*, 340 and n., 427; *R.P.*, iii, 313, 257ff; *C.P.R.*, *1388–92*, 188, 194; *Proceedings and Ordinances*, i, 18 a–b. In 1399 Richard was alleged to have pardoned Gloucester in a chapel at Langley, in the presence of the duke's brothers. There was a royal residence at Langley in Hertfordshire (*R.P.*, iii, 421).

[3] Knighton, *op. cit.*, ii, 313–14; *Polychronicon*, ix, 238–9, 260; Froissart, *Œuvres*, xiv (1872), 150ff; *Expeditions to Prussia and the Holy Land made by Henry, Earl of Derby*, ed. L. Toulmin Smith (Camden Soc., new ser., lii, 1894), xxv ff, 39, 302, 107, 111.

[4] J. J. N. Palmer, 'The Anglo-French Peace Negotiations, 1390–1396', *T.R.H.S.*, 5th ser., 16 (1966), 85ff; *Foedera*, vii, 705–6; *C.C.R.*, *1389–92*, 494; *C.P.R.*, *1388–92*, 476; *C.P.*, xii, part i, 179–80. For Stafford's marriage arrangements and preparations for the crusade, see Account of Nicholas Bradshawe, Stafford County Record Office, D 641/1/2/4.

[5] *R.P.*, iii, 284ff; *Foedera*, vii, 707.

[6] 'A Journal of the Clerk of the Council during the Fifteenth and Sixteenth Years of Richard II', in J. F. Baldwin, *The King's Council in England during the Middle Ages* (Oxford, 1913), 493ff; *Expeditions to Prussia and the Holy Land*, xv ff; *Polychronicon*, ix, 261ff. After putting ashore in Northumberland, Gloucester went to 'castellum . . . de Tyniemutha, velut asylum antiquitus notum sibi; ubi per aliquot dies recreatus' (*Historia Anglicana*, ii, 202). Tynemouth Priory was a cell of St Albans Abbey, a house with which the duke had close links (see above, 82).

[7] 'Journal of the Clerk of the Council', 496; Froissart, *Œuvres*, xiv, 313–15; *Polychronicon*, ix, 264; A. J. Otway-Ruthven, *A History of Medieval Ireland* (London, 1968), 322–3; *cf* B.M., Titus B., xi, fo. 29.

[8] Froissart, *Œuvres*, xiv, 389; *Polychronicon*, ix, 265ff; Knighton, *op. cit.*, ii, 318–19; Carte, *op. cit.*, 156.

[9] Froissart, *Œuvres*, xvi (1872), 5; *Foedera*, vii, 722; *Roll of the Proceedings of the King's Council in Ireland*, ed, J. Graves (R.S., 1877), xiv ff. For the indentures for service in Ireland which the duke made in 1392, see above, 133 and n.

[10] *Foedera*, vii, 30ff; Knighton, *op. cit.*, ii, 319–20; Bird, *op. cit.*, 102ff; *R.P.*, iii, 313; *C.P.*, xii, part i, 180; *Polychronicon*, ix, 281–2. For a reference to Thomas's property in Aquitaine, see above, 88.

[11] *R.P.*, iii, 300ff; *Foedera*, vii, 738–9; Froissart, *Œuvres*, xv (1871), 110ff. For the terms of the contract made by Burgundy, Berry,

Lancaster and Gloucester, see J. J. N. Palmer, 'Articles for a Final Peace between England and France, 16 June 1393', *B.I.H.R.*, xxxix (1966), 18off.

[12] *Foedera*, vii, 746–7; *Johannis de Trokelowe . . . Annales*, ed. H. T. Riley (R.S., 1865), 159ff; J. G. Bellamy, 'The Northern Rebellions in the Later Years of Richard II', *Bulletin of the John Rylands Library*, 47 (1964–5), 261ff.

[13] *Polychronicon*, ix, 281–2; 'Continuatio Eulogii', 369; *R.P.*, iii, 313–14; *C.P.R.*, *1391–6*, 406; *R.P.*, iii, 316–17.

[14] *Trokelowe . . . Annales*, 168–9; *C.C.R.*, *1392–6*, 307, 368; *Anglo-Norman Letters and Petitions*, ed. M. D. Legge (Oxford, 1941), no. 29; Bellamy, *op. cit.*, 267ff.

[15] Otway-Ruthven, *op. cit.*, 326ff; E. Curtis, *Richard II in Ireland* (Oxford, 1927), 26–7, 241, 31–2, 217, 243; Palmer, *op. cit.*, 9off; Knighton, *op. cit.*, ii, 322.

[16] *Foedera*, vii, 802ff; Froissart, *Œuvres*, xv, 148ff, 156ff; Baldwin, *op. cit.*, 135–7, 504–5; Palmer, *op. cit.*, 94; *Œuvres*, xv, 196ff, 237–8, 240, 299ff, xvi, 1ff. For Stury's career, see W. T. Waugh, 'The Lollard Knights', *Scottish Historical Review*, xi (1914), 64ff.

[17] E. Perroy, *L'Angleterre et le grand schisme d'occident* (Paris, 1933), 376ff; *Chronique du religieux de Saint-Denys*, ed. M. L. Bellaguet, ii (Paris, 1840), 456ff; *C.C.R.*, *1396–9*, 73. Froissart alleges that Richard tried to win Gloucester over in 1396 by promising his son Humphrey an earldom endowed with an income of £2,000 *p.a.* and himself a large present if peace was concluded (*Œuvres*, xv, 301).

[18] *Chronica monasterii de Melsa*, ed. E. A. Bond, iii (R.S., 1868), 257; *Chronicque de la Traison*, 1ff; *Trokelowe . . . Annales*, 199, 201ff; Holmes, *op. cit.*, 39; *R.P.*, iii, 338; D. M. Bueno de Mesquita, 'The Foreign Policy of Richard II in 1397: Some Italian Letters', *E.H.R.*, lvi (1941), 628ff.

[19] *Trokelowe . . . Annales*, 201ff; *R.P.*, iii, 436, 418; 'Kirkstall Chronicle', 129ff; *The Chronicle of Iohn Hardyng*, ed. H. Ellis (London, 1812), 345; 'Continuatio Eulogii', 371; *C.P.R.*, *1396–9*, 150.

[20] *C.P.R.*, *1396–9*, 171; *C.C.R.*, *1396–9*, 140, 138; *C.F.R.*, *1391–9*, 219; *C.C.R.*, *1396–9*, 197, 137–8, 208, 144, 147–8; *C.P.R.*, *1396–9*, 241; *Trokelowe . . . Annales*, 206–7.

[21] *C.F.R.*, *1391–9*, 219, 222; *Trokelowe . . . Annales*, 207; *R.P.*, iii, 374ff, 348ff; *C.P.R.*, *1396–9*, 175–6, 186; Usk, *op. cit.*, 157ff; *Trokelowe . . . Annales*, 214ff; *Test. Vet.*, i, 129. For the London Austin friars, patronized by Humphrey de Bohun, Earl of Hereford (d. 1361), and whose prior in 1380 was Ashbourne, see *V.C.H. London*, i, 510ff. Ashbourne's role as controversialist has been established by A. Gwynn, *The English Austin Friars in the Time of Wyclif* (Oxford, 1940), 216–21, 267–8, 274–6.

[22] *R.P.*, iii, 378ff; J. Tait, 'Did Richard II Murder the Duke of Gloucester?' in *Historical Essays*, ed. T. F. Tout and J. Tait (Manchester, 1907), 199ff.

Walsingham considered that the duke's confession had been

doctored, the continuator of the *Eulogium* that the original was so displeasing to Richard that he ordered Nottingham to have him killed. Hardyng says that it was read out in the shires, to counter sympathy for Gloucester (*Trokelowe . . . Annales*, 221; 'Continuatio Eulogii', 373; Hardyng, *op cit.*, 345).

[23] *R.P.*, iii, 430-2, 452-3; *C.C.R.*, *1396-9*, 161; Tait, *op. cit.*, 199ff; A. E. Stamp, 'Richard II and the Death of the Duke of Gloucester', *E.H.R.*, xxxviii (1923), 251; *Foedera*, viii (London, 1709), 20; *C.C.R.*, *1396-9*, 149-50. Gower thought that Gloucester was murdered after his condemnation in parliament ('The Tripartite Chronicle', in *The Major Latin Works of John Gower*, trans. E. W. Stockton, Seattle, 1962, 302-3). It may have been Nottingham who delayed Gloucester's death, if Sir William Bagot's testimony in 1399 is reliable. He alleged that Mowbray told him he had saved Gloucester's life for three weeks and more, against the intent of the king and other lords, and that the king had assigned a man of his own to go with him to Calais and men of other lords, to see that the duke was killed (*Chronicles of London*, ed. C. L. Kingsford, Oxford, 1905, 52-3).

[24] *R.P.*, iii, 436, 379-80; Usk, *op. cit.*, 161-2; *Trokelowe . . . Annales*, 219-20; 'Kirkstall Chronicle', 130; *C.P.R.*, *1396-9*, 339; P.R.O., Ancient Petitions, S.C. 8/221/11037; *C.C.R.*, *1396-9*, 163-4; *Cal. of . . . Papal Registers, Papal Letters, 1396-1404*, 177.

[25] *R.P.*, iii, 353, 355, 382ff; *Chronicque de la Traison*, 12ff. Mowbray was expected to inherit before long the lands of his grandmother, Margaret Marshal, Duchess of Norfolk, who died in March 1399 (*C.P.*, ix, 599ff).

[26] *R.P.*, iii, 353-4; *C.P.R.*, *1396-9*, 360-1, 220-1, 209-10, 213, 467. After Norfolk's forfeiture Exeter was granted Lewes and other Sussex properties, and Salisbury was granted Arundel property in East Anglia which Norfolk had held (*ibid.*, 458, 468).

[27] *C.P.R.*, *1396-9*, 200, 336, 219, 196, 269, 207, 201, 280-1, 220, 211, 213-14, 221.

In September 1398 Beauchamp properties which Norfolk had held were granted to Aumale and Surrey (*ibid.*, 415, 429).

[28] A. Goodman, 'The Countess and the Rebels: Essex and a Crisis in English Society 1400', *Transactions of the Essex Archaeological Soc.*, third ser., ii (1970), 267ff; *C.P.R.*, *1396-9*, 245; *Trokelowe . . . Annales*, 321; Froissart, *Œuvres*, xvi, 82; Usk, *op. cit.*, 180.

[29] *R.P.*, iii, 435-6; *Trokelowe . . . Annales*, 307-8; *Proceedings and Ordinances*, i, 100-1; *Chronicque de la Traison*, 82ff; *C.P.*, xii, part ii, 377ff, i, 245-6, xii, part i, 180-1, ix, 604-5; *Original Letters Illustrative of English History*, ed. Sir H. Ellis, third ser., i (London, 1846), 46ff.

Chapter 4

[1] *R.P.*, iii, 378ff; *C.P.R.*, *1388-92*, 482; G. D. Squibb, *The High Court of Chivalry* (Oxford, 1959), 132; Baldwin, *op. cit.*, 500; *C.C.R.*, *1389-92*, 550; *C.P.R.*, *1391-6*, 367, 533; *C.C.R.*, *1392-6*, 492-3.

Gloucester's reputation for violence is reflected in a charge made on 3 August 1388 before the mayor and aldermen of London. William Ashwell, beadle of Cornhill, was accused of having spread the false rumour that two aldermen, John Churchman and Hugh Fastolf, had been arrested and taken to the Tower by order of the royal council, and that Churchman had had his head broken by the duke (*Cal. of Letter-Books . . . of the City of London, Letter-Book H*, 329–30).

2 *Historia Anglicana*, ii, 226; *C.P.*, ix, 216n., v, 480–1; *Trokelowe . . . Annales*, 309–10, 313–14.

3 *Chronica Monasterii de Melsa*, iii, 219ff, 257; *Trokelowe . . . Annales*, 327ff; Clarke, *op. cit.*, 91. Gloucester's body may have been transferred from Bermondsey to Westminster; Sandford figured his brass in Westminster Abbey (*A Genealogical History of the Kings of England, and Monarchs of Great Britain*, London, 1683, 228, 231; *cf* above, 69).

4 R. Gough, *The History and Antiquities of Pleshy* (London, 1803), Appendix, 81; E. H. Pearce, *William de Colchester* (London, 1915), 68; *C.I.M.*, *1392–9*, no. 372.

5 Froissart, *Œuvres*, ix, 275–7, 280–1, 323ff; 'The Order of Battel in the Court of Chivalry', in *The Black Book of the Admiralty*, ed. T. Twiss, i (R.S., 1871), 300ff. For the Court of Chivalry during Thomas's Constableship, see Squibb, *op. cit.*, 17ff, 25.

6 *R.P.*, iii, 431; *Issues of the Exchequer*, ed. F. Devon, i (Record Comm., 1837), 189.

7 J. S. Roskell, 'Sir Richard de Waldegrave of Bures St. Mary', *Proceedings of the Suffolk Institute of Archaeology*, xxvii, part 3 (1957), 157; *Test. Vet.*, i, 146ff.

8 *Polychronicon*, ix, 77; Froissart, *Œuvres*, xv, 196ff.

9 *Trokelowe . . . Annales*, 204–5; *R.P.*, iii, 378ff; Gough, *op. cit.*, Appendix, 69; Froissart, *Œuvres*, xvi (1872), 27; 'Inventory of the Goods and Chattels belonging to Thomas, Duke of Gloucester', etc., ed. Viscount Dillon and W. H. St John Hope, *Archaeological Journal*, liv (1897), 275ff.

10 *C.I.M.*, *1392–9*, no. 359; *V.C.H. London*, i, 518. In 1367 Agnes Countess of Pembroke willed that she should be buried in the church of the London Minoresses and in 1368 Elizabeth Ferrers, whose sister married the Appellant Warwick, was a nun there (*Test. Vet.*, i, 71–2, 76).

11 *C.P.*, v, 728; *Test. Vet.*, i, 146ff; E. G. Millar and M. R. James, *The Bohun Manuscripts* (Roxburghe Club, 1936), 2n.; C. R. Borland, 'Catalogue of the Medieval MSS. in the Library of the Faculty of Advocates' (1909), 118ff, in The National Library of Scotland. For William of Monkland, the member of the Bohun family who was an outstanding friar in Edward III's reign, see Gwynn, *op. cit.*, 107ff. Duchess Eleanor was buried in Westminster Abbey; her fine surviving brass is figured in J. Evans, *English Art 1307–1461* (Oxford, 1949), 149.

12 *Test. Vet.*, i, 132, 135; *Cal. of . . . Papal Registers, Papal Letters, 1396–1404*, 385, 387; *C.P.R.*, *1401–5*, 248; *C.A.D.*, i, C. 1502. Duchess Eleanor bequeathed to her son 'a cross of gold pendant by a chain, with an image of the crucifix and four pearls round it, with my blessing

as the thing of mine which I have liked best' (*Test. Vet.*, i, 148). Thomas's intentions for Mary de Bohun's future are inferred from *Sir John Froissart's Chronicles*, trans. T. Johnes (Hafod, 1804), 401–2; for a gift from Richard to Isabella, see Account of Keeper of Wardrobe, E. 101/402/10, fo. 30d.

13 *Cal. of . . . Papal Registers, Papal Letters, 1362–1404*, 394; 'Inventory of the Goods and Chattels', 275ff; Clarke, *op. cit.*, 121; *Test. Vet.*, i, 148; *Chronicon Angliae*, xxvi–ii; *C.I.M.*, *1392–9*, no. 372. For the literary patronage of the Bohun earls in the fourteenth century, see L. A. Hubbard, *Mediaeval Romances in English* (New York, 1960), 215, and Gwynn, *op. cit.*, 135ff. A volume of the *Roman de la Rose* was listed in the Pleshey Castle library in 1397 ('Inventory of the Goods and Chattels', 300).

14 *Test. Vet.*, 147–8. Egidius's work and two books 'de vices et vertues' were listed as being at Pleshey in 1397 ('Inventory of the Goods and Chattels', 302–3; *cf The Book of Vices and Virtues*, ed. W. N. Francis, E.E.T.S., 1942). It would be interesting to know whether Gloucester studied Egidius, whose 'royalist' tendencies and useful definition of tyranny may have affected the duke's thought (R. W. and A. J. Carlyle, *History of Mediaeval Political Theory in the West*, Edinburgh, 1937, 70ff).

15 *Test. Vet.*, i, 148. There is a later fourteenth-century version in English of the French epic about the Knight of the Swan (*Chevelere Assigne*, ed. H. H. Gibbs, E.E.T.S., 1868; *cf* Hubbard, *op. cit.*, 239). The combat of the youthful Helyas in defence of his wronged mother made the poem charmingly appropriate reading-matter for the boy Humphrey, supposedly Helyas's descendant (*cf* J. Cherry, 'The Dunstable Swan Jewel', *Journal of the British Archaeological Association*, third ser., xxxii, 1969, 38ff).

16 *The Scrope and Grosvenor Controversy*, ed. N. H. Nicolas (London, 1832), ii, 142ff, 131; *C.P.*, xi, 563ff; *Test. Vet.*, i, 156–7; Devon, *op. cit.*, 245.

In 1415 Henry Scrope left Sibyl de Beauchamp 'unum primerium cum matutinis beatae Mariae Virginis in Anglicis, pro remembrancia'. Duchess Eleanor granted Arnall (Notts.) to Sibyl for life and appointed her an executor (*Scrope and Grosvenor Controversy*, ii, 145; *C.P.R.*, *1399–1401*, 366; *Test. Vet.*, i, 149).

17 *C.C.R.*, *1381–5*, 177; Gough, *op. cit.*, 180.

18 'Liber Benefactorum', ff. 131d, 133; *C.P.R.*, *1381–5*, 492; *Chronicque de la Traison*, 3; Usk, *op. cit.*, 161; *Gesta Abbatum*, iii, 455.

19 Pearce, *op. cit.*, 57; Pearce, *The Monks of Westminster* (Cambridge, 1916), 108; *C.P.R.*, *1388–92*, 291; *ibid.*, *1396–9*, 126, 346; *V.C.H. Essex*, ii, 110ff.

Boniface IX ordered the abbots of Westminster and Waltham (Essex) to assist Gloucester in the foundation of Pleshey College (Gough, *op. cit.*, Appendix, 51).

20 *C.P.R.*, *1391–6*, 363, 367; *V.C.H. Essex*, ii, 193–5; Gough, *op. cit.*, 53. A copy of the college statutes, with impressions from two of the

duke's seals, is in the Public Record Office (D.L. 41/10/31); *cf* Gough, *op. cit.*, Appendix, 69ff.

[21] *C.P.R., 1391–6*, 367; *ibid., 1396–9*, 78, 10; *C.I.M., 1392–9*, no. 311; *C.P.R., 1396–9*, 194. In 1397 Barnston was valued at £12 *p.a.* and in 1393 Bockingfold was valued at 20 *m.*, Whitstable manor at £25 and its advowson at 40 *m.* (*C.I.M., 1392–9*, nos. 243, 26).

[22] *Trokelowe . . . Annales*, 203ff; *R.P.*, iii, 418; Gough, *op. cit.*, 162–3.
The new church, cruciform in plan, and the adjacent college buildings were erected on a site opposite an entrance to the bailey of the castle. The church has been rebuilt to such an extent that very little of Gloucester's work can be seen (*An Inventory of the Historical Monuments in Essex*, ii, Royal Commission on Historical Monuments, 1921, 200–2).

[23] Millar and James, *op. cit.*, 3; 'Inventory of the Goods and Chattels', 275ff; *C.I.M., 1392–9*, no. 372.

[24] Pearce, *William de Colchester*, 57; *Polychronicon*, ix, 260–1; 'Liber Benefactorum', fo. 110.

[25] Froissart, *Œuvres*, xv, 118; *Excerpta Historica, or, Illustrations of English History*, ed. S. Bentley (London, 1831), 24; *Testamenta Eboracensia*, part i (Surtees Soc., 1836), 121–2; *Chronicque de la Traison*, 108–9. Philip of Burgundy gave Gloucester tapestries in 1393 (Evans, *op. cit.*, 93).

Chapter 5

[1] *C.C.R., 1396–9*, 137–8.

[2] P.R.O., D.L. 41/10/31; Palmer, 'Articles for a Final Peace between England and France', 184; *C.P.R., 1370–4*, 472; *C.C.R., 1377–81*, 390ff; *C.P.R., 1374–7*, 337, 407–8. In 1421 Haresfield was given an annual valuation of £20 and Upavon one of £26 13s. 4d. (*R.P.*, iv, 137). Thomas was appointed to head the Essex commission of peace in August 1376 and Essex commissions of array in 1377 (*C.P.R., 1374–7*, 313–14, 496–7; *ibid., 1377–81*, 38, 40).

[3] *C.P.R., 1377–81*, 66–7, 60, 372; Holmes, *op. cit.*, 24; *C.P.R., 1377–81*, 452, 537; *ibid., 1381–5*, 95; *John of Gaunt's Register, 1379–83*, ed. E. C. Lodge and R. Somerville (Camden Third Ser., lvi–ii, 1937), i, no. 556, ii, no. 803; *C.P.*, v, 178.

[4] *C.C.R., 1377–81*, 390ff; *C.P.R., 1377–81*, 502; *C.C.R., 1381–5*, 511ff; *C.F.R., 1383–91*, 91; *C.P.*, ix, 41; P.R.O., 'Cal. of Inquisitions Post Mortem, Richard II', 160–2; *R.P.* iii, 206. In February 1381 the escheator in Herefordshire and the adjacent March of Wales was ordered to partition the castle and town of Bronllys and the whole Lordship of Cantref Selyf, found by the late escheator to be worth £80 *p.a.*, between the Bohun heirs (*C.C.R., 1377–81*, 439–40). For the dispute over these properties between Thomas and Henry of Bolingbroke, see Holmes, *op. cit.*, 24–5.

[5] S.C. 8/222/11029; *C.C.R., 1385–9*, 173; *C.P.R., 1385–9*, 147, 209, 233; *C.C.R., 1385–9*, 224, 662–3; *C.F.R., 1383–91*, 213; S.C. 8/215/10707;

C.P.R., 1388–92, 71, 93, 98. In May 1385 Thomas was granted the custody of St Briavel's Castle and the Forest of Dean, in reversion after the death of Sir Guy Brian the elder. Brian's son Sir William may have served on the 1380 expedition. The 1385 grant was confirmed in 1390, in part satisfaction of the ducal annuity. It was valued in 1390 at £80 *p.a.* and provision was also made for a reversionary grant of 200 *m.* on the issues of Somerset and Dorset, to pay part of the annuity (*C.P.R., 1381–5,* 565, 579; *Foedera,* iv, 91; *C.P.R., 1388–92,* 360, 293).

6 *C.P.R., 1388–92,* 255–6, *ibid., 1391–6,* 575–6. By charter dated 12 November 1390 the king confirmed the comital annuity and specified sums from the profits of alien priories assigned for its payment (*C.P.R., 1391–6,* 575–6). Rutland's attitude towards his uncle is deduced from the accusations made by FitzWalter and Bagot in 1399. For Holderness, see above, 76.

7 *C.P.R., 1388–92,* 381, 391, 429; *Essex Sessions of the Peace 1351, 1377–1379,* ed. E. C. Furber (Essex Archaeological Soc. Occasional Papers No. 3, 1953), 22–3; *C.P.R., 1388–92,* 482, 476; *ibid., 1377–81,* 523; Otway-Ruthven, *op. cit.,* 323; *C.P.R., 1391–6,* 222, 243, 417. In June 1392 the duke and his heirs were granted the reversions of Laughton (Sussex), Bockingfold, Fleet and Whitstable (Kent) and Welbury (Herts.), together with the hundred of Shiplake, and Westdean (Sussex). If the value of these properties exceeded £200 *p.a.,* he was to receive the residue as part satisfaction of the ducal annuity. In November 1393 these reversions were granted in fee simple, probably because the duke intended to use them as endowments for the college he planned to found (*C.P.R., 1391–6,* 98, 347).

8 Account of Nicholas Bradshawe, Stafford County Record Office, D 641/1/2/4; *C.P.,* xii, part i, 179ff; S.C. 8/253; *C.P.R., 1391–6,* 116, 119, 124–7, 129; *C.F.R., 1391–9,* 54; *C.P.R., 1391–6,* 133. Dower was granted to Anne Countess of Stafford in July 1392 and assigned in February 1393 with the assent of Archbishop Courtenay, the earl of Warwick and other friends of the heir William Stafford, and of Anne's guardians John Burton, Thomas Feriby clerks and William Nafferton. In July 1395 Anne was discharged from payment of 300 *m.,* part of a debt to the Crown (*C.P.R., 1391–6,* 133; *C.C.R., 1392–6,* 38–9; *C.P.R., 1391–6,* 304; *cf* Stafford County Record Office, D 641/1/2/4).

9 *C.P.R., 1391–6,* 420; *C.P.,* xii, part i, 180; *C.P.R., 1391–6,* 574; Froissart, *Œuvres,* xvi, 13; *C.P.R., 1391–6,* 111; *Œuvres,* xvi, 6. According to Froissart, Richard promised Gloucester a gift of 50,000 nobles as part of a bribe for his support over the French marriage (*Œuvres,* xv, 301). A noble was worth 6s. 8d.

10 Gough, *op. cit.,* 180; *C.I.M., 1392–9,* nos. 348, 226, 224, 274, 354, 359, 243–4, 267; P.R.O., D.L. 29/42/817 (High Easter), 815 (Waltham), 816 (Wix).

11 *C.P.R., 1381–5,* 334; E. 101/38/2; *C.I.M., 1392–9,* nos. 356, 359; *C.P.R., 1399–1401,* 117. In October 1377 John Clifton was intending to sail in Buckingham's company, and in June 1380 Sir John Clifton;

in 1392 he contracted to serve in the duke's retinue in Ireland
(*Foedera*, iv, 19, 91; E. 101/74/1/43). Identical may be the Sir John
Cliftons who fought in the St-Inglevert tournament, received a pardon
for supporting the Appellants and died fighting for the king at the
battle of Shrewsbury (Froissart, *Œuvres*, xiv, 134–5; C. 67/31, m. 13;
Trokelowe . . . Annales, 369).

12 *Inventory of the Historical Monuments in Essex*, ii, 105; *C.C.R.*,
1377–81, 96; C. 67/30, m. 3; *Foedera*, iv, 19; E. 101/38/2; *C.C.R.*,
1381–5, 394–5; 'Liber Benefactorum', fo. 133; *C.C.R.*, *1381–5*, 384;
ibid., *1385–9*, 392; *C.P.R.*, *1381–5*, 452; *Polychronicon*, ix, 112.

13 *C.C.R.*, *1396–9*, 182–3, 253–4; *C.P.R.*, *1399–1401*, 366; *Test. Vet.*, i,
146ff; Roskell, *The Commons and their Speakers*, 137ff; *C.C.R.*,
1396–9, 222; *ibid.*, *1374–7*, 237, 462–3; *R.P.*, iii, 431; D.L. 29/42/816.
In 1404 John Lightfoot of Roxwell witnessed a grant of Essex properties to a group including some of the duke's former officials—Feriby,
Mils and Hugh Payntour, clerks (*C.C.R.*, *1402–5*, 372).

14 Froissart, *Œuvres*, xvi, 82–3, xv, 269, xvi, 1ff, 72–3; *C.P.R.*, *1396–9*,
311–12; Clarke, *op. cit.*, 109 and n.; C. 67/30, m. 3; E. 101/38/2;
C.C.R., *1381–5*, 598; *C.P.R.*, *1388–92*, 482; *ibid.*, *1391–6*, 512, 533;
Gough, *op. cit.*, Appendix, 88. In 1406 Essex property was granted to
John Bray of Felsted, with the assent of the countess of Hereford,
Sir Gerard Braybrooke, Sir William Marny and Thomas Feriby. In
Felsted church there is a brass commemorating Christine (d. 1420),
wife of John Bray (*C.F.R.*, *1405–13*, 27–8; Mill Stephenson, *History
of the Monumental Brasses in the British Isles*, London, 1926, 118).

15 P. Morant, *History and Antiquities of the County of Essex*, i (London,
1768), 385–6; F. Blomefield, *Essay towards a Topographical History
of Norfolk*, i (Fersfield and Lynn, 1739), 115; *C.C.R.*, *1392–6*, 467–8;
C.F.R., *1391–9*, 143–4, 153; 'Liber Benefactorum', fo. 133; Gough,
op. cit., Appendix, 88; D.L. 29/42/815. For the Heveningham
family's properties in Essex, Norfolk and Suffolk, see *C.I.P.M.* (Record
Comm., 1808, 1821), ii, p. 343 no. 68, iii, p. 181 no. 23. 'Thomas
Hevyngham' was a surety for the countess of Hereford, Sir Gerard
Braybrooke the younger and Feriby in May 1401, when they were
granted custody of the earl of Oxford's properties (*C.F.R.*, *1399–1405*,
125).

16 Gough, *op. cit.*, Appendix, 52; *C.I.M.*, *1392–9*, no. 244; D.L.
29/42/815–16; *C.C.R.*, *1399–1402*, 161ff. For the Marny family see
Scrope and Grosvenor Controversy, ii, 385ff, and Morant, *op. cit.*,
i, 406.

17 E. 101/36/31; *The Antient Kalendars and Inventories of the Treasury
of His Majesty's Exchequer*, ed. Sir F. Palgrave, ii (Record Comm.,
1836), 11–12; *C.C.R.*, *1385–9*, 411–12; *ibid.*, *1389–92*, 27; Aston, *op. cit.*,
317–18; *C.P.R.*, *1388–92*, 98, 482; Gough, *op. cit.*, Appendix, 81.
Feriby was pardoned in 1398 for having supported the Appellants
(C. 67/30, m. 3).

18 *C.C.R.*, *1385–9*, 422; Roskell, *The Commons and their Speakers*,
124ff, 355; 'Cal. of Inquisitions Post Mortem, Richard II', p. 85;

C.C.R., 1385–9, 405–6; *C.P.R., 1391–6*, 319; *Cal. of Select Pleas and Memoranda of the City of London, 1381–1412*, 216–17; 'Liber Benefactorum', fo. 133; *C.C.R., 1392–6*, 295.

19 *C.P.R., 1391–6*, 533; Gough, *op. cit.*, Appendix, 88; Roskell, *The Commons and their Speakers*, 137ff. A witness to Spain's grant was Thomas Lampet, who contracted to go on Buckingham's naval expedition in 1377, was in his retinue on Lancaster's 1378 expedition, and was to receive a pardon for supporting the Appellants (*Foedera*, iv, 19; E. 101/38/2; C. 67/30, m. 3). In 1397, with Doreward and Boys, Lampet was granted property by Sir Thomas Swynbourne of Little Horkesley and was ordered, after the duke's arrest, to appear before the council with Boys (*C.C.R., 1396–9*, 202, 222.)

20 *C.C.R., 1385–9*, 638, 645; *C.P.R., 1391–6*, 533; Roskell, 'Sir Richard de Waldegrave', 154ff; *C.C.R., 1385–9*, 486; *C.P.R., 1385–9*, 441; *C.C.R., 1396–9*, 151, 155, 225, 233, 490–1; *C.P.R., 1396–9*, 260, 539; *ibid., 1399–1401*, 8.

21 Gough, *op. cit.*, Appendix, 69ff, 81; *C.P.R., 1377–81*, 163; Sherborne, *op. cit.*, 738–9 and 738n.; *Anonimalle Chronicle*, 76, 129–30, 132–3, 180, 192; Devon, *op. cit.*, i, 217; *C.P.R., 1377–81*, 495, 586; *ibid., 1391–6*, 240; *ibid., 1377–81*, 350; *C.C.R., 1392–6*, 492–3; *ibid., 1396–9*, 155. For Ivo de Harleston's Essex inheritance, see Morant, *op. cit.*, i, 344–5, 348ff, 491; *cf C.I.P.M.*, iii, p. 297 no. 33.

22 Aston, *op. cit.*, 239 and n.; *John of Gaunt's Register, 1379–83*, i, nos. 97–8, 484; 'Cal. of Inquisitions Post Mortem, Richard II', 24; *C.P.R., 1381–5*, 193; *C.C.R., 1381–5*, 595; *C.P.R., 1381–5*, 494–5; *C.F.R., 1383–91*, 213; *C.P.R., 1385–9*, 549, 553–4; *ibid., 1388–92*, 482; *C.I.M., 1392–9*, no. 244; *C.P.R., 1396–9*, 242, 309; *C.F.R., 1391–9*, 223–4; *C.C.R., 1396–9*, 175, 234; *C.P.R., 1396–9*, 279; *C.C.R., 1392–6*, 359. For Greenwich's service on Gloucester's expeditions, see *Foedera*, iv, 19; Carte, *op. cit.*, 164; *C.P.R., 1391–6*, 487, 490.

23 Clarke, *op. cit.*, 112–13; *C.P.*, xii, part ii, 961–2; C. 67/30, m. 3; E. 101/39/7, nos. 1 and 4; *C.C.R., 1385–9*, 405–6.

24 *Foedera*, iv, 36; *C.F.R., 1383–91*, 280; Squibb, *op. cit.*, 131; *C.P.R., 1391–6*, 71, 589–90; *ibid., 1385–9*, 533; *C.F.R., 1383–91*, 280; *ibid., 1391–9*, 166–7, 194; 'Liber Benefactorum', fo. 133; E. 101/74/1, no. 7; C. 67/31, m. 12d. A John de Lakenheath had Suffolk interests late in Edward III's reign and was a member of the county's commission of peace in 1371 (*C.I.P.M.*, ii, p. 268 no. 16; *C.P.R., 1370–4*, 122).

25 *C.P.*, ix, 215ff; Froissart, *Œuvres*, ix, 245; C. 67/30, m. 3; Carte, *op. cit.*, 164; *C.P.*, i, 417ff; *Trokelowe . . . Annales*, 402; E. 101/38/2; *C.P.*, xi, 503–4; E. 101/74/1, no. 18; *Historia . . . Ricardi II*, 154. Shortly after 10 April 1386 Sir Thomas Mortimer, Gloucester's ally in 1387, married Bardolf's mother (*C.P.*, i, 419).

26 Gough, *op. cit.*, Appendix, 69; Blomefield, *op. cit.*, iv (1775), 307ff; *C.P.R., 1399–1401*, 77; *ibid., 1391–6*, 611, 427–3; Carte, *op. cit.*, 155; *C.P.R., 1388–92*, 188; *C.C.R., 1392–6*, 492–3; *C.P.R., 1396–9*, 185–6, 349, 423, 422

²⁷ A. Goodman, 'Sir Thomas Hoo and the parliament of 1376', *B.I.H.R.*, xli (1968), 144 and n.; *C.P.R., 1385–9*, 320.

²⁸ M. Bassett, 'Knights of the shire for Bedfordshire during the middle ages', *Bedfordshire Historical Record Soc. Publications*, xxix (1949), 20ff; *Scrope and Grosvenor Controversy*, ii, 454ff; A. B. Emden, *A Biographical Register of the University of Oxford to A.D. 1500*, i (Oxford, 1957), 254–5; *C.P.R., 1391–6*, 512; *Test. Vet.*, i, 149; *V.C.H. Buckinghamshire*, iv, 402, 304; E. 101/38/2; *C.C.R., 1385–9*, 405–6; 'Cal. of Inquisitions Post Mortem, Richard II', 160–2; A. Gibbons, *Early Lincoln Wills* (Lincoln, 1888), 59; *C.C.R., 1392–6*, 38–9; *C.I.M., 1392–9*, no. 348.

²⁹ *C.P.*, v, 729. For Gloucester's ambitions for his son, see above, 175.

Chapter 6

¹ Aston, *Thomas Arundel*, 372.

² L. F. Salzman, 'The Property of the Earl of Arundel, 1397', *S.A.C.*, xci (1953), 46–7; Legge, *op. cit.*, no. 30.

³ *Test. Vet.*, i, 129ff, 94ff; *C.I.M., 1392–9*, no. 237; *C.P.*, i, 245; *V.C.H. Sussex*, ii, 64ff. For the renaming of Shrawardine, see R. W. Eyton, *Antiquities of Shropshire*, x (London, 1860), 97–8; *C.P.R., 1381–5*, 1–2; *C.I.M., 1392–9*, nos. 236–7.

⁴ Salzman, *op. cit.*, 32ff; *C.P.R., 1374–7*, 129; *Test. Vet.*, i, 94–5.

⁵ Aston, *Thomas Arundel*, 140 and n.; *C.P.R., 1377–81*, 92, 151, 402, 494; *C.C.R., 1381–5*, 311.

⁶ *C.P.R., 1381–5*, 38, 66; *V.C.H. Sussex*, ii, 108–9; N. R. Ker, *Medieval Libraries of Great Britain* (London, 1941), 3; E. W. Tristram, *English Wall Painting of the Fourteenth Century* (London, 1955), 135; M. A. Tierney, *History and Antiquities of the Castle and Town of Arundel* (London, 1834), 747ff, 772. Bishop Rede left thirteen books to the college, with 20 *m.* to be spent on chaining them firmly in the library (*V.C.H. Sussex*, ii, 109).

⁷ *V.C.H. Sussex*, ii, 97–8, 82–3; *C.P.R., 1377–81*, 351; *ibid., 1381–5*, 578. For recent excavations, see K. J. Evans, 'The Maison Dieu, Arundel', *S.A.C.*, cvii (1969), 65ff.

⁸ Salzman, *op. cit.*, 33ff; B.M., Harleian MS. 4840, fo. 303; *Chronicon Angliae*, 270; *C.C.R., 1377–81*, 426; *C.P.R., 1377–81*, 618–19; *Cal. of Select Pleas and Memoranda of the City of London, 1381–1412*, 155; *C.F.R., 1391–9*, 227; Salzman, *op. cit.*, 45. For recent appraisal of Arundel's properties, see introduction to *Two Estate Surveys of the FitzAlan Earls of Arundel*, ed. M. Clough (Sussex Record Soc., lxvii, 1969).

⁹ *Chronicon Angliae*, 168, 270–1; W. Dugdale, *The Baronage of England*, i (London, 1675), 317; *R.P.*, ii, 348, iii, 95, 211.

¹⁰ *C.P.R., 1370–4*, 308; *ibid., 1377–81*, 42–3; *C.C.R., 1381–5*, 74; *C.P.R., 1381–5*, 119, 259; Salzman, *op. cit.*, 44–5. For Sussex convictions of conspiracy against Arundel's servant John Stephens, see *C.P.R., 1388–92*, 264.

[11] *C.A.D.*, iii, D. 805; John Stow, *A Survey of London*, ed. C. L. Kingsford (Oxford, 1908), i, 235–6.

[12] *C.P.R., 1396–9*, 209, 270; *C.C.R., 1385–9*, 411–12.

[13] *C.I.M., 1392–9*, nos. 367, 334, 280–1; *C.P.R., 1385–9*, 91; *V.C.H. Wiltshire*, viii, 256. In May 1383 Arundel had granted John Bonham a life tenure in Bulkington (*C.I.M., 1392–9*, no. 280).

[14] *V.C.H. Buckinghamshire*, iii, 451, 455; *C.I.M., 1392–9*, nos. 245, 242; *C.P.R. 1396–9*, 255; *ibid., 1385–9*, 359, 382; *C.I.M., 1392–9*, no. 280; *C.P.R., 1385–9*, 415.

[15] *C.I.M., 1392–9*, no. 263; *C.P.R., 1385–9*, 440.

[16] *C.I.M., 1392–9*, *passim*; *C.P.R., 1377–81*, 539, 624; *ibid., 1385–9*, 25–6. For Arundel's Marcher lordships see also *The Extent of Chirkland (1391–1393)*, ed. G. P. Jones (London, 1933); W. J. Slack, *The Lordship of Oswestry 1393–1607* (Shrewsbury, 1951); B. Evans, 'A Grant of Privileges to Wrexham (1380)', *B.B.C.S.*, xix (1962), 42ff. For the earl's Shropshire properties, see *C.I.M., 1392–9*, no. 236 and Clough, *op. cit.*, introduction.

[17] *C.P.R., 1388–92*, 19; Bellamy, *op. cit.*, 261ff; S.C. 8/88/4387. For comments on the lawlessness of Marcher inhabitants, particularly of Cheshiremen, see *R.P.*, iii, 42–3, 62, 81, 139, 201, 308. In August 1395 the king commanded the sheriff of Cheshire to arrest disturbers of the peace, of whom, it was alleged, there were great numbers, emboldened by lack of punishment ('Welsh Records: Cal. of Recognizance Rolls of the Palatinate of Chester', 98, in *Thirty-Sixth Report of the Deputy Keeper of the Public Records*, London, 1875). A letter to Thomas Earl of Arundel (1399–1415) from one of his officials predicts a Cheshire raid on the Lordship of Yale and Bromfield (Legge, *op. cit.*, no. 308).

[18] *C.P.*, xii, part i, 354–5; *C.C.R., 1377–81*, 226; *C.P.R., 1385–9*, 4; H. Le Strange, *Le Strange Records* (London, 1916), 337; *C.C.R., 1381–5*, 147; *C.P.R., 1385–9*, 415; *ibid., 1391–6*, 548. For Arundel's connections with Grey and Glyn Dŵr, see above, 34: in 1394 Grey and Burnell were among the earl's sureties at Lambeth (*C.C.R., 1392–6*, 368). In 1388 Gloucester had appointed Burnell his deputy as justice of Chester ('Welsh Records', 76). For the latter's connections with Warwick, see S.C. 6/1123/5; *C.I.M. 1392–9*, no. 306; *C.A.D.*, i, A. 658.

[19] *C.P.R., 1364–7*, 237–8; Salzman, *op. cit.*, 33; *C.C.R., 1369–74*, 448; *C.P.R., 1374–7*, 283, 395. In 1344 Edward St John was the earl of Arundel's bachelor (*Cal. of Ancient Correspondence Concerning Wales*, ed. J. G. Edwards, Cardiff, 1935, 248–9).

[20] 'Cal. of Inquisitions Post Mortem, Richard II', 3ff; *C.F.R., 1377–83*, 278; *C.A.D.*, iii, D. 805; E. 101/40/33; C. 67/3, m.

[21] *C.P.R., 1377–81*, 230; *C.C.R., 1377–81*, 226; *C.P.R., 1381–5*, 35; *C.C.R., 1381–5*, 537; L. F. Salzman, 'Tregoz', *S.A.C.*, xciii (1955), 51–3.

Two knights called Edward St John may have been confused in the above account, for one of that name was listed in Arundel's 1387 naval retinue (E. 101/40/33).

[22] *Scrope and Grosvenor Controversy*, i, 164–5, ii, 370ff; *C.P.R., 1377–81*, 286–7, 459; The Marquis Curzon of Kedleston, *Bodiam Castle Sussex* (London, 1926), 25ff; *C.F.R., 1377–83*, 270–1; *C.P.R., 1381–5*, 35; Somerville, *op. cit.*, 380; *C.C.R., 1381–5*, 459, 482–3.

[23] *C.P.R., 1377–81*, 292, 611; *ibid.*, *1385–9*, 42, 98, 123; E. 101/40/33; E. 101/41/4; *C.P.R., 1396–9*, 341; *ibid.*, *1385–9*, 415; K. Fowler, *The Age of Plantagenet and Valois* (London, 1967), fig. 38, 123.

[24] *C.P.R., 1388–92*, 102, 118, 214, 232; Bird, *op. cit.*, 102ff; Knighton, *op. cit.*, 319–20; *C.P.R., 1391–6*, 37, 388.

[25] E. 101/40/33; *Expeditions to Prussia and the Holy Land*, 304; *C.P.R., 1396–9*, 573, 341; Curzon, *op. cit.*, 28–9; L. F. Salzman and H. Whistler, 'Sir John Dalyngrigge and Robertsbridge Abbey', *S.A.C.*, lxxviii (1937), 266; *Test. Vet.*, i, 132.

[26] *C.P.*, v, 250ff; *C.P.R., 1381–5*, 35; E. 101/33/40; *C.P.R., 1385–9*, 283, 407, 384, 547.

[27] Baldwin, *op. cit.*, 494–5; *C.P.*, v, 252, vi, 484ff; E. 101/40/33; C. 67/30, m. 3; *C.P.R., 1385–9*, 449; E. 101/41/5; J. A. Tuck, 'The Cambridge Parliament, 1388', *E.H.R.*, lxxxiv (1969), 233; *Test. Vet.*, i, 163; Curtis, *op. cit.*, 123.

[28] *C.P.R., 1381–5*, 181; *C.C.R., 1381–5*, 392–3; *C.A.D.*, iii, D. 805; *Test. Vet.*, i, 133; *C.P.R., 1391–6*, 548; *ibid.*, *1396–9*, 596; L. Lyell, *A Mediaeval Postbag* (London, 1934), no. 93.

[29] *C.P.*, xi, 328–9; E. 101/40/33.

[30] *C.P.*, ii, 506–8; *C.P.R., 1367–70*, 368; Froissart, *Œuvres*, ix, 248; *C.C.R., 1396–9*, 84; Mill Stephenson, *op. cit.*, 517. On the 1380 expedition Camoys served in the retinue of Lord Latimer, with whom Arundel had links (see above, 169), and after Latimer's death his wool houses at Calais were to be divided between his widow and Camoys (*Foedera*, iv, 87; 'Cal. of Inquisitions Post Mortem, Richard II', 158). In 1387 Camoys was perhaps no friend to the Lords Appellant, for they expelled him from court (*Polychronicon*, ix, 116).

[31] *C.C.R., 1385–9*, 218; Salzman, 'The Property of the Earl of Arundel, 1397', 33; *C.C.R., 1385–9*, 633; *C.P.R., 1381–5*, 35; *ibid.*, *1391–6*, 548; *Test. Vet.*, i, 133–4.

[32] *C.P.*, xi, 328–9; *Foedera*, iv, 69–70; Devon, *op. cit.*, i, 234; *C.P.R., 1385–9*, 123, 177, 306.

[33] Tuck, *op. cit.*, 233; *C.P.R., 1388–92*, 264; *ibid.*, *1385–9*, 501; *C.P.*, x, 662ff; *C.P.R., 1381–5*, 35; *ibid.*, *1388–92*, 210.

[34] E. 101/40/33; *C.P.R., 1385–9*, 440; *C.C.R., 1396–9*, 84; *C.P.R., 1396–9*, 242; C. 67/30, m. 2; *C.C.R., 1399–1402*, 107–8; Roskell, *The Commons and their Speakers*, 137ff.

[35] *C.P.R., 1385–9*, 82–3; *ibid.*, *1370–4*, 370; *ibid.*, *1385–9*, 91; E. 101/40/33.

[36] *C.P.R., 1385–9*, 401; E. 101/41/4; *Test. Vet.*, i, 133–4; *C.P.R., 1391–6*, 548; *ibid.*, *1396–9*, 380. For Publow's connection with Arundel, see also *ibid.*, *1381–5*, 35, 116; *C.F.R., 1383–91*, 4.

[37] *C.I.M., 1392–9*, nos. 229, 235; Mill Stephenson, *op. cit.*, 513. In November 1397 David Eyton was described as late constable and Sir

John de Nevill as late receiver of Holt, John Whethales as late constable of Chirk and steward of Oswestry. William Banastre had been keeper, Alan Thorpe receiver, Roger Glaas and John de Pole constables of the Lordship of Oswestry. Welshmen had been employed mainly as deputies—John ap William had been lieutenant at Chirk. In Henry IV's reign Glyn Dŵr's adherent Gruffydd ap Dafydd ap Gruffydd aspired to the offices of master forester and bailiff of Chirkland (*C.I.M.*, *1392–9*, nos. 229, 233–6; J. Beverley Smith, 'The Last Phase of the Glyndwr Rebellion', *B.B.C.S.*, xxii (1967), 250ff).

³⁸ Salzman, 'The Property of the Earl of Arundel, 1397', 34; *C.P.R.*, *1381–5*, 35, 116; *C.I.M.*, *1392–9*, no. 233; *C.P.R.*, *1385–9*, 548. Herdewyke acted as Arundel's attorney in connection with his ward Lord Charlton's majority ('Cal. of Inquisitions Post Mortem, Richard II', 268).

³⁹ *C.P.R.*, *1381–5*, 116; *ibid.*, *1385–9*, 280; *ibid.*, *1396–9*, 199; Beverley Smith, *op. cit.*, 251–2.

⁴⁰ *C.P.R.*, *1385–9*, 433; *Scrope and Grosvenor Controversy*, i, 256–7, ii, 266; *Foedera*, iii, part ii (Record Comm., 1830), 1013–14; *ibid.*, iv, 91; Froissart, *Œuvres*, ix, 70; E. 101/40/33; 'Welsh Records', 497, 61; *C.P.R.*, *1391–6*, 489.

Chapter 7

¹ Froissart, *Œuvres*, viii (1869), 392–3; *C.P.R.*, *1374–7*, 487; E. 101/36/31; *Historia . . . Richardi II*, 4; *Chronicon Angliae*, 171–2, 191–2; *Anonimalle Chronicle*, 116–17, 188–9; *Foedera*, iv, 36; Holmes, *op. cit.*, 33–4; A. F. Alexander, 'The War with France in 1377' (London Ph.D. thesis, 1933), 209ff. For his own wages and those of his retinue Buckingham was paid in October 1377 a total of £2,175 14s. 11d., (E. 101/36/31).

² R. Delachenal, *Histoire de Charles V*, v (Paris, 1931), 228, 211 and n.; *C.P.*, xi, 388ff; E. 101/36/32; *Chronicon Angliae*, 201. For the Courtenay brothers' unfortunate encounter with Castilian ships when putting out on the expedition led by Salisbury and Arundel, see *Historia . . . Ricardi II*, 6.

³ Armitage-Smith, *John of Gaunt*, 232–4 and notes; *Foedera*, iv, 45; E. 101/38/2; *Chronicon Angliae*, 204–6; Froissart, *Œuvres*, ix, 67ff, 89ff; *Anonimalle Chronicle*, 131ff. Warwick and Stafford served on Lancaster's expedition (*Historia . . . Ricardi II*, 7). For Lancaster's possible motives for wishing his brother to go overseas in 1380, see above, 89.

⁴ Sherborne, *op. cit.*, 731–2; *Foedera*, iv, 87–8, 91–2; *Anonimalle Chronicle*, 132; *Chronicon Angliae*, 266. For the text of Buckingham's appointment as lieutenant, see Gough, *op. cit.*, 14n.; for Harleston, above, 99.

⁵ Sherborne, *op. cit.*, 731–2. The earl later arranged for the celebration of anniversaries for all those who died on his expedition between 8 July 1380 and 2 May 1381 (Gough, *op. cit.*, 179–80).

6 *Anonimalle Chronicle*, 132–3; *Chronicon Angliae*, 267, 272ff; Sherborne, *op. cit.*, 732–3; Froissart, *Œuvres*, ix, 241ff, 292ff, 303ff, 314ff, 331ff; Delachenal, *op. cit.*, v, 367ff; *Foedera*, iv, 107; *C.P.R.*, *1377–81*, 606–7, 609; 'Continuatio Eulogii', 351. For arrangements reducing the profits available to soldiers on the expedition, see K. Fowler, 'Les finances et la discipline dans les armées anglaises en France au XIVe siècle', *Les Cahiers Vernonnais*, no. 4 (1964), 66–7. In December 1383, at Buckingham's petition, an assignment of £1,416 on the wool subsidy was made to Knolles and John Philpot, part of a sum which the earl owed them for war payments on the Breton expedition (*C.P.R.*, *1381–5*, 361). The translated passage from Froissart is taken from Pynson's edition of *The Cronycles of Englande, Fraunce, Spaygne* (etc.), fo. cclxxxiii.

7 *C.P.R.*, *1381–5*, 72–3; *Chronicon Angliae*, 315ff; A. Réville, *Le soulèvement des travailleurs d'Angleterre en 1381* (Paris, 1898), cxv ff.

8 M. Aston, 'The Impeachment of Bishop Despenser', *B.I.H.R.*, xxxviii (1965), 127ff.

9 *Polychonicon*, ix, 32; Knighton, *op. cit.*, ii, 203.

10 N. B. Lewis, 'The Last Medieval Summons of the English Feudal Levy, 13 June 1385', *E.H.R.*, lxxiii (1958), 1ff; *Polychronicon*, ix, 64–5; Froissart, *Œuvres*, x (1870), 395ff; Sherborne, *op. cit.*, 731n.

11 'Continuatio Eulogii', 358–9; *C.P.R.*, *1385–9*, 176; Carte, *op. cit.*, 153–4; P.R.O., Issue Roll, E. 403/515, *passim*.

12 *Handbook of British Chronology*, 130; *Chronicon Angliae*, 373–4; Carte, *op. cit.*, 155; E. 101/40/33. For the number of soldiers, sailors and ships under Arundel's command in 1387, see J. W. Sherborne, 'The English Navy. Shipping and Manpower 1369–1389', *Past and Present*, 37 (1967), 174.

13 *Polychronicon*, ix, 91–3; Knighton, *op. cit.*, ii, 234–5; *Chronicon Angliae*, 374–5; Froissart, *Œuvres*, xii, 67ff; *The Great Chronicle of London*, ed. A. H. Thomas and I. D. Thornley (London, 1938), 46; *Historia Anglicana*, ii, 146; Baldwin, *op. cit.*, 507ff. For Cryse's retinue and ship, see E. 101/40/33 and *C.P.R.*, *1385–9*, 266. Ships captured by Arundel's fleet included the *Seint Johan* and *Seint Marie* of San Sebastian, the *Gracedieux* of Santander, the Flemish *Seint Marie Cogge* and the *Holygost* (*C.P.R.*, *1385–9*, 302, 308, 364, 338).

14 Myres, *op. cit.*, 20ff; *Polychronicon*, ix, 110ff; Aston, *Thomas Arundel*, 342 and n.; Knighton, *op. cit.*, ii, 252ff; *Historia . . . Ricardi II*, 94ff; 'Continuatio Eulogii', 365; Usk, *op. cit.*, 145. For the Lechlade incident, see above, 31–2. Gower and Froissart treated Gloucester as the victor ('Tripartite Chronicle', 293; *Œuvres*, xii, 282ff).

15 Froissart, *Œuvres*, xii, 152ff, xiii, 99ff, 109–10, 146ff, 273ff, 297–8; *R.P.*, iii, 228; *Foedera*, vii, 578–9; N. H. Nicolas, *History of the Royal Navy*, ii (London, 1847), 326–9; Carte, *op. cit.*, 158; Tuck, *op. cit.*, 233; *Polychronicon*, ix, 187–8; *Historia Anglicana*, ii, 175; *C.P.R.*, *1388–92*, 12. For Gloucester's correspondence with Burgundy, see above, 49. For Arundel's account and muster rolls for the expedition,

E. 101/41/nos. 4, 5 and 7. The force was considerably larger than the one which he took to sea in 1387 and a large number of victualling ships were employed (Sherborne, 'The English Navy', 174). I owe thanks to Dr Kenneth Fowler for his information about Lancaster's diplomacy.

16 *Foedera*, vii, 706; Carte, *op. cit.*, 164.

17 E. 101/74/nos. 1–52; E. 101/69/1/289; Legge, *op. cit.*, no. 154; J. F. Lydon, 'Richard II's Expeditions to Ireland', *Journal of the Royal Society of Antiquaries of Ireland*, xciii (1963), 135ff.

18 Froissart, *Œuvres*, xiv, 314–15, 384, xvi, 3. When Brest, which Thomas had occupied in 1378, was surrendered to the duke of Brittany in 1397, it ill became him to reproach Richard with never having captured a town, as he had failed to take Nantes in 1380 (*Chronicque de la Traison*, 1ff).

Chapter 8

1 *Chronicon Angliae*, 255; *Polychronicon*, ix, 105; P.R.O., Ministers' Accounts, S.C. 6/1123/5.

2 *C.P.*, iii, 292, xii, part i, 177–9; Dugdale, *Baronage*, i, 235ff. For Basset's attitude in 1387, see above, 24.

3 Holmes, *op. cit.*, 39; Usk, *op. cit.*, 161.

4 *R.P.*, iii, 326; *C.C.R.*, *1389–92*, 563; *ibid.*, *1392–6*, 368.

5 *C.P.R.*, *1377–81*, 89; *C.C.R.*, *1381–5*, 163; *ibid.*, *1385–9*, 53.

6 *C.P.R.*, *1391–6*, 167–8, 430–1; *C.C.R.*, *1392–6*, 104, 64; *R.P.*, iii, 326.

7 *C.P.R.*, *1381–5*, 268, 580; *V.C.H. Warwickshire*, ii, 124ff, iii, 111; W. Dugdale, *The Antiquities of Warwickshire* (London, 1656), 322, 345. Brasses commemorating the earl and countess are in St Mary's at Warwick (*Antiquities of Warwickshire*, 324; Mill Stephenson, *op. cit.*, 525).

8 *Test. Vet.*, i, 153–5; *C.I.M.*, *1392–9*, nos. 306–7; *C.P.R.*, *1396–9*, 315; T. D. Kendrick, *British Antiquity* (London, 1950), 28–9; Dugdale, *Baronage*, i, 235–6; *Antiquities of Warwickshire*, 322. Among the earl's goods was a 'silver-gilt "surgon" for green ginger' (*C.I.M.*, *1392–9*, no. 307). For the romances of Guy and Reynbrun, see Hubbard, *op. cit.*, 127ff. There is a conflict of evidence as to how far Warwick was responsible for the castle works (*V.C.H. Warwickshire*, viii, 456).

9 *C.I.M.*, *1392–9*, nos. 305, 302; *C.C.R.*, *1381–5*, 409; *ibid.*, *1385–9*, 569, 627–8; *C.P.R.*, *1388–92*, 80; C. D. Ross, 'Forfeiture for Treason in the Reign of Richard II', *E.H.R.*, lxxi (1956), 563–4; *V.C.H. Worcestershire*, iii, 401ff. For Warwick's nomination of a sub-sheriff of Worcestershire, see B. Wilkinson, *The Chancery under Edward III* (Manchester, 1929), 35 and n.

10 *C.I.M.*, *1392–9*, *passim*; *C.P.*, ii, 3; *C.C.R.*, *1389–92*, 203–5.

11 *V.C.H. Hertfordshire*, ii, 199; A. Steel, *The Receipt of the Exchequer 1377–1485* (Cambridge, 1954), 424; *C.P.R.*, *1396–9*, 196; *ibid.*, *1399–1401*, 472; *V.C.H. Buckinghamshire*, iv, 358.

[12] *C.I.M.*, *1392–9*, nos. 339, 346–7, 280, 283. For Chedworth, see S.C. 6/1123/5.

[13] *C.I.M.*, *1392–9*, nos. 249–50, 252, 255–7, 228; Holmes, *op. cit.*, 48–9.

[14] *C.I.M.*, *1392–9*, *passim*; S.C. 6/1123/5; C. Ross, *The Estates and Finances of Richard Beauchamp Earl of Warwick* (Dugdale Soc., 1956), 14–15.

[15] S.C. 6/1123/5; *C.I.M.*, *1392–9*, nos. 307, 231; *C.P.R.*, *1388–92*, 80.

[16] *C.I.M.*, *1392–9*, nos. 305, 302; *C.C.R.*, *1381–5*, 410; 'Liber Benefactorum', fo. 129d; *C.F.R.*, *1383–91*, 233; Dugdale, *Baronage*, i, 235; *C.C.R.*, *1396–9*, 422; Carte, *op. cit.*, 156; *Polychronicon*, ix, 172; *C.P.R.*, *1388–92*, 372–3.

[17] *C.P.R.*, *1381–5*, 238; *ibid.*, *1391–6*, 465–6, 31; *ibid.*, *1396–9*, 166.

[18] Holmes, *op. cit.*, 114; *C.I.M.*, *1392–9*, no. 305; R. H. Hilton, *Ministers' Accounts of the Warwickshire Estates of the Duke of Clarence 1479–80* (Dugdale Soc., 1952), x; *V.C.H. Warwickshire*, v, 169; *C.I.M.*, *1392–9*, no. 272.

[19] Hilton, *op. cit.*, xvii–iii; Holmes, *op. cit.*, 77; *C.I.M.*, *1392–9*, nos. 305–6, 256, 258, 298, 249.

[20] *C.I.M.*, *1392–9*, no. 241; *C.C.R.*, *1385–9*, 411–12; *C.I.M.*, *1392–9*, no. 228. On 9 October 1397 Aldebury's estate as warden of the Hospital of St Michael at Warwick was confirmed (*C.P.R.*, *1396–9*, 199).

[21] W. Dugdale, *The History of St Paul's Cathedral in London* (London, 1658), 54; Beltz, *op. cit.*, 48; *C.P.*, ii, 50–1; *C.P.R.*, *1354–8*, 416; *Warwickshire Feet of Fines*, ed. L. Drucker, iii (Dugdale Soc., 1943), no. 2097; *C.P.R.*, *1367–70*, 24; *C.C.R.*, *1369–74*, 69, 108–9, 322, 441–2, 453ff; *Registrum Simonis de Sudbiria*, ed. R. C. Fowler, i (Canterbury and York Soc., 1927), 289; *C.C.R.*, *1381–5*, 258, 386. In 1355 the earl of Warwick rewarded a yeoman for his good service. Among the witnesses were the earl's sons Guy, Thomas and Reynbrun and the earl's steward Richard Piryton, clerk (*C.A.D.*, iv, A. 7203).

[22] *V.C.H. Warwickshire*, iv, 61–2; J. T. Driver, 'The Knights of the Shire for Worcestershire', *Transactions of the Worcestershire Archaeological Soc.*, 40 (1963), 48; *C.C.R.*, *1369–74*, 330; *ibid.*, *1381–5*, 598; *C.P.*, ii, 49–50; *C.C.R.*, *1369–74*, 453ff; Holmes, *op. cit.*, 77 and n.; 'Cal. of Inquisitions Post Mortem, Richard II', 188–9; 'Liber Benefactorum', fo. 131d.

[23] *C.C.R.*, *1381–5*, 410; 'Liber Benefactorum', fo. 129d; *C.P.R.*, *1377–81*, 89; *C.C.R.*, *1396–9*, 346–7; S.C. 6/1123/5; *C.I.M.*, *1392–9*, no. 306; *Test. Vet.*, i, 153–5; *C.C.R.*, *1396–9*, 161.

[24] *C.C.R.*, *1381–5*, 410; Dugdale, *Baronage*, i, 235; *C.C.R.*, *1377–81*, 332; *Warwickshire Feet of Fines*, no. 2256.

[25] *Warwickshire Feet of Fines*, iii, no. 2214; *C.C.R.*, *1369–74*, 330. In 1375 a release of properties in Budbrooke and elsewhere in Warwickshire was made to the earl. The witnesses included Sir Henry Arderne and Sir William Breton (Beauchamp Cartulary, B.M., Add. MS. 28,024, fo. 21).

[26] *C.P.R.*, *1388–92*, 341; *ibid.*, *1396–9*, 346–7; *C.C.R.*, *1396–9*, 157; *C.I.M.*, *1392–9*, no. 302. Spernore sat as knight of the shire for

Warwickshire in 1395 and for Worcestershire in 1393, 1394 and 1399 (Driver, *op. cit.*, 48, 57).

[27] *C.C.R., 1381–5*, 409–10; 'Liber Benefactorum', fo. 132; *C.F.R., 1383–1391*, 233; *Test. Vet.*, i, 78; *C.P.R., 1396–9*, 346–7.

[28] *C.P.R., 1381–5*, 157; *C.I.M., 1392–9*, nos. 249, 252; S.C. 6/1123/5; *C.C.R., 1396–9*, 125. Gough cites the inscription in the church at Necton, Norfolk (a Beauchamp manor) to Sir Guy Beauchamp's wife Philippe: she died on 5 August 1383 (*Sepulchral Monuments in Great Britain*, i, London, 1786, 147).

[29] *C.I.M., 1392–9*, nos. 346–7, 306; *C.P.R., 1396–9*, 207, 257, 321.

[30] *C.P.R., 1381–5*, 277–8; *ibid., 1391–6*, 465–6; *ibid., 1396–9*, 166; 'Cal. of Inquisitions Post Mortem, Richard II', 188–9; *C.P.R., 1396–9*, 418; *V.C.H. Warwickshire*, ii, 127; S.C. 6/1123/5; *Estates and Finances of . . . Warwick*, 8.

[31] Steel, *Receipt of the Exchequer*, 424; *C.P.R., 1381–5*, 157; *C.F.R., 1383–91*, 173–4; *C.I.M., 1392–9*, no. 303; *Foedera*, vii, 565, 581–2. For Say's acquisition of the Butler inheritance, see *C.P.*, ii, 232–3.

[32] Carte, *op. cit.*, 155–6; *C.P.R., 1388–92*, 80; *C.I.M., 1392–9*, no. 272.

[33] Tout, *op. cit.*, iv (1928), 13–14; *C.P.R., 1396–9*, 317; D.L. 41/5/1; *Warwickshire Feet of Fines*, iii, no. 2221; 'Liber Benefactorum', fo. 129d; *C.P.R., 1377–81*, 89; *C.C.R., 1385–9*, 494, 405–6; *Expeditions to Prussia and the Holy Land*, 306–7.

[34] *C.I.M., 1392–9*, nos. 306, 302; *C.C.R., 1396–9*, 157; *C.P.R., 1396–9*, 215; 'On Richard's Ministers', in *Political Poems and Songs*, ed. T. Wright, i (R.S., 1859), 364; *C.P.R., 1396–9*, 350; *Chronicque de la Traison*, 17; *C.P.R., 1396–9*, 494. Bagot bought Baginton Castle from Sir Richard Harthill. There are a few remains of it (*V.C.H. Warwickshire*, vi, 22–3). Richard may have stayed at Caludon Castle near Coventry, which Bagot was holding of the duke of Norfolk (see above, 159).

[35] Usk, *op. cit.*, 180 and n.; *Trokelowe . . . Annales*, 303–5, 308; *Chronicles of London*, ed. C. L. Kingsford (Oxford, 1905), 51ff; *R.P.*, iii, 458; Mill Stephenson, *op. cit.*, 519. According to one version of Bagot's testimony in the 1399 parliament, earlier that year he had sent a messenger to Henry in France to warn him that Richard did not intend him to have seisin of the Lancastrian inheritance (*Chronicles of London*, 53).

[36] Driver, *op. cit.*, 48; 'Liber Benefactorum', ff. 129d, 132; *C.P.R., 1385–9*, 138–9; *ibid., 1388–92*, 341, 307; *ibid., 1391–6*, 269; S.C. 6/1123/5.

For Henry Bruyn of Worcester, see *C.I.M., 1392–9*, no. 302. Borguyllon and John Catesby held the majority of Warwickshire sessions of the peace whose records survive from the period 1377–97 (*Rolls of the Warwickshire and Coventry Sessions of the Peace 1377–1397*, ed. E. G. Kimball, Dugdale Soc., 1939, xxxi–ii).

[37] *C.A.D.*, i, A. 658; *Test. Vet.*, i, 153–5; *C.P.R., 1405–8*, 219.

[38] *C.P.R., 1388–92*, 325; *ibid., 1399–1401*, 2, 343, 209, 212; *ibid., 1396–9*,

396; *C.I.M., 1392–9,* no. 301; *C.P.R., 1401–5,* 126, 128, 287; *ibid., 1405–8,* 153–4, 199–200.

[39] Mill Stephenson, *op. cit.,* 541; *C.C.R., 1381–5,* 410; *C.P.R., 1381–5,* 238; *ibid., 1385–9,* 372, 446; *ibid., 1388–92,* 71; *ibid., 1391–6,* 366. A Sir John Russell took part in the St-Inglevert tournament and the Tunis Crusade (Froissart, *Œuvres,* xiv, 106, 114–15, 245). A John Russell 'de Wykewane' took out a pardon for supporting the Appellants (C. 67/30, m. 1).

[40] *C.P.R., 1391–6,* 269; *ibid., 1396–9,* 222, 314, 359; *ibid., 1391–6,* 482–3, 549; S.C. 8/221, nos. 11010, 11021; *Chronique du religieux de Saint-Denys,* ii, 710; *C.P.R., 1396–9,* 589; *ibid., 1399–1401,* 566; Mill Stephenson, *op. cit.,* 541.

Chapter 9

[1] Somerville, *op. cit.,* 67; *C.P.,* iv, 204; Usk, *op. cit.,* 157–8. For Henry's role in 1387, see above, 28–9, 130. The previous year, when giving evidence before the Court of Chivalry, he had alluded modestly to his youth and inexperience: 'we are young and have been armed only for a short while' (*Scrope and Grosvenor Controversy,* i, 50).

[2] *Anonimalle Chronicle,* 106; 'Liber Benefactorum', fo. 129 d; *John of Gaunt's Register, 1379–83,* i, p. 11n.

[3] *John of Gaunt's Register, 1379–83,* i, p. xl; Somerville, *op. cit.,* 131–2, 385; 'Liber Benefactorum', ff. 129d–130; *Register,* i, nos. 308a, 706; Somerville, *op. cit.,* 67–8 and 68n.; Holmes, *op. cit.,* 25.

[4] Somerville, *op. cit.,* 132–3; *C.C.R., 1385–9,* 411–12.

[5] Somerville, *op. cit.,* 385–6; *C.P.R., 1396–9,* 70–1; C. 67/30, m.2. For Buckton's career, see E. P. Kuhl, 'Chaucer's "My Maistre Bukton" ', *P.M.L.A.A.,* xxxviii (1923). Thomas Totty esquire, of Rolleston (Staffs.), was one probable servant of Derby who took out a pardon in 1398 for the support he had given to the Appellants. By letters patent dated Kenilworth, 17 October 1388, the earl appointed him porter of Brecon Castle for life and in 1389 granted him and his wife for their lives the reversion of property in the Lordship of Brecon. In 1392 Lancaster granted Totty 10 *m.* per annum as a reward for his services to Derby. In October 1398 Totty was first-named on the commission to collect ships for Hereford's voyage into exile (C. 67/30, m. 19; *C.P.R., 1396–9,* 122, 440).

[6] *Chronicque de la Traison,* 63; *Expeditions to Prussia and the Holy Land,* lxxxvi ff; Froissart, *Œuvres,* xvi, 106–8, 110–11, 132, 136–7, 162ff.

[7] *Trokelowe . . . Annales,* 168; *Diplomatic Correspondence,* no. 229a; Accounts of the Clerk of Derby's Great Wardrobe, D.L. 28/1/5; D.L. 28/1/6; *Chronicque de la Traison,* 45–6; Devon, *op. cit.,* i, 252. Mary de Bohun's alabaster effigy is in Trinity Hospital, Leicester (A. Gardner, *Alabaster Tombs of the Pre-Reformation Period in England,* Cambridge, 1940, 93).

[8] Froissart, *Œuvres,* xvi, 139, 141ff.

[9] D.L. 28/1/5; Froissart, *Œuvres*, xvi, 95–6; Bueno de Mesquita, *op. cit.*, 635–6; *Œuvres*, xvi, 115–16, 141; *Chronique du religieux de Saint-Denys*, ii, 700ff; *Œuvres*, xvi, 169, 147–8.

[10] F. Ll. Harrison, *Music in Medieval Britain* (London, 1958), 220–1; John Capgrave, *Liber de Illustribus Henricis*, ed. F. C. Hingeston (R.S., 1858), 100; J. H. Fisher, *John Gower* (London, 1965), 68, 37–8; *Chaucer Life-Records*, ed. M. M. Crow and C. C. Olson (Oxford, 1966), 275; *History of the King's Works*, ii, 935–6.

[11] *C.P.*, ix, 383–5, 780–1; *C.F.R.*, *1369–77*, 8–9; *C.P.R.*, *1377–81*, 456; *Anonimalle Chronicle*, 106, 114; *C.I.M.*, *1377–88*, nos. 50, 123; *Polychronicon*, ix, 30.

[12] *C.P.*, ix, 601, 603–4; *C.P.R.*, *1381–5*, 236, 229.

[13] Froissart, *Œuvres*, xvi, 90; *C.C.R.*, *1396–9*, 258–9; *Polychronicon*, ix, 30.

[14] Tout, *op. cit.*, iv, 2, 20n.; *Chronique du religieux de Saint-Denys*, i (1839); 676ff; *Polychronicon*, ix, 236; Clarke, *op. cit.*, 288.

[15] *C.P.R.*, *1385–9*, 45; *ibid.*, *1391–6*, 579, 721; *ibid.*, *1396–9*, 254; *V.C.H. Sussex*, ii, 60ff; C. 67/30, m. 2.

[16] *V.C.H. Lincolnshire*, i, 158; E. M. Thompson, *The Carthusian Order in England* (London, 1930), 218ff; *C.C.R.*, *1396–9*, 27; *Chronicque de la Traison*, 17; *C.P.R.*, *1396–9*, 420.

[17] *C.I.P.M.*, xi, no. 144, xii, no. 397; *C.I.M.*, *1392–9*, nos. 387–96. Thirsk and the surrounding country, which had belonged to the earl's ancestors in the twelfth century, was known as the Vale of Mowbray (*V.C.H. Yorkshire, North Riding*, ii, 62).

[18] Curtis, *op cit.*, 26 and 27 n.; *C.I.M.*, *1392–9*, nos. 387–96; *R.P.*, iii, 384, 255; *C.I.M.*, *1392–9*, nos. 392, 388; *V.C.H. Warwickshire*, viii, 121; *C.P.R.*, *1391–6*, 348; *C.C.R.*, *1399–1402*, 334. The reason that remedy was sought from the Crown in 1388 for the condition of Bramber Castle was that the earl's lands were still in royal wardship, remaining so until February 1389 (*C.C.R.*, *1385–9*, 580).

[19] *C.I.M.*, *1392–9*, nos. 388, 392; *C.P.R.*, *1399–1401*, 90.

[20] *C.P.R.*, *1391–6*, 363.

[21] *C.P.R.*, *1396–9*, 565; *C.I.M.*, *1392–9*, nos. 391, 387; *C.C.R.*, *1399–1402*, 9–10.

Nottingham may have been generous to his servants at this time in anticipation of his acquisition of Gower. In May 1397 he was granted the wardship of properties of Gilbert, son and heir of Sir Richard Talbot (*C.F.R.*, *1391–9*, 211–12).

[22] *C.I.M.*, *1392–9*, no. 388; *C.C.R.*, *1399–1402*, 16; *C.P.R.*, *1399–1401*, 259.

[23] *C.C.R.*, *1399–1402*, 30, 48. Hopcroue received a pardon for his support of the Appellants (C. 67/30, m. 3).

[24] E. 101/41/7; *C.F.R.*, *1383–91*, 258–9; *C.I.M.*, *1392–9*, no. 387; *C.C.R.*, *1385–9*, 411–12; *C.P.R.*, *1396–9*, 107, 200.

[25] *C.C.R.*, *1396–9*, 123–5. Rome, Yokflete, Brunham, Rees and Dalby were among the attorneys appointed by Mowbray in 1394 and in a letter dated Windsor, 9 June 1398, the latter mentioned Dalby as one of his attorneys in a Chancery suit (*C.P.R.*, *1391–6*, 506; *S.C.*

1/56/124). In May 1399 Rome, a king's clerk, was granted an annuity of £40 at the Exchequer, confirmed the following October (*C.P.R.*, *1396–9*, 564; *ibid.*, *1399–1401*, 50).

[26] C. 67/30, m. 3; *C.P.R.*, *1388–92*, 231, 242; Froissart, *Œuvres*, xiv, 124–5; Carte, *op. cit.*, 172; *Test. Vet.*, i, 161–2.

[27] R. Thoroton, *History of Nottinghamshire*, republished by J. Throsby, iii (London, 1797), 61ff; C. 67/30, m. 3; *C.C.R.*, *1396–9*, 157; *ibid.*, *1399–1402*, 381–2; *Trokelowe . . . Annales*, 369–70; Gardner, *op. cit.*, 96. Goushill was pardoned in 1390 at Mowbray's petition on the indictment that in 1387 he had ordered a murder to be carried out in his presence at Chesterfield (Derbyshire) and had rescued and harboured the murderers. Sureties, including servants of Mowbray, swore his innocence in Chancery (*C.P.R.*, *1388–92*, 231).

[28] Tout, *op. cit.*, iv, 12–13; *C.P.R.*, *1377–81*, 456; *C.I.M.*, *1377–88*, no. 299; *Trokelowe . . . Annales*, 308; *C.F.R.*, *1383–91*, 258–9; *Cal. of Letter-Books . . . of the City of London, Letter-Book H*, 376; C. 67/30, m. 19; C. 67/31, m. 12d; *C.P.*, iii, 314–15. Bagot was appointed on the 1380 commissions to enquire into waste in Mowbray properties. In 1394 and 1396 the Earl Marshal appointed him as an attorney (*C.I.M.*, *1377–88*, no. 123; *C.P.R.*, *1391–6*, 506; *Foedera*, vii, 844).

[29] C. 67/30, m. 3; *C.P.R.*, *1396–9*, 255; *C.F.R.*, *1383–91*, 258–9; *C.C.R.*, *1396–9*, 123ff; Roskell, *The Commons in the Parliament of 1422*, 194ff; Froissart, *Œuvres*, xiv, 120.

[30] *R.P.*, iii, 452–3; 'Welsh Records', 117; Legge, *op. cit.*, no. 386; 'Welsh Records,' 97; *C.P.R.*, *1391–6*, 404, 573. For Colfox, see J. L. Hotson, 'Colfox vs. Chauntecleer', *P.M.L.A.A.*, xxxix (1924).

[31] Carte, *op. cit.*, 164, 172, 170; *Cal. of Select Pleas and Memoranda of the City of London 1381–1412*, 161; *C.P.R.*, *1391–6*, 668.

In June 1396 Nottingham was pardoned for persistently failing to have works executed at Roxburgh Castle, which as keeper he had twice indented to do in 1389 (*C.P.R.*, *1391–6*, 723).

[32] *C.P.R.*, *1396–9*, 422; *C.C.R.*, *1392–6*, 32. In an undated letter the Earl Marshal wrote to his 'friend and cousin' Rauf Baron de G. requesting him and his company to join the earl's retinue on the king's proposed expedition to Scotland. The baron refused, explaining that he had agreed to serve in Lancaster's retinue for two years (Harleian MS. 388, ff. 41d–42). The baron may have been the Border landowner Ralph Lord Greystoke.

[33] Curtis, *op. cit.*, 75–85; *C.P.R.*, *1396–9*, 422; *R.P.*, iii, 384. Calveley had been an Appellant supporter (C. 67/30, m. 3).

[34] E. 101/41/7; *R.P.*, iii, 377; *C.P.*, xii, part ii, 441–3. For Bardolf and Morley, see above, 101–2.

[35] *C.C.R.*, *1392–6*, 429; *Trokelowe . . . Annales*, 321; *Chronicles of London*, ed. Kingsford, 52–3. For the treatises (B.M., Nero D vi) which Nottingham probably had compiled in his capacity as Marshal, and the possible implications of the inclusion of the 'Modus Tenendi Parliamentum' among them, see M. V. Clarke, *Medieval Representation and Consent* (London, 1936), 352ff.

Select Bibliography

I MANUSCRIPT SOURCES

Public Record Office

'Calendar of Inquisitions Post Mortem, Richard II', incomplete.
C. 67/30–31   Chancery, Pardon Rolls.
D.L. 28   Duchy of Lancaster, Accounts Various.
D.L. 29   Duchy of Lancaster, Ministers' Accounts.
D.L. 41   Duchy of Lancaster, Miscellanea.
E. 101   Exchequer, King's Remembrancer, Accounts Various.
S.C. 1   Special Collections, Ancient Correspondence.
S.C. 8   Special Collections, Ancient Petitions.

British Museum

The Beauchamp Cartulary, Additional MS. 28,024.
Letter-writing Formulary, Harleian MS. 3988.
'Liber Benefactorum' of St Albans Abbey, Cottonian MS. Nero D. vii.

Staffordshire County Record Office

Account of Nicholas Bradshawe, Receiver-General of Thomas Earl of Stafford (1390–1), D. 641/1/2/4.

The National Library of Scotland

Psalter and Hours of Eleanor de Bohun, MS. 18.6.5.

II PUBLISHED DOCUMENTS

Anglo-Norman Letters and Petitions, etc., ed. M. D. Legge (Oxford, 1941).
Calendar of Select Pleas and Memoranda of the City of London, 1381–1412, ed. A. H. Thomas (Cambridge, 1932).

Calendars of Close Rolls, Edward III, vol. xiii, to Henry IV, vol. i (H.M.S.O., London, 1911–27).
Calendars of Fine Rolls, x–xiii (H.M.S.O., London, 1929–33).
Calendars of Inquisitions Miscellaneous, iv–vi (H.M.S.O., London, 1957–63).
Calendars of Patent Rolls, Edward III, vol. x, to Henry IV, vol. iii (H.M.S.O., London).
Catalogue des rolles francois, ed. T. Carte (London, 1743).
Catalogue of Ancient Deeds, i–iv (H.M.S.O., London, 1890–1902).
The Diplomatic Correspondence of Richard II, ed. E. Perroy (Camden Third Ser., xlviii, 1933).
Expeditions to Prussia and the Holy Land Made by Henry Earl of Derby, ed. L. Toulmin Smith (Camden Second Ser., lii, 1894).
The Extent of Chirkland (1391–1393), ed. G. P. Jones (London, 1933).
Foedera, Conventiones, etc., ed. T. Rymer, vii–viii (London, 1709); Record Commission edition, iii parts ii and iv (London, 1830–69).
'Inventory of the Goods and Chattels belonging to Thomas, Duke of Gloucester, and seized in his Castle at Pleshy', etc., ed. Viscount Dillon and W. H. St John Hope, *Archaeological Journal*, liv (1897).
Issues of the Exchequer. ed. F. Devon, i (Record Comm., 1837).
John of Gaunt's Register, 1371–75, two vols., ed. S. Armitage-Smith (Camden Third Ser., xx–xxi, 1911).
John of Gaunt's Register, 1379–83, ed. E. C. Lodge and R. Somerville, two vols. (Camden Third Ser., lvi–ii, 1937).
Proceedings and Ordinances of the Privy Council of England, ed. Sir H. Nicolas, i (Record Comm., 1834).
Rotuli Parliamentorum, etc., ii–iii (London, 1783).
The Scrope and Grosvenor Controversy, ed. N. H. Nicolas, two vols. (London, 1832).
Testamenta Vetusta, ed. N. H. Nicolas, two vols. (London, 1826).
Two Estate Surveys of the FitzAlan Earls of Arundel, ed. M. Clough (Sussex Record Soc., lxvii, 1969).

III NARRATIVE SOURCES

Anonimalle Chronicle, ed. V. H. Galbraith (Manchester, 1927).
Chronica monasterii de Melsa, ed. E. A. Bond, iii (R.S., 1868).
Chronicles of London, ed. C. L. Kingsford (Oxford, 1905).

Chronicon Adae de Usk, ed. E. M. Thompson (London, 1904).

Chronicon Angliae, ed. E. M. Thompson (R.S., 1874).

Chronicon Henrici Knighton, ed. J. R. Lumby, ii (R.S., 1895).

Chronicque de la Traison et Mort Richart Deux, etc., ed. B. Williams (London, 1847).

Chronicque du religieux de Saint Denys, ed. M. L. Bellaguet, i–ii (Paris, 1839–40).

Eulogium (historiarum sive temporis), ed. F. S. Haydon, iii (R.S., 1863).

Favent, T., 'Historia...mirabilis parliamenti', etc., ed. M. McKisack, *Camden Miscellany XIV* (1926).

Froissart, J., *Œuvres . . . Chroniques*, ed. Kervyn de Lettenhove, viii–xvi (Brussels, 1869–72).

Gower, J., 'The Tripartite Chronicle', in *The Major Latin Works of John Gower*, trans. E. W. Stockton (Seattle, 1962).

Historia Vitae et Regni Ricardi II Angliae Regis, ed. T. Hearne (Oxford, 1729).

Johannis de Trokelowe . . . Annales, ed. H. T. Riley (R.S., 1865).

'The Kirkstall Chronicle, 1355–1400', ed. M. V. Clarke and N. Denholm-Young, *Bulletin of the John Rylands Library*, 15 (1931).

Polychronicon Ranulphi Higden, ed. J. R. Lumby, viii–ix (R.S., 1882–6).

IV SECONDARY AUTHORITIES

Aston, M., *Thomas Arundel* (Oxford, 1967).

Barron, C. M., 'The Tyranny of Richard II', *B.I.H.R.*, xli (1968).

Bellamy, J. G., 'The Northern Rebellions in the Later Years of Richard II', *Bulletin of the John Rylands Library*, 47 (1964–5).

Bird, R., *The Turbulent London of Richard II* (London, 1949).

Chrimes, S. B., 'Richard II's Questions to the Judges, 1387', *Law Quarterly Review*, lxxii (1956).

Clarke, M. V., *Fourteenth Century Studies*, ed. L. S. Sutherland and M. McKisack (Oxford, 1937).

Cokayne, G. E., *The Complete Peerage*, ed. V. Gibbs and others (London, 1910–59).

Curtis, E., *Richard II in Ireland* (Oxford, 1927).

Dugdale, W., *The Baronage of England*, i (London, 1675).

Gough, R., *The History and Antiquities of Pleshy* (London, 1803).

Handbook of British Chronology, ed. Sir F. M. Powicke and E. B. Fryde (London, 1961).

Holmes, G. A., *The Estates of the Higher Nobility in Fourteenth-Century England* (Cambridge, 1957).

Bueno de Mesquita, D. M., 'The Foreign Policy of Richard II in 1397: Some Italian Letters', *E.H.R.*, lvi (1941).

Millar, E. G., and James, M. R., *The Bohun Manuscripts* (Roxburghe Club, 1936).

Myres, J. N. L., 'The Campaign of Radcot Bridge in December 1387', *E.H.R.*, xlii (1927).

Palmer, J. J. N., 'The Anglo-French Peace Negotiations, 1390–1396', *T.R.H.S.*, Fifth Ser., 16 (1966).

Roskell, J. S., *The Commons and their Speakers in English Parliaments 1376–1523* (Manchester, 1965).

Ross, C., *The Estates and Finances of Richard Beauchamp Earl of Warwick* (Dugdale Soc., 1956).

Ross, C. D., 'Forfeiture for Treason in the Reign of Richard II', *E.H.R.*, lxxi (1956).

Otway-Ruthven, A. J., *A History of Medieval Ireland* (London, 1968).

Salzman, L. F., 'The Property of the Earl of Arundel, 1397', *S.A.C.*, xci (1953).

Sherborne, J. W., 'Indentured Retinues and English Expeditions to France, 1369–1380', *E.H.R.*, lxxix (1964).

Armitage-Smith, S., *John of Gaunt* (London, 1904).

Somerville, R., *History of the Duchy of Lancaster*, i (London, 1953).

Mill Stephenson, *History of the Monumental Brasses in the British Isles* (London, 1926).

Storey, R. L., 'The Wardens of the Marches of England towards Scotland, 1377–1489', *E.H.R.*, lxxii (1957).

Tait, J., 'Did Richard II Murder the Duke of Gloucester?' in *Historical Essays*, ed. T. F. Tout and J. Tait (Manchester, 1907).

Tierney, M. A., *The History and Antiquities of the Castle and Town of Arundel*, two vols. (London, 1834).

Tout, T. F., *Chapters in the Administrative History of Mediaeval England*, iii–iv (Manchester, 1928).

Victoria History of the Counties of England.

Index

Index

Index

Beaufort, John, Earl of Somerset, Marquess of Dorset, brother of Henry, 67, 71

Beaumont, John, Lord, 19, 48, 53, 54, 63, 128, 171

Bedford, 39, 159

Beeding, Sussex, 159

Beeston, Norfolk, 38, 112

Bellamy, J. G., 113

Benhale, Suffolk, 101

Beoley, Worcs., 140, 142, 143, 148

Berkeley, Thomas, Lord, 125

Berkswell, War., 140

Bermondsey Priory, Surrey, 69, 177

Berners, Sir James, 41, 54, 92

Berry, Duke of, *see* John, Duke of Berry

Berwick, Essex, 95

Berwick-upon-Tweed, 49, 53, 127

Bewbush, Sussex, 159

Bidlington, Sussex, 117

Bigot, Sir Ralph, 38

Billingshurst, Sussex, 38

Bill of Appeal (1397), 67ff.

Bishopston, Glam., 137

Black Prince, *see* Edward, Prince of Wales

Blisland, Cornwall, 142, 144

Blockley, Worcs., 130

Blois, 131

Blois, Jean de, 148

Blount, Sir John, 151

Blounts, Essex, 145

Bockingfold, Kent, 83, 179, 180

Bodiam, Sussex, 38, 116, 117

Boethius, 156

Bohun family, 178

Bohun, Eleanor de, daughter of Humphrey, *see* Gloucester, Duchess of

Bohun, Elizabeth de, sister of Humphrey, *see* Arundel, Countess of

Bohun, Humphrey de, Earl of Hereford, 4, 5, 12, 29, 78, 80, 81, 83, 85, 88, 98, 100, 103, 169

Bohun, Joan de, Countess of Hereford, wife of Humphrey, 5, 77, 79, 83, 89, 90, 96, 98, 99, 103, 181

Bohun, Mary de, daughter of Humphrey, *see* Derby, Countess of

Bohun, William de, Earl of Northampton, father of Humphrey, 81

Bolingbroke, Lincs., 153

Bolton, Robert, 25

Bonde, William, 37

Bonham, John, 38, 112, 184

Boniface IX, 178

Bordeaux, 2

Borguyllon, Robert, 150, 190

Boston, Lincs., 154

Bosyate, Simon, 31

Botiller, Sir John, 44

Boucicaut, Marshal of France, 155

Bourbon, Louis de, 57

Bourchier, John, Lord, 57, 124

Bourton-on-the-Hill, Glos., 130

Boys, Sir John, 96, 97, 182

Bradshawe, Nicholas, 93, 100

Brailes, War., 140, 144

Bramber, Sussex, 34, 159, 192

Bramber, Sir Nicholas, 7, 18, 25-7, 31, 42, 44, 45, 172

Brantingham, Thomas, Bishop of Exeter, 52, 53

Braundeston, Richard, 42

Bray, John, 97, 181

Braybrooke, Sir Gerard, 43

Braybrooke, Sir Gerard, son and heir of Gerard, 43, 100, 103, 181

Braybrooke, Robert, Bishop of London, brother of Sir Gerard snr, 21, 23, 43, 47, 54, 64, 75, 79, 83, 96, 148, 172

Brecon, 89, 153, 154, 191

Brest, 30, 54, 101, 117, 122, 129, 131, 148, 174, 188

Brétigny, Treaty of, 59, 88

Breton, Sir William, 146, 189

Brian, Sir Guy, 180

Brian, Sir William, 180

Brightford, Sussex, 159

Bristol, Glos., 36, 60

Brittany, 2, 100, 120, 121, 123-5, 127, 130, 131

Brittany, Duke of, *see* Montfort

Brocas, Sir Bernard, 131

Brocas, John, 115

Broes, Sir Hues, 120

Bromfield, Salop, 34, 113, 184

Bromley, Richard, 146, 147

Bronllys, Breck., 154, 179

Broun, Philip, 111

Browe, Sir Hugh, 38, 43, 120, 121

Bruges, 2, 3

Brugge, Edmund de, 150

Brunham, Thomas, 160, 161

Bruyn, Henry, 150, 190

Buckby, Northants., 141

Index

Index

Index

Index

Index

205

Index

Index

Index

Index

Walsall, Staffs., 141
Walsh, Sir Thomas, 44
Walsingham, Thomas, 6, 7, 9, 11, 12, 22, 33, 53, 55, 66–70, 75, 110, 123, 132, 135, 136, 163, 175, 176
Waltham, Essex, 89, 90, 95, 96, 98
Waltham, Essex, Abbot of, 178
Waltham Holy Cross, Herts., 26
Waltham, John, Bishop of Salisbury, 22, 52, 53, 117, 172
Walthamstow, Essex, 141
Walton, Ralph, 43
Walworth, Sir William, 31
Warbleton, Sussex, 119
Warburton, John, 119
Wardenships of the Marches towards Scotland, 48–52, 55, 162
Wardieu, John, 116
Warwick, 9, 67, 71, 72, 135, 137–40, 143, 144, 147, 148, 188
Warwick, Earls of, see Beauchamp
Warwick the Kingmaker, 134
Washington, Sussex, 159
Waterford, 62
Waterton, Sir Hugh, 153, 154
Waverley, Surrey, Abbot of, 36
Wayland, Norfolk, 141
Wedgenock Park, War., 140
Welbury, Herts., 83, 180
Welles, Eleanor, wife of John, 163
Welles, John, Lord, 163
Wenlock, William, 150
Wenzel, King of the Romans, 66
West, John, 26
Westdean, Sussex, 180
West Hatch, Wilts., 159, 160
Westminster, 26–8, 36, 46, 51, 52, 55, 58, 137, 164, 170–2
Westminster Abbey, 45, 69, 82, 84, 85, 177
Westminster, Abbot of, 178; see Litlyngton
Westminster Chronicler, 10, 11, 18, 23, 29, 32, 42, 45, 50, 52, 54, 56, 58–60, 85, 114, 130, 135, 136
Westminster, monk-recluse of, 29, 82
Westmorland, Earl of, see Neville
Weston by Cherrington, War., 160
Westwycombe, John, 102, 103
Wethersfield, Essex, 96
Wheatenhurst, Glos., 88, 90, 95
Whethales, John, 186
Whitchurch, William, 142
White, Sir John, 38, 43

Whitehed, Thomas, 94, 96
Whitstable, Kent, 83, 180
Whyte, William, 108
Wick, Worcs., 140
Wickham, William, Bishop of Winchester, 36, 42, 47, 52, 53, 56
Wicklow, 62
Wickwar, Glos., 150
William, John ap, 186
William of Hainault, Count of Ostrevant, 155
William of Jülich, Duke of Guelders, 59, 102, 148
Willington, Beds., 159, 160
Wilmington Priory, Sussex, 116
Winchelsea, Sussex, 7, 132
Winchester, Hants, 60, 150, 151
Windsor, Berks., 17, 21, 28, 32, 55, 58, 60, 93, 153, 192
Windsor, Sir William, 124
Wing, Bucks., 112, 159
Witney, Oxon., 130
Wix, Essex, 89, 90, 95, 96, 98
Wodcok, John, 26
Wodelond, William, 111
Wolston, Essex, 112
Wonderful Parliament, see Merciless Parliament
Woodham Walter, Essex, 91
Woodstock, Oxon., 23
Woolmer Forest, Hants, 115
Worcester, 140
Worcester Cathedral, register of, 130
Wrexham, Denb., 120
Wryght, John, 37
Wyche, see Wick
Wydeville, John, 43
Wydeville, Thomas, 39
Wymondeswold, William, 160
Wyndham, Sussex, 159
Wynter, William, 148
Wyre Piddle, Worcs., 140, 143

Yale, see Bromfield
Yardley, Worcs., 39, 140
Yarmouth, Norfolk, 160
Yattere, John, 111
Yevele, Henry, 125
Yokflete, Thomas, 160, 161, 192
York, 36, 50, 127
York, Duke of, see Edmund of Langley; Richard, Duke of, 14, 33, 74

Zwin, 128, 129

212